WITHDRAWN
FROM STOCK
QMUL LIBRARY

QMC   626412 4

a30213 006264124b

DATE DUE FOR RETURN

THE TRADITIONS OF
FRENCH PROSE STYLE

THE TRADITIONS
OF FRENCH PROSE
STYLE ～ A Rhetorical Study

JOHN PORTER HOUSTON

Louisiana State University Press
Baton Rouge and London

218612

Copyright © 1981 by Louisiana State University Press
All rights reserved
Manufactured in the United States of America

Designer: Albert Crochet
Typeface: VIP Palatino
Typesetter: G&S Typesetters, Inc.
Printer and binder: Thomson-Shore, Inc.

LIBRARY OF CONGRESS CATALOGING IN PUBLICATION DATA

Houston, John Porter.
    The traditions of French prose style.

    Includes bibliographical references and index.
    1. French prose literature—History and criticism.   2. French language—
Rhetoric.   I. Title.
PQ611.H6   848'.08   80-27871
ISBN 0-8071-0858-8

QUEEN MARY
COLLEGE
LIBRARY

For Jeremy

Contents

Introduction

French prose has enjoyed the greatest reputation among the stylistic traditions of modern languages. Nietzsche, for example, considered its cultivated rhetoric to be on a plane with that of classical literature. The last broad historical treatment of French prose was, however, Gustave Lanson's *L'Art de la prose* (1908), and I have thought it valuable to reexamine this side of French literature from a specific point of view, that of rhetoric. This work is not, strictly speaking, a history of French prose: many books are omitted from the discussion, and, in the case of the eighteenth century, a whole period is covered fairly briefly, not because the eighteenth century was not one of excellent prose—on the contrary—but because relatively few new kinds of prose were created then. Some minor texts, such as *L'Astrée*, are brought in because they were once admired for their style and show something curious about the evolution of prose. On the other hand, the major writers are treated somewhat unevenly, depending on the amount and quality of what has been written about their prose. Montaigne is an important case in point; his style has been well studied, and I have confined myself to those aspects of his prose which are most interesting for the developing picture of French style. This brings me to what I consider an important aim of this book: to permit one, in studying an individual author, to situate his prose historically. Otherwise useful studies of style are often impaired for want of any terms of comparison in the prose writers of the same or the preceding period. For this reason, I have devoted attention more to authors than to general movements, unlike the only recent book attempting to establish some broad perspective on the history of prose style: Ian A. Gordon's *The Movement of English Prose* (London: Longman's, 1966).

The commonest way of studying style in France has been the psychological method, which tries to determine general traits of the author's mind, often employing statistical information. Obviously, this kind of approach is of limited value if one does not consider literature to be above all an expression of personality or if one believes that the apparent author of a work is a fiction more or less consciously created by the real author, as was the brilliant rhetorician of sixteenth- and seventeenth-century ornamented prose. I find the study of how literary effects are created, that is, the study of rhetoric, to be of superior relevance. Rhetoric was, of course, the dominant aspect of practical literary studies in schools until well into the nineteenth century and marked even those who, under the sway of romantic ideas, disdained it. A rhetorical study, furthermore, is concerned primarily with significant texts, not with statistics about a writer's whole work and how often he uses a certain word, much as that information may be of incidental value in working out a rhetorical characterization. Finally, a rhetorical study deals with more than simply the occurrence of figures like anaphora or metonymy; levels of style and the relation of genre to style are central to it.

There has been a great renewal of interest in rhetoric in the last two decades or so, but this work is the first rhetorical study concerning such a lengthy period, from the sixteenth to the early twentieth century. The basis of the book is the body of theory most importantly represented by Aristotle in his *Rhetoric*, the *Rhetorica ad Herennium*, Cicero's *Orator* and *De Oratore*, and Quintilian's *Institutio*. The first principle is what is called in French the *écart* theory of style, which considers literary language to be defined by a discrepancy with speech. "Sweet is amazement," says Aristotle (*Rhetoric* III, 2)— amazement that comes from making language strange: *poieîn xénen ten diálekton*. At the same time, there is a hidden art which suffices for strangeness: all rhetoric does not rely on extraordinary words or constructions. Prose literary language has another quality, an ambiguous one: it is neither metric nor rhythmless (*méte émmetron . . . méte árrythmon*), but has a distinctive structure (*schêma*) of its own. Prose grows out of elements of speech but is not identifiable with it; the intonational phrases of French and the fall at the end of the sentence have been turned by writers into distinctive patterns differing from the same ones in speech. Nonspeech constructions, such as inversion or a long adverb at the beginning of the sentence, play a significant role. The history of these effects may be considered a somewhat limited fashion of approaching prose, which, after all, represents in many cases an intellectual as well as an esthetic achievement, but Buffon suggested that style itself has "beautés intellectuelles," which are forms of truth more precious and enduring than the ideas of any period.

In charting the directions of French prose, I shall make some contributions toward the discussion of literary modes and periods such as the baroque and neoclassical. The examination of prose permits one to see with especial clarity the presence or absence of some of the broad categories customarily invoked in the study of such matters. I have seen fit, furthermore, to establish some points of comparison between French prose and that of other modern literatures, especially English and Italian. Through ignorance of the larger picture of European literature, some have been led to make extraordinary remarks, such as Albert Thibaudet's to the effect that only French of the modern languages has a true prose. The character of French prose will emerge more clearly if we see it in relation to other major traditions. Such a notion as vernacular Ciceronianism, for example, simply cannot be discussed with any soundness or cogency unless one resorts to comparative stylistics. To understand seventeenth-century literary distinctions, one must, like the people who made the distinctions, be acquainted with contemporary Italian and Spanish literature. At the same time, of course, I am not attempting to present a coherent survey of English or any other prose, but only to touch upon those aspects most illuminating for French.

The history of French as a language has been more closely studied than that of other modern languages, and certain aspects of it are pertinent to style. The great *Histoire de la langue française* by Ferdinand Brunot and Charles Bruneau is of major help, as are specialized studies such as Alf Lombard's *Les Constructions nominales dans le français moderne* (Uppsala: Almqvist, 1930). French styles have also been more frequently studied in a literary fashion than those of any other modern language. Appropriate references will be made in the following pages, without, however, any attempt to indicate the merits, considerably varying, of individual studies. Editions of works are only mentioned when they are of some significance. Finally, the value of certain scholarly studies like Erich Auerbach's *Mimesis*, Daniel Mornet's *Histoire de la clarté française*, and Morris Croll's essays on sixteenth- and seventeenth-century prose has been much greater than footnotes can really indicate.

I ❧ FROM HUMANISM TO THE END OF NEOCLASSICISM

1 Rabelais and the Middle French Background

In anthologies, Rabelais ordinarily stands as the first great French prose writer; however, he belongs in many ways more to the final stage of Middle French than to the first phase of the modern language. By this I do not mean that he necessarily spoke Middle French, for the term usually indicates less an imperfectly known form of colloquial French than a stylistic complex, encompassing both some peculiarities of oral language from the fourteenth to the early sixteenth centuries and some resources of vocabulary and sentence structure that were to be found exclusively, no doubt, in the more learned forms of writing. It is made of erudite vocabulary, complicated sentence structure, and varied forms, now medieval, now modern. That Middle French style was capable of diverse and rare forms of beauty is seen from the fact that both Rabelais and Scève are exponents of it; the *Délie* differs from Pléiade poetry on a number of points of basic historical linguistics as well as by its conception of versification and imagery.

It is important that we have some perspective on Rabelais' language and realize its relation to the literary syntax, vocabulary, and stylistic aspirations of the preceding century or so. One of the expository writers, Christine de Pisan, shows the new attempts in Middle French at a fairly convoluted sentence form.

> Dit Aristote que art ou science est percepcion ou percevance qui donne certaineté et raison d'aprendre, et pour tant que la matiere sus dicte me reduit à memoire de plus longuement dire, comme il soit expedient me semble, sur le fait cy devant touchié, c'est assavoir que ne soient vallables en fais d'armes ne mes les hommes excitéz et apris en ce, sembleroit grant merveille, et non sans cause, qu'en cestui royaume qui tout autre de toute

3

haultesse precede et passe, ne se excercitassent plus meismes en temps de
paix les nobles en la buisson du hernoiz et des armes que ne font afin qu'en
temps et au besoing y fussent si maistres et prests que d'autres y occuper
ne fust besoings.[1]

Sembleroit is the main verb, preceded by three subordinate clauses;
the subjunctive with *comme* is a Middle French mannerism (after the
model of Latin *cum*); and the positioning of the verbs represents the
fusion of Old French freedom in verb placement with the Latinizing
tendency to postpone finite verb forms. The word order in general
strives for a kind of learned elegance.

The syntactic doublings belong to a complex phenomenon.[2] The
doubling of nouns and adjectives occurs in Old French and seems
sometimes to represent a fondness for emphatic set phrases, sometimes a metrical convenience. Classical Latin doublings were ascribed
by Cicero to the need for fuller expression in the absence of a satisfactory conceptual vocabulary; however, we gather from Cicero's own
practice that doublings are, more than anything else, a means of giving weight, and sometimes even grandeur, to style. They are, along
with antithesis, a major figure of symmetry. Christine's *percepcion ou
percevance* derives from the practice of Nicole Doresme, who, in the
preceding century, translated some of Aristotle's works from Latin
into French and often found it convenient to pair new forms (*percepcion*) with normal French words (*percevance*). Unquestionably, *art ou
science* comes from Doresme as well and belongs to the large category
of doublings wherein the terms are not entirely synonymous but
overlap somewhat. Finally, *precede et passe*, like *percepcion ou percevance*, has a satisfying alliteration. The prevalence of doublings in
legal or administrative language, both Latin and French, is sometimes said to have been an influence on other styles in this respect,
but, of course, the motivation for legal doublings is precisely the
same love of emphasis and redundance as elsewhere.

1. Christine de Pisan, *The "Livre de la Paix" of Christine de Pisan*, ed. Charity Cannon
Willard (The Hague: Mouton, 1958), 134. Christine (*ca.* 1364–*ca.* 1430) wrote in verse
and prose and has been called a humanist for her interest in education and politics. *Ne
mais*: except.
2. For an analysis and a bibliography, see Alexandre Lorian, *Tendances stylistiques
dans la prose narrative du XVIe siècle* (Paris: Klincksieck, 1973), 65–92.

A certain legalistic air is given Christine's text by *sus dicte, cy devant*, and *c'est assavoir*. The specific function of these expressions is clearly to link this chapter opening with what has gone before. The same concern for explicitness is found in the second sentence of the chapter.

> Car si que dist Tulles, pou vallent les armes dehors se le conseil n'en est dedans, c'est assavoir la science de combatre, et à dire de mectre en ceste chose ordonnance comme elle fust moult convenable et bonne, y convendroit pourveoir par le roy, c'est assavoir qu'il ordonnast par commandement expres que tous les nobles hommes de son royaume taillez à porter armes, et ses fealx hommes liges, fussent tousjours et en tous temps tres bien garnis de hernois, bien tenus et prests à toute heure que mandé leur seroit de venir, et de ce en eust la certaineté par monstres chascum an à certain jour es contrees dont ilz seroient et fussent partis les pays par dyoceses.

The title of this thirteenth chapter of Part II of *Le Livre de la paix* is "Cy dit des manières bonnes à tenir afin que les nobles soient en tous temps exercitez aux armes." In other words, the title clearly sets the problem which is answered by *c'est assavoir qu'il ordonnast*. We have a curious mixture in this and the preceding sentence of tight reasoning (the connection made with an earlier chapter and the solution to the question being made quite specific) and seemingly idle amplification in the manner urged by medieval rhetoricians: Aristotle and Tully are really of little relevance, as is the superiority of France; *dire de mectre . . . ordonnance* and *qu'il ordonnast par commandement* are so redundant that only a rather complicated syntactic arrangement permits the use of both expressions in the same sentence. Some of the problem arises from the basic difficulties of adapting to French expression and to the habits of thinking in that language the kind of formal expository writing that can be called treatise style.

The first, most obvious contribution of a writer of treatises like Christine to Middle French style and ultimately to Rabelais' work is the taste for complex sentences. Here is Rabelais on affairs of state, deploying the same ceremonious and mildly legalistic language as Christine.

> Pantagruel, avoir [after having] entierement conquesté le pays de Dipsodie, en icelluy transporta une colonie de Utopiens en nombre de 987654-

3210 hommes, sans les femmes et petitz enfans, artizans de tous mestiers, et professeurs de toutes sciences liberales, pour ledict pays rafraichir, peupler et orner, mal autrement habité et desert en grande partie. Et les transporta non tant pour l'excessive multitude d'hommes et femmes qui estoient en Utopie multipliez comme locustes . . . non tant aussi pour la fertilité du sol, salubrité du ciel et commodité du pays de Dipsodie, que pour icelluy contenir en office et obéissance par nouveau transport de ses antiques et feaulx subjects, les quelz de toute memoire autre seigneur n'avoient congneu, recongneu, advoué ne servy, que lui . . .[3]

One senses, I think, in both Christine and Rabelais an immense pleasure in spinning out this exuberantly pleonastic style—a pleasure that may be independent of the degree of the writer's success in manipulating syntax. While it is never the case of Rabelais, I believe, there are many examples to be found in Middle French of incomplete mastery of grammar, which should not be dignified with the name of anacoluthon. The second aspect of the treatise as an informer of styles other than purely expository lies in the quest for organization above the level of the sentence: short chapters embodying a single event, like the single topic of the treatise chapter, are an important feature of Middle French narrative, and in Rabelais' work, narrative is intermittently matched and supplemented by presentation of facts and opinions in little essays. These aspects of the treatise have a considerable interest in that the genre runs from antiquity to the time when, in France, Montaigne and Descartes proposed other ways of handling the exposition of ideas.

The Greeks and Romans used the straightforward treatise as an alternative to the Platonic dialogue. This form was not so utilitarian, however, that its style was neglected; for example, one of Cicero's most widely read works, *De Officiis*, is a treatise on moral duty written with his customary care. There are, furthermore, some recurrent characteristics that commonly inform the detail of style and concern the organization of the material; sentences abound on the order of: "This subject has four parts. The first one is . . ." The general problem of classifying and ordering imposes such writing. Often quite

3. *Tiers Livre*, Chap. 1. The second sentence, which has been cut, is the longest in the first three books of Rabelais. The latter is quoted from *Oeuvres complètes* (2 vols.; Paris: Garnier, 1962).

short chapters subdivide the work for, at least theoretically, a maximum of clarity. Sometimes, as in the case of Quintilian's *Institutio Oratoria*, the chapter headings may go back to the author's copy and not be merely a scribal addition, as others probably are. In certain cases, there is no question of the chapter divisions' authenticity, since they are written into the very text, as with the *Rhetorica ad Herennium*, the second oldest extant Latin prose work.

The *Rhetorica*, which remained a classic throughout the Middle Ages, exemplifies another characteristic of chapters in the treatise style: the very short chapters allow the author fully to develop material, close off the argument, and return to the main line of discussion without there seeming to have been an unplanned digression, any more than the subcategories of an outline form are digressive. Thus seven chapters (thirteen pages) of the *Rhetorica* are devoted to examining the question of from where the author should derive his examples. (The proportions are suggested by the fact that Part IV of the *Rhetorica* consists of fifty-six chapters in ninety-one pages.) The great explicitness and peculiar neatness of this expository mode may seem fatiguing to us, who are accustomed to the more elliptical essay style of writing. But the *Rhetorica* is nothing compared with the highest example of treatise style and its adherence to outline form: Saint Thomas' *Summa Theologica* overwhelms the modern reader by its full enumeration of all parts of a question and their interrelations.[4] This bewildering excess of clarity does not, I should imagine, conceal the irrelevant and capricious leaps of argument that we sometimes find in lesser writers of treatises. Of these, the Europeans writing in the vernacular often show weaknesses that we should perhaps ascribe not only to personal failings but also to the lack of a highly developed logical tradition in the modern languages: Dante's Latin *De Vulgari Eloquentia*, for example, brings order and an odd kind of lucidity to often outlandish ideas, whereas Du Bellay's *Deffense et Illustration de la langue françoise*, also in treatise style, seems deplorably confused in expression and method, even though its content is basically more

4. Its "clarification for clarification's sake" is discussed in Erwin Panofsky, *Gothic Architecture and Scholasticism* (Latrobe, Penn.: Archabbey Press, 1951). The *Summa's* three parts contain 512 questions subdivided into 2,669 articles. The latter have reasons for and against, solutions, and answers to objections.

within our ken than is Dante's. (It is significant that Du Bellay's poems are often highly organized: prose always seems to lag behind verse.)

Despite the disproportion of Saint Thomas' work and Christine de Pisan's little chapter (the two sentences I have quoted constitute about half of it), we notice in Christine attempts at logical movement not unrelated to the great scholastic outlines of the *Summa Theologica*; authorities are invoked as part of the reasoning process, and the movement is from the general to the particular: Christine manages to progress from Aristotle to yearly demonstrations of readiness to arms. There is also a certain point where we cannot clearly distinguish between logical concern for the full exposition of various sides of a question and the medieval rhetorical doctrine of amplification.[5] Panofsky's comparison between scholastic method and Gothic architecture is interestingly ambiguous in this respect, since Gothic looked to its later detractors like an excess of ornamentation—the latter being exactly what rhetoric sought. Probably the best way of analyzing Christine's chapter opening is as a decorative exordium in the form of a general maxim or piece of wisdom. Later on, her attempts at full articulation (*matiere sus dicte, fait cy devant touchié*) and definition (*c'est assavoir . . .*) are merely redundancies striving to achieve the condition of logical stages. The title of her chapter is answered at the end of the second passage quoted, and everything intervening is merely filler. The elaborateness of the sentence is a kind of pretense at complex thought, attractive in places but rather unsatisfying.

There also existed in antiquity and in European literature a third expository mode, which, though called a dialogue, resembled Socratic colloquy not at all, for one person actually spoke uninterrupted, and the dialogue situation was scarcely developed. Such were Cicero's dialogues, based for their form on the lost ones of Aristotle. Actually, all dialogue has in potential the occasions for rather formal and uninterrupted speeches, such as Socrates' account of Diotima in the *Symposium*, and in the special form of Aristotle and Cicero's dialogues, this merely increased. Boethius' *Consolation* with its personification of philosophy transposed the speechifying dialogue into a

---

5. Medieval amplification was lengthening, whereas classical amplification was heightening or intensifying.

dreamlike or symbolic setting, suggesting a dialogue of prosopopeias or allegorical figures. The concern for stylistic effectiveness, for an oratorical note even, made this kind of dialogue a happy pretext for those whose rhetorical abilities could not always, or even at times, be exercised in political speeches or theatrical form. Alain Chartier's *Quadrilogue invectif* (1422), with its harangues on the part of France, Le Peuple, Le Chevalier, and Le Clergé is just such a work—political, hortatory, and commonly said to be the first monument of French *éloquence*.[6]

Chartier worked out basic principles of sentence structure, which, refined, were to serve many writers of speeches after him.

> Comme les hautes dignitez des seigneuries soient establies soubz la divine et infinie puissance qui les eslieve en florissant, en prosperité et en glorieuse renommee, il est a croire et tenir fermement que, ainsi que leurs commencemens et leurs accroissances sont maintenues et adrecees par la divine providence, ainsi est leur fin et leur detriment par sentence donnee ou halt conseil de la souveraine sapience, qui les aucuns verse du hault trosne de imperial seigneurie en la basse fosse de servitude et de magnificence en ruine et fait des vainqueurs vaincus et ceulz obeir par crainte qui commander souloient par autorité. Mais quant doulce misericorde estremeslee avecques droituriere justice donne sur les princes et sur le peuple le decret de plus attrempee punicion, l'orgeuil de trop oultrecuidié povoir qui se descognoist est rabaissié par puissance ennemie, la superfluité des biens mondains, qui est nourrice de sedicions et de murmure, est chastiee par sa mesmes nourreture et l'ingratitude des dons de Dieu est punie sur les hommes par sustracion de sa grace que aprés bon amendement et loiale correction a renvoyé et redrecié les seigneuries et les peuples en parfaitte paix et restitucion de leur disposicion premiere.[7]

The comparative clauses are a major device in classicizing oratory, and the movement of the whole is directed by the traditional principles of similarity and antithesis. Chartier's well-developed sentence forms, or periods, consist essentially of an introductory subordinate clause, two or three parallel main clauses, and a concluding subordinate section. This arrangement provides the clear articulation into

---

6. Alain Chartier (*ca.* 1390–*ca.* 1440) was a diplomat, the author of *La Belle Dame sans merci* (1424), and an early humanist in respect to his interest in Latin oratorical prose.

7. Alain Chartier, *Le Quadrilogue invectif*, ed. E. Droz (Paris: Champion, 1950), 1–2. *Oultrecuidé*: overweening; *se descognoist*: does not know its place; *ingratitude des dons de Dieu*: ingratitude toward God for his gifts.

principal and subsidiary ideas associated with persuasive passages in oratory. Such an impression is intensified for the reader in that Chartier uses the normal modern word order, the one which seems the most direct to us and which may already have been the customary spoken one of Chartier's day. However, the phrases, which seem to be much the same from both the grammatical and intonational point of view, tend to be longer than what oral delivery can regularly accommodate. The importance of polysyllabic words is matched by the dominance of phrases whose average length is twelve syllables. This fact brings us to an interesting question: long sentences are usually associated with oratory, but there is a length beyond which the elements of the sentence cannot go, if they are to be readily spoken. A comparison with a letter in Rabelais shows the latter's phrases to average only nine syllables, whereas a passage from an *oraison funèbre* of Bossuet's, a work we know to have been delivered before a large audience, indicates that Bossuet's average phrase length is just under seven syllables. We must conclude that Chartier was giving an impression in the *Quadrilogue invectif* of the harmony of elegant proportions and division of the whole—concinnity—such as he gathered it from classical speeches; the sentences have the look of it without truly conforming to declamatory exigencies. The gradual adjustment of prose to oral delivery is one of the important developments in French style in the earlier centuries.

To illustrate, by contrast, the form true oratorical phrasing may take, here is the exordium, or opening, of Gargantua's grand address to the defeated in the *guerre picrocholine*: "Nos peres, ayeulx et ancestres de toute memoyre ont esté de ce sens et ceste nature, que, des batailles par eulx consommées, ont, pour signe memorial des triumphes et victoires, plus voluntiers erigé trophées et monumens es cueurs des vaincus par grace, que, es terres par eulx conquestées, par architecture: car plus estimoient la vive souvenance des humains, acquise par liberalité, que la mute inscription des arcs, colonmes et pyramides, subjects es calamitez de l'air et envie d'un chascun" (*Gargantua* 50). The fourteen phrase divisions are quite varied in length; Rabelais, furthermore, likes the elegant suspension effect of prepositional expressions interrupting the syntactic flow, a device of the complicated treatise style. These are elements of style we shall be meeting again, and Chartier's sentences seem rather routinely constructed in comparison. Basically, the rhetorical structure in both the Chartier and the Rabelais consists of an antithesis or analogy being worked out; this kind of prolonged tension is a favorite syntactico-stylistic pattern in elaborate rhetorical writing, and its origins are to be found in the classical use of analogy as both ornament and logical device. Chartier's duller and less intricate sentence structure seems to arise from an external, artificial handling of analogy, whereas Rabelais' antithesis appears to be essential to the train of thought; such would seem to be a reason for the greater rhythmic tightness and elegance in the Rabelais.

I have dwelt on expository and oratorical writing in Middle French rather than on the narrative writers, since the former seems to me to represent the more sophisticated stylistic side of late medieval literature. Although their success is not unqualified, Christine and Chartier show the emergence of a Latinizing, humanist ideal of prose, both on the level of the individual sentence and on that of larger formal organization. Rabelais is much more the heir of the treatise and dialogue styles than of fifteenth-century fiction.

Hypotaxis and grandiloquent delivery have only a limited compatibility. While all Rabelais may be comfortably read aloud, thanks to his skillful handling of phrase lengths, his work contains many periods that are not conceived of primarily as oratory but that seek rather to employ hypotaxis in the most effective manner. A number of sentence types emerge from the confluence of Latin and Middle and Modern French tendencies in the early sixteenth century, and their combinations make for an elegantly varied texture. The important thing about these sentence types is that, unlike Christine de Pisan's periods, their shape is clear and readily grasped, their articulations well-defined, their concinnity striking.

We have just seen a passage based on the rather-this-than-that kind of comparative formula; its bipartite character is only partly manifested in sentence structure, but there are many other periods in which the working out of an analogy, condition, cause, result, con-

sists of parallel clauses, a principal and a subordinate one. There
is suspension of sense in these constructions, the characteristic of
the classical period. Here is the opening of Grandgousier's letter to
Gargantua.

> La ferveur de tes estudes requeroit que de long temps ne te revocasse de
> cestuy philosophicque repous, sy la confiance de noz amys et anciens con-
> federez n'eust de present frustré la seureté de ma vieillesse. Mais, puis que
> telle est ceste fatale destinée que par iceulx soye inquieté es quelz plus je
> me repousoye, force me est de te rappeler au subside des gens et biens qui
> te sont par droict naturel affiez.
>
> Car, ainsi comme debiles sont les armes au dehors si le conseil n'est en la
> maison, aussi vaine est l'estude et le conseil inutile qui en temps oportun
> par vertus n'est executé et à son effect reduict. (*Gargantua* 29)

Here we can observe not only the general correspondence in sense of
the clauses but also parallel details of vocabulary: *repous/seureté; fatale
destinée/force . . . me est; debiles/vaine.* The notion of structuring prose
with two parallel, sometimes antithetical, clauses belongs to the oldest theory of artistic prose, that named for the Sophist Gorgias, a contemporary of Plato's. Gorgian prose risks being rather mannered, and
here Rabelais compounds its artificiality by using abstract words (*fer-
veur, repous, confiance*) instead of concrete ones or personal pronouns
as the subject and object of verbs; this is a kind of synecdoche—the
state of mind representing the person—to be found in Latin and especially Ciceronian rhetoric and which, in sixteenth- and seventeenth-century French, belongs to high style. The passage quoted
above is appropriately followed by clipped antitheses, preserving the
formal, highly wrought manner: "Ma deliberation n'est de provoc-
quer, ains de apaiser; d'assaillir, mais defendre; de conquester, mais
de guarder . . ."

The bipartite period of the type we have just seen, composed of a
subordinate protasis followed by the main clause or apodosis, affords
an example of how the vernacular can approximate the form of the
Latin period, which is to postpone the primary nucleus of the sentence until near the end. The at least limited suspension of sense and
the possibility of parallelism or antithesis explain the frequency of
such sentences in elaborate writing. Conditional sentences in particular enjoy a favor quite incommensurate with any strict logical neces-

sity for them; *if* expressions are created for the sake of suspensional effects.

There exists one kind of period characteristic of the modern languages with the principle subject and verb in the middle. Our example from Gargantua's speech to the defeated illustrates how in such a period the central section (*ont . . . erigé*) may be technically subordinate but nevertheless bears the main weight of sense, as indeed is normal in sentences beginning with expressions like *it seems that.* Otherwise, the structure consists of a main clause introduced and followed by subordinate ones as in this passage from a letter, this time Gargantua's to Pantagruel: "Entre les dons, graces et prerogatives desquelles le souverain plasmateur, Dieu tout puissant, a endouayré et aorné l'humaine nature à son commencement, celle me semble singuliere et excellente par laquelle elle peut, en estat mortel, acquerir une espece de immortalité, et, en decours de vie transitoire, perpetuer son nom et sa semence. Ce que est faict par lignée yssue de nous en mariage legitime" (*Pantagruel* 8). This passage is an excellent example of prose that does not flow but rather achieves its effect through carefully and irregularly spaced pauses, putting words and expressions in relief. The final sentence, so closely linked in sense to what precedes it that its grammatical independence is a moot point, illustrates the ambiguity we sometimes encounter in Latin and French prose, wherein the exact extent of a period can be uncertain: the relative pronouns, when used as sentence connectives, seem to create superperiods.

The varied phrase groups in our example—so different from the symmetrical ones of some later writers—are reflected in a specific case of irregularity that is not uncharacteristic of sixteenth-century prose: the main clause is shorter than the preceding and following ones. The importance presupposed by its syntactic role is belied by its slightness; the weak predicate nominative contrasts with the multiple subordinate active verbs, and nothing shows better the sixteenth-century obsession with hypotaxis than this unbalanced use of it. If we rewrite the sentence somewhat, we can see perhaps better the function of Rabelais' grammar: "Entre les dons, graces, et prerogatives dont Dieu a endouayré l'humaine nature, la lignée des enfans issue de nous nous permet d'acquerir une espece d'immortalité." This sentence obviously demands that its statement be continued in further sentences; it initiates a series of *raisonnements*. Rabelais' period, however, is self-contained; its information is not information at all but elegant phrases referring to what one already knows more or less. While it may seem that the most important things are being said in subordinate clauses, the fact of being relegated to a relative or adverbial clause assures that such material cannot lead on to a new step in a ratiocinative process. Rabelais' editors frequently put sentences like this one into paragraphs by themselves: they are complete. The passing of judgment suffuses the whole sentence with an affirmative mood, and we are merely to contemplate the rightness of the familiar state of things. This might be called an epideictic period, after that type of rhetoric whose aim is to praise rather than to deduce; it is opposed to the argumentative judicial or deliberative functions of complex syntax.

Another peculiarly sixteenth-century period, the sentence in which the main verb comes early and the bulk of the material later, can be seen in the same letter in *Pantagruel.*

> Non doncques sans juste et equitable cause je rends graces à Dieu, mon conservateur, de ce qu'il m'a donné povoir veoir mon antiquité chanue refleurir en ta jeunesse; car, quand, par le plaisir de luy, qui tout regist et modere, mon ame laissera ceste habitation humaine, je ne me reputeray totallement mourir, ains passer d'un lieu en aultre, attendu que, en toy et par toy, je demeure en mon image visible en ce monde, vivant, voyant, et conversant entre gens de honneur et mes amys, comme je souloys, laquelle mienne conversation a esté, moyennant l'ayde et grace divine, non sans péché, je le confesse (car nous pechons tous, et continuellement requerons à Dieu qu'il efface noz pechez), mais sans reproche.

Here we have an extreme case of breaking the sentence into small rhythmic units, a practice joined with a taste for massive forms or juxtapositions of grammatical tool words: *non doncques sans*; *car, quand, par*; *moyennant*; *laquelle mienne conversation*. The first two examples recall Latin periodic style and illustrate the grandeur that was sometimes ascribed in antiquity to weighty opening expressions such as *quandoquidem*. This and our preceding quotation also show the great beauty that could be derived from the use of *lequel*, so widespread in Middle French. Interestingly enough, the clatter of *qui* and *que*,

which Flaubert so deplored in earlier French prose, is barely perceptible in many of Rabelais' long sentences: the frequent syntactic and
intonational breaks, along with ample use of *lequel*, seem to diminish
the obtrusiveness of the commoner relative pronouns.

Somewhat concealed by the frequent pauses in the sentence is the
fact that after *attendu que* . . ., the second clause (*de ce qu'il* . . .) is re-
stated and leads by an almost incidental word (*conversant*) into a
clause (*laquelle mienne conversation* . . .) quite distant in meaning from
the general sense of the whole. The *laquelle mienne* . . . exemplifies
additive structure, in which tangential movement can take the sense
in any direction the author chooses. The notion of a subordinate
clause as contributing directly to the main one is abandoned, and development is grammatical but not logical. The terms "loose" and "descending" have been used of this kind of sentence structure because
it does not build toward a semantic and grammatical culmination.[8]
However, like the period we just examined above, this one is characteristic of sixteenth-century prose in that the author seems to aim at a
unit which is a whole discourse in itself; there is no thrust toward the
next sentence. One might contrast the conception of this sentence
with that of the well-developed Ciceronian period—ratiocinative, deliberative, or contentious—in which the main verb, placed at the end,
informs the whole, creates a vigorous climax, and points to the next
sentence.

Finally, in our enumeration of basic structures in complex sentences—a series of variations that is relevant to the analysis of writers
as different as Bossuet and Proust—we encounter the sentence in
which the main clause is comparatively short and comes at the end.
In the following period, still from Gargantua's letter, the main clause
is double, each section being brief: "Mais, encores que mon feu pere,
de bonne memoire, Grandgousier, eust adonne tout son estude à ce
que je proffitasse en toute perfection et sçavoir politique, et que mon
labeur et estude correspondit très bien, voire encores oultrepassat
son desir, toutefoys, comme tu peulx bien entendre, le temps n'estoit
tant idoine ne commode es lettres comme est de present, et n'avoys

---

8. See Aldo Scaglione, *The Classical Theory of Composition from its Origins to the Present: A Historical Survey* (Chapel Hill: University of North Carolina Press, 1972), 174.

copie de telz precepteurs comme tu as eu." We have already seen one classical type of period in French, wherein the sentence begins with a subordinate clause opening with *si, quand,* or something of the sort. There, however, the principal and subordinate clauses are single in number and parallel, and ideally would have the same structure and length. Here, on the other hand, the introductory clause leads into other subordinates; there is a leisurely development with a number of pauses before the principle clause is reached. This is a distinctly classicizing period characterized by amply suspenseful grammar and sense; one is constantly impelled forward in search for a point of repose; there is a dynamism absent from the loose or descending sentence.

In the detail of the clause much variation is possible in Rabelais: modern syntactic arrangements were quite customary in his time, and he makes ample use of them; but, in addition, he draws generously on the ones Middle French inherited from Old French and which doubtless had a certain Latin feeling for him, even when no precise equivalent is normally found in Latin prose. Subject and verb can be separated, and even, rarely, a pronoun subject is found at some distance from the verb: "Il en cette façon son tonneau tempestait pour, entre ce peuple tant fervent et occupé, n'estre veu seul cessateur et ocieux." The separation of infinitive and *pour* is occasionally found as well, but the finite transitive verb following its direct object, as here, is rare in Rabelais; the sentence just quoted comes from the prologue to the *Tiers Livre,* which contains many exceptional effects of style. Generally speaking, infinitives can precede or follow at a distance the auxiliary verb, as can the past participle: "Doncques merveille n'est si le roy Grandgousier, mon maistre, est à ta furieuse et hostile venue saisy de grand desplaisir et perturbé en son entendement. Merveille seroit si ne l'avoient esmeu les excès incomparables qui en ses terres et subjectz ont esté par toy et tes gens commis, esquelz n'a esté obmis exemple aulcun d'inhumanité, ce que luy est tant grief de soy, par la cordiale affection de laquelle tousjours a chery ses subjectz, que a mortel homme plus estre ne sçaroit" (*Gargantua* 31). This is from Ulrich Gallet's address in classical oration form, which makes the hyperbaton, or displacement of words, especially appropriate. The principle underlying all the syntactic arrangements I have been detailing is, of course, suspension, in small units as well as in the larger form of the period. This is why a device that is not especially Latinate, if it involves a suspended grammatical relation, fits in with the classicizing effects. (Such, for example, is the separation of auxiliary verb and past participle.)

While the classical orators recognized the existence in the fully developed formal speech of a section called the narrative, we associate artful devices of language perhaps more with expositional oratory than the recounting of events in sequence. It is nevertheless remarkable that Rabelais obtains impressive effects with fairly ordinary narrative constructions. Here is the participial sentence connective (*Quod rex audiens . . . Vespere igitur veniente . . .*) that is so frequent and monotonous in medieval Latin and French narration: "Les lettres dictées et signées, Grandgousier ordonna que Ulrich Gallet, maistre de ses requestes, homme saige et discret, duquel en divers et contencieux affaires il avoit esprouvé la vertu et bon advis, allast devers Picrochole pour luy remonstrer ce que par eux avoit esté decreté." The formality of the absolute participial construction is underscored and matched by the solemn and ceremonious appositions and relative clause modifying Gallet's name. The absolute construction is often consonant with the public, official, and even kingly character of the subject at hand. Much the same is true of other sentence connectives which contribute to the overall stately movement of the prose: "A tant son pere aperceut que vrayement il estudoit très bien et y mettoit tout son temps, toutesfoys qu'en rien ne prouffitoit et, que pis est, en devenoit fou, niays, tout resveux et rassoté. De quoy se complaignant à Don Philippe des Marays, vice roy de Papeligosse, entendit que mieulx luy vauldroit rien aprendre, car leur sçavoir n'estoit que besterie et leur sapience n'estoit que moufles, abastardissant les bons et nobles esperitz et corrompent toute fleur de jeunesse" (*Gargantua* 15). As we see here, the use of reported speech in Rabelais has an especially important role. It may be denser than direct speech, of course, but straightforward reported speech is exceedingly monotonous with its constant repetitions of conjunctions: *dire que . . . que . . . que*. Rabelais' solution to the problem is to summarize at the same time that he reports speech, adding dignity and weight to it by both lexical and syntactic means, such as the infinitive clause after verbs like *dire*, the use of the dense contractions *es* and *on*, and the choice of *ou* for *en le*. Furthermore, this summarized speech blends with the narrative period and its wealth of logical and temporal indications. The sophistication of Rabelais' device is suggested by the fact that nineteenth-century novelists use it. Rabelais' way of mingling narrative and discourse is a synthetic style that can encompass the essential of each; here orders are reported: "Puis ceulx qui là estoient mors il feist honorablement inhumer en la vallee des Noirettes et au camp de Bruslevieille. Les navrés il feist panser et traicter en son grand nosocome . . ." (*Gargantua* 51). The unusual construction object-subject-verb, which we have called generally unworkable in French, shows the characteristic concern for variation in sentence structure in passages mingling narrative and summarized speech.

The expressive superiority of the prose in the preceding examples over prose contemporary with it lies in a very high sense of order excluding idle repetition and conveying a dignified pomp. While there is less antithesis and fewer conditional sentences in the narrative proper than in expository passages, the feeling of reasoned discourse obtains in the frequent, typical division of the sentence into a main clause and a subordinate one with *car*, with *de sorte que*, or with a *que*-clause after *tellement*, *tant*, or *si*: "Mais accidens bien divers leurs en advindrent, car à tous survint au corps une enfleure très horrible"; "Es aultres tant croissoit le nez qu'il sembloit la fleute d'un alambic" (*Pantagruel* 1). These sentences with result clauses form one of the most characteristic types of sixteenth-century narrative texture. Temporal clauses and absolute participial constructions are the other common features of narrative hypotaxis, which, if articulated as clearly as in Rabelais, conveys lucidity and order.

In Rabelais' particular historical linguistic situation, he had an exceptionally large variety of sentence forms at his disposal. These were not some impersonal creation of the mass of French speakers but depended on the elaboration of syntax by writers and on Rabelais' seeing the possibilities in the general sixteenth-century attitude toward style as well as in the devisings of his predecessors. The classical principle of variation in periodic structure had to be actualized and not simply believed in, and Rabelais' consciousness of sentence patterns was unique in the domain of French vernacular humanism.

If we think of style as consisting primarily in lexico-semantic choices, then not only do Rabelais' word order and periodic form seem imposed at a secondary stage on his language, but the sound of the words appears to be a tertiary consideration. While this oversimplifies the act of choice, the sporadic occurrence in Rabelais' prose of certain sound figures suggests, as does the same phenomenon in classical writings, that when it is convenient, rime, alliteration, and so forth are brought into the stylistic texture, but that primary choices of wording are not governed by these figures. They are, in any case, perhaps the most remote effect from our esthetic expectations and need some brief commentary.

Here is a passage from the oration made by Ulrich Gallet in *Gargantua* 31: "Quelle furie doncques te esmeut maintenant, toute alliance brisée, toute amitié conculquée, tout droict trespassé, envahir hostilement ses terres, sans en rien avoir esté par luy ny les sien endommagé, irrité ny provocqué? Où est foy? Où est loy? Où est raison? Où est humanité? Où est crainte de Dieu? Cuyde tu ces oultraignes estre recellés es esperitz eternelz et au Dieu souverain qui est juste retributeur de nos entreprinses?" The brief exclamatory phrases are of the kind called *commata* in rhetorical theory and form a customary, intermittent alternance with periods; they are strictly in accordance with the Ciceronian theory of oratorical style. The most striking feature of the passage, however, is the repetition of sounds: the consonance of grammatical endings known as homeoteleuthon (*brisée, conculquée, trespassé*), the rime (*foy, loy*), and the more subtle interplay of sounds in *estre recellés es esperitz eternelz*. It would be ingenuous to imagine these repetitions to be accidental, or silly by intention; there is no place where one needs more to be on guard against anachronistic interpretations, seeing "satire" in whatever one dislikes.

There is a long tradition, classical and medieval, of sound plays in prose—originating, of course, at a time when such effects were not a regular part of verse—and though they may strike the modern

number of striking rimes or puns in the prologue to the *Tiers Livre*,
generally one of the densest examples of Rabelais' rhetoric.

> Je pareillement, quoy que soys hors d'effroy, ne suis toutesfoys hors
> d'esmoy, de moy voyant n'estre faict aulcun pris digne d'œuvre . . .

> . . . que je n'entre en l'opinion du bon Heraclitus, affermant guerre estre
> de tous biens pere: et croye que guerre soit en Latin dicte belle non par
> antiphrase, ainsi comme ont cuydé certains repetasseurs de vieilles fer-
> railles latines parce qu'en guerre gueres de beaulté ne voyoient . . .[14]

> Par doncques n'estre adscript et en ranc mis des nostres en partie offen-
> sive, qui me ont estimé trop imbecille et impotent, de l'autre, qui est defen-
> sive, n'estre employé aulcunement, feust-ce portant hotte, cachant crotte,
> ployant rotte, ou cassant motte, tout m'estoit indifferent . . .

If we read this in a simplistic modern context of esthetics of prose, we
will see only a kind of silly joke. But we must see what elegance it has
in common with Saint Augustine's description of his youth, which is
not usually considered comic: "Quid enim miserius misero non mise-
rante se ipsum et flente Didonis mortem, quae fiebat amando Ænean,
non flente autem mortem suam, quae fiebat non amando te, deus,
lumen cordis mei et panis oris intus animae meae et virtus maritans
mentem meam . . . et haec non flebam, et flebam Didonem extinctam
ferroque extrema secutam, sequens ipse extrema condita tua relicto
te, et terra iens in terram: et si prohiberer ea legere, dolerem, quia
non legerem quod dolerem" (*Confessions*, I, 13).[15] Saint Augustine's
florid prose carries conviction; the loftiness of the language guaran-
tees the author's capacity of judgment. Rabelais' general aim is not
simply to amuse the reader, but to control, if necessary overwhelm,
him with eloquence. We should remember the way plays on sound
and words often function in Shakespeare: they represent a competi-
tion in which one character tries to outwit and silence another. A superior gift for the manipulation of words is not always prized today—

----

14. The etymology of *bellum* from *bellus* by antiphrasis is, for classical and hence humanist grammarians, a perfectly reasonable and not altogether rare type of derivation.

15. "What is more wretched than a wretch that does not pity his own wretchedness,
than a man who laments the death of Dido, which came about by loving Aeneas, and
does not lament his own death, which came about by not loving thee, O God, light of
my heart and bread of the inward mouth of my soul and virtue marrying my soul."

we are afraid that *verborum ac rerum copia*, in Erasmus' phrase, really means *copia verborum et rerum egestas*—but in a culture so dominated by rhetoric as that of the sixteenth century, the person who could discourse with brilliant embellishments on Diogenes and antiquity had achieved a high version of the humanist ideal.

The organization of Rabelais' well-thought-out prose into chapters is one of his greatest achievements; he had no models in prose fiction for the sophisticated shaping of his material. While he used the customary short sections, he also borrowed the brief chapters of expository writing to arrange his subject into small, discrete units, since he tells numerous more or less self-contained anecdotes and employs a frankly expository method in presenting Pantagruel's origins, life at the Abbey of Thélème, the significance of Gargantua's blue and white clothes, and so forth. The highly thematic character of his narrative (the episode of the *écolier du Limousin*, for example, has a purely thematic interest and no cumulative plot significance) favors the use of small building blocks, which are further differentiated in many cases by stylistic elements. Sometimes it is a peculiar rhetorical device or a cluster of them that sets off a chapter; sometimes a fictional technique like the use or avoidance of dialogue. Rabelais seems, in any case, to have had the utmost awareness of elements of design in the juxtaposition of dissimilar techniques.

Pantagruel is less elaborately composed than *Gargantua* but still has many of the same kinds of stylistic variations. Chapters 1 and 2 feature enumerations, including a genealogy, sentences with very unusual numbers of subordinate clauses, and an expository movement with organization by topic sentences. The first words spoken in *Pantagruel* are puns and jokes at the end of Chapter 2. In Chapter 3, initial hypophora (the author raises a question and answers it) is followed by Gargantua's speeches, first one in deliberative rhetoric, then a series of *carpe diem* topoi. Chapter 4, without speech, contains authorial interventions, occupatio ("I shall not speak of . . ."), hypophora, and extensive hypotaxis. Chapter 5, finally, enumerates the universities of France and their characteristics. Except for Chapter 7, which has the peculiarity of being largely a list, Chapters 6–13 contain special kinds of speech. The other chapters include the episode of the *écolier du Limousin*, the letter from Gargantua, in elaborate expository style, Panurge's speaking in various languages, and Pantagruel's Solomonic first deed as an adult hero: with complex, logically formed sentences devoid of meaning, litigants plead before him, and, in the same style, but enhanced with legal touches, he renders his judgment.

Chapter 16 is the first Panurge chapter with no dialogue; in 17 the authorial persona, Alcofribas, comes forward and recounts, with dialogue, an anecdote about Panurge. Chapters 18–20 return to the linguistic theme and present the disputation in sign language, which involves highly complicated descriptions. In Chapter 23 there is a traditional kind of learned anecdote: the etiological story in which a present phenomenon is accounted for through origins in a distant past event. The war chapters contain a variety of stories and a good deal of dialogue, the most interesting sections for style being the epic invocation, the reformist prayer of Pantagruel, and the Homeric single combat, with the traditional sanguinary detail (end of 28, 29); such imitative style is fairly uncommon. The Homeric *nekuia*, or descent to hell (Chapter 30), is enumeratory, partially in the form of a list. Chapters 32–34 emphasize the authorial first-person, Alcofribas. And homeoteleuthonic lists, puns, and invented words make a splendid conclusion. Rabelais comes back in the last chapters to the theme of Pantagruel as giant, so that, even though it is not quite so fine a work as *Gargantua*, *Pantagruel* certainly shows a great stylistic ingenuity and care for design.

The prologue to *Gargantua* is so different from the relatively simple one to *Pantagruel* that we are immediately aware of the greater invention of the later work. The massive opening sentence ends with the verb and its complement *Silenes*; *Silenes*, followed by a verb, opens the second and very lengthy period. So unusual a pattern for the eye and ear gives way to extraordinary lists before the narrator enters into the invitation to read his book for its marrow. The greater wit and ease of the narrator of Rabelais' second book is shown directly by his scoffing at allegory, which the reader was preparing at his promptings to find in *Gargantua*. "Croiez vous en vostre foy qu'oncques Ho-mere, escrivent *l'Iliade* et *Odyssée*, pensast es allegories lesquelles de luy ont calfreté Plutarche, Heraclides Ponticq, Eustatie, Phornute, et ce que d'iceulx Politian a desrobé?" This is like some imperfect form of logic in which we are asked to look for hidden meanings or to reject systematic allegory; in fact, the reader can neither ignore the religious and political allusions in *Gargantua* nor find a sustained allegory. And if Rabelais did indeed deny the validity of the customary allegorizing of the *Odyssey* (which was normally printed with it until the eighteenth century, so generally was the allegory accepted), he, like most contemporaries, certainly regarded the Homeric poems as laudative, exemplary, and didactic. But the point is, of course, that the alternatives of no allegory or total allegory are impossible. This dilemma is designed to form a symmetry with the last chapter of *Gargantua*, in which we are invited to see the poetic "enigme en prophetie" as dealing with either the evangelical movement or a game of tennis, whereas, in fact, both interpretations have an intermittent validity.

The narrative persona is much in evidence in the opening chapter of *Gargantua*, as he participates in the investigation of the giant's origins and offers for our inspection an ancient poem imperfectly preserved. Like the list, the series of scholarly references, the concluding "Enigme," the letter, the classical oration, this poem written on elm bark shows Rabelais' increasing sense of the possibilities of the document, in the form of language taken from life or lying outside the limits of narrative style. (The newspaper clippings used by various modern novelists are of the same order.) Chapter 3 is a short medical treatise in the manner of the compilations (Gellius' *Noctes Atticae*, Erasmus' *Adages*, Macrobius' *Saturnalia*) that Rabelais seems especially to have enjoyed reading.

In the account of the tripe eating in Chapter 4 we find a kind of heroicomic tone introduced by the rare and ostentatious figure called anadiplosis: "L'occasion et maniere comment Gargamelle enfanta fut telle, et, si ne le croyez, le fondement vous escappe! Le fondement luy escappoit une après dinée, le iije de febvrier, par trop avoir mangé de gaudebillaux. Gaudebillaux sont grasses tripes de coiraux. Coiraux sont beufz engressez à la creche et prez guimaulx. Prez guimaulx sont . . ." Much verbal play occurs during the first dialogue of *Gargantua*, which occupies all Chapter 5, "Les Propos des bien yvres." Generally we find less of the miraculous-legendary in the account of Gargantua's birth than of Pantagruel's, and a greater presence of the narrator. The obstetric Chapter 6 contains the narrator's digression on strange births, which we must not overlook as simply being a somewhat loosely connected passage: digression was recognized as an ornament in medieval rhetoric (though more in the form of description), and it is a capital device for characterizing a narrator, that of *Gargantua* being highly learned in out-of-the-way matters. Chapters 9 and 10 will be given over to a digression on color symbolism. It is important, in any case, to emphasize that *Gargantua* is not written in some impersonal mode but is recounted by a persona as versed in the secrets of elegant style as in everything else.

Rabelais' narrator is no buffoon, as some try to make him out to be. Here, just before an authorial intervention, is an example (from Chapter 7) of beautiful sentence liaison, progressively elaborated syntax, and carefully devised variations in phrase length.

> En cest estat passa jusques à un an et dix moys, onquel temps, par le conseil des medecins, on commenca le porter, et fut faicte une belle charrette à beufs par l'invention de Jehan Denyau. Dedans icelle on le pourmenoit par cy par là joyeusement; et le faisoit bon veoir, car il portoit bonne troigne et avoit presque dix et huyt mentons; et ne crioit que bien peu; mais il se conchioit à toutes heures, car il estoit merveilleusement phlegmaticque des fesses, tant de sa complexion naturelle que de la disposition accidentale que luy estoit advenue par trop humer de purée septembrale. Et n'en humoyt goutte sans cause, car, s'il advenoit qu'il feust despit, courroussé, fasché ou marry, s'il trepignoyt, s'il pleuroit, s'il crioit, lui apportant à boyre l'on le remettoit en nature, et soubdain demouroit coy et joyeulx.

The narrator's intervention continues in the same vein with the added grace of anastrophe.

> Une de ses gouvernantes m'a dict, jurant sa fy, que de ce faire il estoit tant coustumier, qu'au seul son des pinthes et flaccons il entroit en ecstase, comme s'il goustoit les joyes de paradis. En sorte qu'elles, considerans ceste complexion divine, pour le resjouir, au matin, faisoient davant luy sonner des verres avecques un cousteau, ou des flaccons avecques leur

toupon, ou des pinthes avecques leur couvercle, auquel son il s'esguayoit, il tressailloit, et luy mesmes se bressoit en dodelinant de la teste, monochordisant des doigtz et barytonant du cul.

In these paragraphs, we see the elegant way *cest, icelle, n'en, de ce faire, en sorte que* provide a continuous movement from one period to the next, and the *onquel temps* and *auquel son* serve a similar inner function. Within each period, the lucid, rationalized character of the narrative is stressed by the result clauses with *tant* and the nexuses *sans cause, car, si*, and *en sorte que . . . considerans . . . pour*. With these devices and the varying arrangement of the elements of the period, Rabelais creates that effect of high syntactic decorum so frequently encountered in his work. It is the dignified sentence structure here and elsewhere in Rabelais that holds together the shifting, dissonant classes of words; the continuously strong and well-defined periods actually emphasize, with their many pauses, the varying nature and sonorities of unusual words, while joining them together. The sustained eloquence of the sentence permits the characteristic passage back and forth from the comic-gigantic to the serious-humanist, although, in regard to the latter, of course, Rabelais tends to be a laughing philosopher like Democritus. Essentially, all this linguistic paradox—the familiar word in a sentence learned in structure, the treating of rare words on the same plane as ordinary ones—contributes both to our image of the narrative characters and our sense of a narratorial personality.

The heroicomic tone so frequent in *Gargantua* is made of grandeur in sentence form, together with a kind of detail in vocabulary the rhetorical mold had not been made to accommodate. The peculiar thing about heroicomic effects in Rabelais is that they result from the depiction of giants, and great stature is identified with the heroic from the *Iliad* on. This is why, unlike the neoclassical mock epic, for example, *Le Lutrin* or *The Rape of the Lock*, which, as Boileau pointed out, enlarges the mediocre, Rabelais' fantasy of giants has nothing, in its essentials, to do with satire; this is why the lofty and comic so readily commingle. His two giants are not even ordinary men with their failings writ large; Gargantua and Pantagruel as adults are even-tempered and elevated in thought.

The enumeration of set expressions in Chapter 11 is one of Rabelais' most surprising plays on language and very near to the imaginings of Ionesco. Many of the expressions are no longer current, but enough are, so that one seizes immediately the bizarre mechanism by which, in juxtaposition, the literal sense obtrudes in *songe creux, cracher au bassin, faire le sucré, retourner à ses moutons, tirer les vers du nez,* and so forth. Anecdotes follow; then the discussion of Gargantua's education, of which we have seen a part; and finally his departure for Paris. Carefully worked out individual characteristics are to be found in each chapter. For example, the journey to Paris, in which monstrosity and gigantism suddenly become important once more, is built around an etymology of *Beauce;* like the etiological story, this is a traditional form of rhetorical embellishment. The great speech of Janotus de Bragmardo in Chapter 19 is preceded and followed by chapters with limited or no direct discourse, the better to set it off. The speech itself, an attempt to record the inchoate and shapeless, is one of the most amazing things in Rabelais, when one reflects that before the early seventeenth century in France, in the highly rhetorical culture of the renaissance, the language of writing was dissociated from speech, and certainly from pathological (if only drunken) forms of it. This is not merely the medieval nonsense style, as in the *coq-à-l'âne* chapter in *Pantagruel.* Chapters 21–24 are a total contrast, bare largely of discourse and constituting enormous enumerations on different grammatical levels (noun, verb, sentence). Except for the day as planned by the sophist or theologian, the interest of these chapters is highly intellectual and appeals to the same fascination for great expanses of detail that Rabelais obviously felt with Pliny the Elder's natural history, the *Digesta,* or those other works recurrent in footnotes to Rabelais, which it is important to look at in order to see the kind of material that stimulated him.

The war is a much more complexly depicted one than the campaign against the Dipsodes in *Pantagruel,* and the chapters are far more differentiated. The one introducing Frère Jean is a perfect example of using a series of special effects to draw attention to its importance. The opening sentence has an unusual movement: "Tant feirent et tracasserent, pillant et larronnant, qu'ilz arriverent à Seuillé, et

detrousserent hommes et femmes, et prindrent ce qu'ilz peurent
. . ." (Chapter 27). Much is made of monks' Latin, since their only
thoughts are ones that can be formulated by using bits of the missal.
Frère Jean's sarcasms directed at those who think of the *service divin* to
the exclusion of the *service de vin* are many and brilliant. The great
portrait of him hangs on one slim verb, rather unlike Rabelais' usual
syntactic practice, but this is an altogether exceptional piece of writing: "En l'abbaye estoit pour lors un moine claustrier, nommé Frere
Jean des Entommeures, jeune, guallant, frisque, de hayt, bien à
dextre, hardy, advantureux, deliberé, hault, maigre, bien fendu de
gueule, bien advantaigné en nez, beau despescheur d'heures, beau
desbrideur de messes, beau descroteur de vigiles, pour tout dire
sommairement vrai moyne si oncques en feut depuys que le monde
moynant moyna de moynerie; au reste clerc jusques es dents en matiere de breviaire." The enumeratory sentence is, from Rabelais on, one
of the most characteristic forms of showy writing in French; the terms
are here arranged into categories: manner, appearance, and monklike
traits, with the unexpected occurrence of sound patterns. The effect
depends on the rise from seeming miscellany to a brilliant climax of
repeated syllables. More distinctive material is found in a battle passage, inspired by the anatomical detail of classical epic in such matters: "Es uns escarbouilloyt la cervelle, es aultres rompoyt bras et jambes, es aultres deslochoyt les spondyles du cou . . ." Often, as here,
when a chapter is not dominated by one device in particular, like a
self-contained anecdote or an enumeratory overall pattern, Rabelais
aims at density of varied kinds of language.

The deliberative speech of Grandgousier (Chapter 28) and his letter
to Gargantua (Chapter 29) lead us to more philosophical aspects of
warfare, and in Gallet's address to Picrochole (Chapter 31) we find a
six-part oration in classical form: 1) exordium, a commonplace ("Plus
juste cause . . ."); 2) narration, setting forth the facts ("Doncques
merveille . . ."); 3) definition, the nature of Picrochole and Grandgousier's alliance ("Plus y a"); 4) amplification, proof that Picrochole's
mind and fortunes are declining ("Quelle furie . . ."); 5) refutation of
possible objections ("Si quelque tort . . ."); and 6) peroration, the
order to desist from war ("Depars d'icy . . ."). A wandering mono-

logue on Frère Jean's part (Chapter 39) and Gargantua's speech to the vanquished in very grand style (Chapter 50) stand out in later chapters. There is also much discussion of monkery (Chapter 40), the basis upon which, by contrast, the Abbey of Thélème is erected. Among the many enumeratory features here, the detailed exposition of measures and building materials would seem derived, for its minute manner, from the directions for the building of the Temple in Exodus 25–30.

The formal variations in *Gargantua* and *Pantagruel* suggest the complexity of interpretation: the interweaving of levity and the fruit of mature reflection must be approached with the care used in reading other renaissance writers whose tone is problematic, such as Ariosto or Donne. The tradition, unfortunately, in Rabelais studies is to assume that wit is always satire, that humor is usually directed *against* something, and that parody is necessarily disrespectful (as if Boileau and Pope found epics silly, because they wrote *Le Lutrin* and *The Rape of the Lock*). Usually some general all-embracing principle has been put forth—the popular spirit, *incroyance*, Catholic orthodoxy—which is supposed to inform the books relentlessly. This goes along with another assumption, that Rabelais should have observed consistency and development of "character" in the manner of a nineteenth-century novelist, as though coherence of this sort were an esthetic necessity. Intermittent use of the giant imagery is criticized, as, more frequently, is the failure of the Abbey of Thélème section to serve as a generally valid book of rules for life, whereas, in reality, those chapters are meaningless apart from the preceding discussion of monkery. Rabelais is also charged with violating principles of realism or truthfulness to self: theologians spoke better Latin than Janotus de Bragmardo; Rabelais praised Cicero but unaccountably failed to write in the same style, and so forth.

Selective discontinuity of theme and style, and the importance of the context of chapters to any development are governing principles in Rabelais' esthetics, and they apply to such subjects as the evangelical movement, the contempt for scholastic thought and language, the symbolism of wine, the politics of Charles V, and the new learning.

The plan of *Gargantua*, and, to a lesser extent, of *Pantagruel*, is based on the topics of praise codified by late antique rhetoricians and studied in the renaissance as the basis for epics and panegyrics. The traditional sequence of topics is lineage, birth, education, and the edifying deeds of the prince, especially at arms, which allows introduction of the heroic note. The epic genre is, in this way of thinking, a poem of praise.[16] Rabelais embellishes epideictic style with displays of real wisdom, and a mingling of the marvelous and grotesque results from his giant imagery. This late antique basis for Rabelais' composition is, of course, perfectly consonant with the encyclopedic taste, the looking back to high ages of culture so characteristic of the compilers— Aulus Gellius and all the others Rabelais borrowed from.

It would be tempting to see the influence of late antiquity at work also in the detail of Rabelais' style, his Middle French as an imitation of Apuleius' "African" Latin with its large and difficult body of rare expressions. Actually, however, the problem is much broader. While his vocabulary was varied on a scale never previously attempted in a modern language, the analogy with the dialect variations of Homer, choral poetry, and tragedy, among the Greeks, and the range of poetic words, archaisms, and familiar terms in Latin literature, from Cicero and Catullus to Tacitus, is sufficient to demonstrate Rabelais' classical and even high classical affinities; there is good reason to see the literature of the great periods in Greece and Rome as differing considerably from the European ideal of stylistic "classicism," such as it was understood between the late sixteenth and eighteenth centuries. Rabelais imitated a very important and soon to be neglected feature of ancient literary art. At the same time, his lexicon is richer than that of most prose writers of any period. It has been observed of Rabelais' own Latin prose that he drew on the most varied sources, including poetry;[17] he was, in a special sense, an anti-Ciceronian, for he in no wise confined himself to Cicero's usage, unlike contemporary Italian humanists. In a way, therefore, Rabelais had a synchronic and all-embracing view of Greco-Roman literary language as a model

16. O. B. Hardison, *The Enduring Monument* (Chapel Hill: University of North Carolina Press, 1962), 72–76.
17. See Rabelais, *Oeuvres complètes*, II, 471n.

but not an unduly perverse or idiosyncratic view, we should note, since the last four centuries of lexicographic and related studies were not at his disposal; and he lived in an age that, in any case, was less concerned than later periods with historical linguistic distinctions.

Beyond the analogies with the ancient languages, we must remember that Rabelais was inventing a language when there was the double possibility of typically Middle French and typically Modern French word order and constructions, when dialectal differences were normal among French speakers, and when people spoke and wrote many kinds of Latin as well, ranging from the Ciceronian down to *Tu dormivisti hodie pinguem matutinum.*[18] Auerbach went so far as to say of Rabelais' French vocabulary, "There is no esthetic standard; everything goes with everything."[19] I think, however, we can distinguish two standards, of classical origin, in Rabelais' style. One is richness of sentence forms, the Ciceronian characteristic; the other is abundance and variety in expression, which Quintilian praises in the *Institutio Oratoria.* We can see that Rabelais' created language is the fullest esthetic flowering of the tendencies generally identified as Middle French. The sentence links through relatives and participles, which characterize Middle French expository prose especially; the absence of personal pronouns, prepositions, and articles where we find them today, which creates density of texture; the suspenseful syntax; and the free adaptation to French of polysyllabic Latin words, in answer to Erasmus' summons to copia—all these features were largely to disappear in the coming great age of neoclassical prose.[20] The case of Rabelais is an extraordinary example of the realization in a particular writer of the esthetic potential in a general period of linguistic evolution.

18. Rickard, *Langue française*, 2. Bad Latin was so ubiquitous it came to form a new genre in Italy, the "maccheronic" poem.

19. Erich Auerbach, *Mimesis: The Representation of Reality in Western Literature*, trans. Willard Trask (Garden City: Doubleday, 1957), 244.

20. See Desidarius Erasmus, *On Copia of Words and Ideas* (*De Utraque Verborum ac Rerum Copia*), trans. Donald B. King and H. David Rix (Milwaukee: Marquette University Press, 1963). For the general question of style, see Floyd Gray, *Rabelais et l'écriture* (Paris: Nizet, 1974), and Marcel Tetel, *Etudes sur le comique de Rabelais* (Florence: Olschki, 1964).

2 The Period in Modern French

It is most interesting to note what seventeenth-century neoclassical French critics saw as the beginnings of French prose style: Chartier was known as the father of French oratory, but they dated the appearance of a truly formed kind of prose from the second half of the sixteenth century. Amyot's Plutarch began the movement, which was continued by the orator of the religious wars, Du Vair; by Cardinal Du Perron, whose *œuvre* is quite varied; and by Coeffeteau, chiefly in his *Histoire romaine*.[1] The modern era definitively began with Guez de Balzac. The criteria by which Du Vair, Du Perron, and Coeffeteau deserved nomination were double: sentences had to be divided into clear units of reasonable length, and, more important, authors were judged on the degree to which they anticipated the nature of seventeenth-century vocabulary and grammar and thus participated in the general evolution of French. These criteria are characteristic of the modernist, neoclassical identification of French political and literary hegemony under Louis XIV with linguistic maturity, against which all writing should be judged.

Amyot took great care with his style in his translation of Plutarch, actually modernizing it in successive editions as he felt French was evolving.[2] La Bruyère was later to ask, rhetorically, whether any of Amyot's contemporaries were still read, whereas the *Vies des hommes*

1. See, for example, Dominique Bouhours, *Les Entretiens d'Ariste et d'Eugène* (Paris: Armand Colin, 1962), 113–16; Jean de La Bruyère, *Les Caractères*, "Des ouvrages de l'esprit," 60; and Antoine Adam, *Histoire de la littérature française au XVIIe siècle*, I, "L'Époque d'Henri IV et de Louis XIII" (Paris: Domat, 1956), 259–60. Montaigne seems not to be mentioned with the others because his style is not judged contributory to the "regular" prose of the seventeenth century.
2. See René Sturel, *Jacques Amyot, traducteur des Vies parallèles de Plutarque* (Paris: Champion, 1908).

illustres and Plutarch's moral writings continued to serve as a great summa of classical cultùre on into the eighteenth century. One is justified in discussing Amyot's version of Plutarch on the same plane as original works because of his particular treatment of the Greek text, which he often rendered rather freely, adding words to fill out unduly economical expressions and changing sentence structures in small but significant ways. Undoubtedly he was hampered by the lack of the scholarly tools one would have today, but there is sufficient coherence and method in his work to incline one to believe that absolute stylistic principles were at work, beyond any specific problems with the Greek text. Here is a passage from the life of Pericles, where, characteristically, the doublet *convenable et conforme* is an addition and the long *efficace . . . à prouver* explains just one unusual Greek word.

> Pericles doncques se voulant former un stile de parler, et une façon de langage comme un outil convenable et conforme à la maniere de vivre et à la gravité qu'il avoit prise, y employoit à tous propos ce qu'il avoit appris de Anaxagoras, coulourant ses raisons de philosophie naturelle par l'artifice de rhetorique: car ayans acquis par l'estude de ceste philosophie une haultesse de conceptions, et une efficace de venir à bout de tout ce qu'il prenoit à prouver, avec ce que de nature il estoit doué de bon entendement, comme escrit le divin Platon, et en tirant ce qui convenoit à son propos, qu'il accoustroit puis après par artifice d'eloquence, il se rendit de beaucoup plus excellent orateur que nul autre de son temps: au moyen de quoi luy fut, comme lon dit, imposé le surnom d'Olympien, qui vault autant à dire comme, celeste ou divin: encore que quelques uns veuillent dire, que ce fut à cause des beaux ouvrages et edifices publiques, dont il embellit la ville d'Athenes et d'autres à cause de la grande authorité et puissance qu'il avoit au gouvernement tant en guerre qu'en paix.[3]

The huge period—there are over thirty intonational phrases, not always marked by the punctuation in this prerevolutionary edition of the *Vies des hommes illustres*—can be divided at *car* and *au moyen de quoi* into three clauses, each one corresponding to one of the sentence types we have seen in Rabelais. In the first the verb comes near the middle; in the second, subject and verb are at the end; and the third begins with verb and subject. In this early period of Modern French the range of sentence forms is still close to Rabelais' Middle French

3. Jacques Amyot, *Vie des hommes illustres*, "Pericles" 13. This is Chapter 8 in the Guillaume Budé series edition with translation.

but differs from it, nevertheless, by generally using less inversion, less suspenseful syntax, and less rhythmic segmentation. As for the overall sentence structure, Plutarch's Greek actually has sentence divisions where Amyot uses *car*, *au moyen de quoi*, and *encore que*; but Amyot felt that subordination of all the material after the finite verb was preferable from the logical point of view, even if the resulting period reaches toward the limits of what the reader can readily take in without a syntactic break. Plutarch's Greek prose is at this point distinctly looser in continuity of sense than modern usage generally allows. Another difference between the Greek and French is that the cola, or phrases, are increased in number in the translation. This is what I would call the French renaissance paragraph-period rather than a classical one,[4] which, Cicero suggested, averages only about four cola per period. And the fact that Amyot's construction resembles a paragraph in function gives rise to another characteristic: it belongs to an essentially unoratorical, expository concept of prose. Although Amyot's period can be read aloud without awkwardness, and divisions into manageable phrases are explicit or easily sensed, the length and content of the period discourage any true declamation. This distinction between reading periods and oratorical periods is far more modern than classical, and finally, in the early seventeenth century, a French writer on *éloquence*, La Motte le Vayer, made it clear that modern rhetoric is normally conceived with a written style in mind. Much is clarified in French periodic prose by this distinction.

Besides the fact that it encompasses so much more than the individual Greek sentences out of which it was put together, Amyot's period has another curious syntactic quality, which we have already found in Rabelais' language but to a lesser degree. The verbs, finite and participial, are not very strong. Indeed, one could convert much of the clausal period into the nominal style used by Saint-Simon over a century later, as I have done here: "Avec un style de parler comme un outil convenable à sa manière de vivre, une philosophie apprise d'Anaxagoras avec les artifices de la rhétorique, une hautesse de conceptions avec une efficace de tout prouver, son bon entendement

---

4. It has been said that the sixteenth century tended to lengthen the sentence while shortening the paragraph. See Alexandre Lorian, *Tendances stylistiques dans la prose narrative du XVIe siècle* (Paris: Garnier, 1962), 159.

joint à l'artifice de l'éloquence, Périclès fut le meilleur orateur de son temps . . ." The convertibility of Amyot's clauses suggests that his is, in effect, a pseudoperiod, an artificial imposition of clausal periodic structure by the employment of weak verbs. The result is a static construction, at first seemingly complicated but readily reducible to a list of nominal elements with none of the active relationships created by dynamic verbs. The possibility of turning one into the other suggests, furthermore, to what degree clausal and nominal constructions may be optional, ungoverned by sense. This element of choice in the use of clauses is not, of course, unrelated to Amyot's combining Greek sentences into a larger period: we begin to see the peculiar Frenchness of the ample period, which is by no means, as it is nearly always said to be, some casual, superficial imitation of the classical languages.

Elaborate clausal constructions are not without certain problems in French, however. Some consideration of a Latin narrative period and related French passages will illustrate this. Here Livy is describing an incident from before the founding of Rome itself.

> Forte et Numitori, *cum* in custodia Remum haberet audissetque geminos *esse* fratres, *comparando* et aetatem eorum et ipsam minime servilem indolem tetigerat animum memoria nepotum, *sciscitandoque* eodem pervenit, *ut* haud procul esset *quin* Remum agnosceret. Ita undique regi dolus nectitur. Romulus non cum globo iuvenum—*nec enim* erat ad apertam vim par—, sed aliis alio itinere *iussis* certo tempore ad regiam *venire* pastoribus, ad regem impetum facit, et a domo Numitoris alia *comparata* manu adiuvat Remus. Ita regem obtruncant. Numitor inter primum tumultum hostis *invasisse* urbem atque *adortos* regiam *dictitans*, *cum* pubem Albanam in arcem praesidio armisque *obtinendam* avocasset, *postquam* iuvenes *perpetrata* caede *pergere* ad se *gratulantes* vidit, extemplo *advocato* concilio scelus in se fratris, originem nepotum, *ut* geniti, *ut* educati, *ut* cogniti essent, caedem deinceps tyranni seque eius auctorem ostendit.[5]

The text is a demonstration of Latin's capacities for subordination. There are twenty-three (italicized) subordinate constructions or the

---

5. Livy, *Ab urbe condita*, I, 5–6. "As it happened, Numitor as well, when he had Remus in custody and had learned that the brothers were twins, noticed their age and Remus' scarcely servile nature, and was struck with the thought of his grandsons. His inquiries led to the same conclusion, and he was on the point of recognizing Remus. Thus the plot was woven against the king from all sides. Romulus did not mass his men—he was not up to open violence—but ordered his shepherds to come to the pal-

equivalent, falling into ten types: *cum* clause, infinitive clause, gerund, *ut* clause, *quin* clause, ablative absolute, present participle, gerundive, *postquam* clause, and a *nec enim* parenthetical clause. Relatives are not even represented, nor is *quod*. As French equivalents, there are scarcely more than the stiff absolute participial construction, the participle in *-ant*, and the words in *k-* (excluding the relatives): *quand, car, que, comme*, and *que* compounds such as *après que*. Using these French forms to hold together Livy's lengthy periods, a translator would come out with something not unlike Amyot's abundant use of *-ant* and *que* constructions. But the monotony of French subordinating constructions is not the whole issue, since, within the system of one language, one does not always perceive repetitions brought about by morphological and syntactic necessities to be so grave (the recurrent declensions of Latin or the constant vowel endings of Italian do not oppress one except in the course of a comparison between languages). What is an additional stylistic problem in a period like Amyot's is that there are so many indicative finite verbs, whereas in Livy's Latin there are, with the exception of the *postquam* clause, no indicative verbs other than the principal ones about which the periods are constructed: *tetigerat, pervenit, adiuvat, ostendit*. One cannot get lost in subordinate clauses that do not differ in verb mood or word order from main ones. The brief and dramatic short sentences—*nectitur, obtruncant*—stand out, creating that alternation of period and brief sentence characteristic of Latin periodic style and not at all of a writer like Amyot. The basic periodic idea of a main verb around which subordinates cluster is far more effective in Livy's syntax than in Amyot's.

The order of syntactic elements is another essential consideration in periodic style. At a later stage in the evolution of French prose than

---

ace at an appointed time by diverse routes. Supported by Remus with another party procured from Numitor's house, he attacked and killed the king. At the beginning of the tumult, Numitor shouted that an enemy had invaded the city and attacked the palace and so had drawn the armed Alban men off to serve as a garrison in defense of the citadel. When he saw the young men coming to congratulate him after they had slain the king, he immediately called an assembly and set forth his brother's crimes against himself and the history of his grandchildren, how they had been born, reared, and discovered; he then made known the death of the usurper and his own responsibility for it."

Amyot's, Malherbe, translating Book 33 of Livy, in a version of which
he was proud, still uses the *-ant* and *qu-* forms, but his sentences are
shorter, more perspicuous.

> Cet exploit ayant été figuré à Philippe plus à son avantage qu'il n'estoit, et
> de moment en moment lui étant rapporté que les Romains avoient
> l'épouvante et qu'ils s'enfuyoient, il se résolut de mettre toute son armée
> en bataille. Quintus par nécessité plutôt que par élection, en fit de même.
>
> Philippe, qui avec quelques gens de pied et de cheval étoit monté sur la
> plus haute de ces buttes pour considérer ce qui se faisoit à la main gauche,
> comme il vit tous ses gens en fuite, et que de quelque part qu'il se tournât il
> ne paroissoit que les armes et les enseignes des Romains, il se retira lui-
> même hors du combat. Quintus, qui alloit après les fuyards, ayant vu les
> Macédoniens hausser leurs piques, et ne sachant ce que cela vouloit dire,
> s'arrêta tout court; puis ayant appris que c'étoit un signe que ceux de cette
> nation avoient accoutumé de faire lorsqu'ils se vouloient rendre, il eut
> opinion de les sauver.[6]

The positioning of the main verb at or near the end of the sentence,
especially when the subject is stated right at the beginning, is Latinate, and I call this period, for convenience, the classical one, thereby
differentiating it from the customary modern syntactic patterns. The
frequence of the classical period, ingeniously varied, gives Malherbe's Livy a special stylistic color. We sense at once Malherbe's seventeenth-century purism and, despite it, his reluctance to abandon a
certain suppleness in sentence structure. When this translation was
made, "natural" word order was already, with Vaugelas' theorizing,
becoming an issue;[7] according to this doctrine the insertion of adverbial matter or even unduly long adjectival elements between subject
and verb violates not only proportion but the very sequence of elements that is identical with the French sentence. While it is not really
surprising that Amyot, along with Rabelais, preserves the classical
habit—also illustrated by my quotation from Livy in Latin—of beginning a period with a noun, only much later to have it connected with
the main verb, Malherbe's taste for this sentence form runs counter to

6. François de Malherbe, *Oeuvres* (5 vols.; Paris: Hachette, 1862–69), I, 404, 406.
7. Claude Favre, sieur de Vaugelas (1585–1650), was the most influential gram-
marian of his day, his ideas being communicated mostly by word of mouth, since he
published his *Remarques sur la langue françoise* (1647) only near the end of his life.

the whole movement of seventeenth-century French theory of style. Obviously, he felt there were enormous advantages in the irregularly shaped sentence: all the material is held in a tensional span between subject and verb; there is none of the uncertainty one may find in an ordinary sentence as to where it is going after the main verb. But Malherbe's periods have to be said to employ such dislocation of word order as to constitute the figure of hyperbaton, so limited were the possibilities of the word order that was beginning to prevail in French.

Hyperbaton like Malherbe's is a precious stylistic resource and one that major prose writers were never entirely to give up, whatever their theoretical acquiescence to natural word order might be. Another resource that is less precisely counter to natural word order but of similar tensional value consists in prolonging an initial subordinate clause, especially one using *bien que, quelque . . . que, si,* or some similar effect of suspending resolution: "S'il y a quelqu'un d'entre vous, Messieurs, ou de ceux qui assistent à ce jugement, qui trouve estrange, que moy, qui ai faict toute ma vie profession d'employer mon eloquence pour la conservation de plusieurs, et n'en abuser jamais à la ruine de personne, ayant changé de coustume, je vienne maintenant à briguer une accusation, je m'asseure, s'il cognoist une fois le merite de ceste cause, qu'il approuvera mon dessein, et jugera qu'en la poursuitte que je fay, nul autre accusateur ne me doit estre preferé."[8] This is from Du Perron's translation of Cicero's *First Verrine Oration* and, like the Malherbe version of Livy, makes available to Modern French some of the same elegant features of Latin prose as Rabelais' rapidly aging style already had. In the detail of both the first and main clauses a multitude of modifiers destroys the easy syntactic sequentiality of simpler sentences. Such grammar is more in opposition to the spirit than to the letter of natural word order, which does not exclude modifiers but tends to demand that the reader always know precisely where he is in a syntactic structure. Periods like this one lend themselves to various effects of tone—such as grandeur in Rabelais or insidious logic in Pascal—which the seventeenth-century

8. Jacques Davy du Perron, *Oeuvres diverses* (3rd ed.; 2 vols.; Geneva: Slatkine, 1969 [1633]), II, 713.

partisans of natural grammar seemed to ignore. When the initial adverbial clause is carried to extreme lengths in comparison with the main clause, I count it as hyperbatic in that grammatically subordinated material is not subordinate in respect to the distribution of verbal mass.

A third violation of natural word order grows out of spoken French and consists in the use of absolute nouns, which are then caught up by reprise pronouns. In the following it helps relieve the monotony of indirect discourse, which is generally more laborious in French than in the classical languages (the relevant nouns and pronouns are italicized).

> Aussi est-ce l'œuvre de toutes celles de Pericles, pour laquelle ses envieux et malveuillans luy porterent plus d'envie, et dont ilz le calumnierent plus crians contre luy en toutes les assemblées du conseil, que le peuple d'Athenes estoit diffamé pour avoir transporté les deniers comptans de toute la Grece, qui estoient en depost dedans l'isle de Delos: et encore que *la plus honneste excuse* que lon eust pour couvrir ce faict, en disant que c'estoit pour la crainte des Barbares, à fin de le mettre en lieu fort, où il fust en plus seure garde, Pericles *la* leur avoit ostée, et que c'estoit une trop grande injure faitte à tout le demourant de la Grece, et un tour de manifeste tyrannie, attendu qu'elle voit devant ses yeux que *l'argent* que lon luy a fait contribuer à force pour les affaires de la guerre contre les Barbares, nous *l'*employons à faire dorer, embellir et accoustrer nostre ville, ne plus ne moins qu'une femme glorieuse, qui veult estre parée de riches joyaulx et de pierres precieuses, et *en* faisons faire des images, et bastir des temples d'une excessive despense. ("Pericles" 13)

We see why Rabelais and nineteenth-century writers prefer summarized discourse to this lengthy kind of texture. Amyot attempts to relieve it with the reprise pronoun; the absolute noun construction with reprise constitutes a way of endowing Modern French with an equivalent to the Old and Middle French sentence order object-subject-verb. Highly individual and inventive writers like Pascal, Saint-Simon, and Proust seem especially to favor it.

The period can be described not only by clausal structure but also by the relations of sense between its parts. Traditionally, the classical period is said to be a circle, because each subordinate section points back to the main clause; the end-position verb then ties up the structure with its reference back to the subject at the beginning. Obviously, not many sentences in Modern French are like this; the normal balanced type of period would be binary or something like those we have seen in Rabelais wherein a subordinate clause precedes and follows the central main clause. In narrative, however, the periodic style differs from the expository type: there appears to be a temporal progression, a sequence of actions recorded in the period rather than a static subordination of all elements to one. The Roman historians used progressive periods, as in our Latin quotation from Livy; in Rabelais, we commonly find purpose or result clauses (with *de sorte que, tant . . . que,* or something of the sort) prolonging the action and creating a bipartite period. The progressive period is sometimes grammatically more coherent than it is from a strict temporal-logical viewpoint; *L'Astrée* contains good examples: "Mais se levant en sursaut, elle se fût mise dans un petit cabinet, pour n'estre vue ainsi déshabillée, s'il ne l'eût retenue par sa robe, et puis se jetant à genoux devant elle, il la pria et supplia tant, qu'elle revint où elle estoit, commandant toutefois à Andronire de reculer les chandelles en lieu qu'elle eût moins de honte de se voir en habit."[9] The conditional expression, result (*tant . . . que*), and purpose (*en lieu qu'elle eût*), along with participles, are merely elaborate, periphrastic ways of putting a simple sequence of events: she got up, started for the cabinet to hide; he caught her skirt, fell on his knees, spoke to her; she gave an order, came back. The taste for hypotaxis has provided what from the chronological standpoint is a plain sequence with an artificial series of relations, by using the logical form of the period with subordinate elements. *Se levant* and *se jetant*, for example, are not chronologically correct (the correct form would be *s'étant levée, s'étant jeté*); the first implies a cause and result, and the second is essentially circumstantial. The period therefore is not only progressive like the Latin period of Livy's we have seen earlier, but it presents more rationalized action, with lucidity of motive counting for as much as the sequence of actions. It is obvious that we are dealing here, as in the global paragraph-period, with a quite naturally European renaissance con-

9. Honoré d'Urfé, *L'Astrée* (4 vols.; Lyon: Masson, 1926), IV, 520.

ception of the function and value of hypotactic style—one that is
somewhat independent of Latin antecedents.

In characterizing periods by the sense relations of their clauses,
one finds, besides the progressive-narrative type, a large variety of
expository periods in which facts are aligned in a grammatically coherent but logically tangential fashion. Often relative clauses, which
have no necessarily logical value, are the syntactic device.

> Pericles donques pour obvier à ce que le peuple ne se saoulast de luy, s'il le
> voyoit continuellement, ne s'approchoit de luy, et ne se presentoit devant
> luy que par intervalles, ny ne parloit pas de toutes manieres, et ne sortoit
> pas en public, ains se reservoit ne plus ne moins que lon gardoit à Athenes
> la galere Salaminiene, comme dit Critolaus, pour les matieres de grande
> consequence: et ce pendant manioit les autres affaires de moindre impor-
> tance par l'entremise de quelques orateurs qui estoient ses familiers, entre
> lesquelz Ephialtes, à ce que lon dit, en estoit l'un, celuy qui osta l'authorité
> et la puissance à la cour d'Areopage, et donna trop grande et trop effrenée
> licence au peuple, ainsi que le dit Platon: à l'occasion de laquelle, ce disent
> les poëtes comiques, il devint si insolent qu'on ne le pouvoit plus tenir non
> plus qu'un jeune cheval qui n'a point de bride, et prit une audace telle,
> qu'il ne voulut plus obeïr, ains mordit l'isle d'Euboee, et saulta dessus les
> autres isles. ("Pericles" 13)

We have seen an additive period in Rabelais, but this one is much
more significant, as it represents a choice in translation. Here Amyot
put together two Greek sentences (the second beginning, "Some say
Ephialtes was one of them, he who . . .") to form this period, an excellent example of subordination that is false and agglutinative, since
the Ephialtes material is completely independent of the relations of
Pericles himself with the populace. Again, the European feeling for
the period is independent of classical practice.

In the above example, subject and main verbs occupy the first half
of the period; often in the additive period the main clause takes up
only the first words, and the rest of the development is devoted entirely to an accumulation of details of slight-seeming relevance, as in
a long, incremental sentence of Rabelais' we have seen, taken from
Grandgousier's letter. This is the "loose sentence" as distinguished
from the real period in some terminologies, or the descending sentence structure, in which tensions of grammar and sense steadily di-

minish. But such false subordination is characterized often by rhythmic and syntactic wholeness and sometimes even elegance, so that we have no immediate impression of an afterthought.

If logic were the only criterion for sentence structure, a good deal of French periodic writing would have to be rejected. The casual period seems very much a part of French taste and by no means a learned artifice of humanism; its significance in the world of letters is suggested by its privileged place in the novel, an essentially courtly genre. The *grande période de roman*, as Sévigné called it, uses hypotaxis less for its logical functions than to tie together large numbers of short clauses. Its weak pauses and fluent syntax make it infinitely preferable, in the renaissance esthetic, to a sequence of independent constructions; it avoids abruptness for a much admired *mollesse de style*. This elegant middle style is an interesting European exception to the general classical practice of employing elaborate hypotaxis primarily in the grand oratorical style. Here is a passage from the model of seventeenth-century novels, d'Urfé's *L'Astrée*.

> Elle commence donc de faire bonne chère à Téombre, luy parle, et montre de se plaire à tout ce qu'il dit et qu'il fait, et quand elle voit que je n'en prens garde, c'est alors qu'elle en fait plus de cas, et qu'elle a plus de secrets à luy dire. Je remarquay incontinent ce renouvellement d'amitié, et le dis à Dorinde, qui en rioit avec moy, voyant que Téombre s'y rembarquoit; et d'autant que Florice ne voyoit point que je revinsse comme elle s'estoit figurée, elle augmenta les faveurs qu'elle lui faisoit; de sorte que plusieurs ne pouvant approuver cette vie, le dirent à ses parents, d'autant que le bruit de cette affection estoit si grand, qu'il ne se pouvait plus cacher, à quoi elle avoit esté contrainte, parce que pour me faire voir ses actions, il fallut qu'elle en fit de grandes demonstrations, et qu'au lieu de les cacher, comme c'est l'ordinaire, elle les descouvrit à la vue de chacun, voire s'estudia de les faire paraître, autrement elles m'eussent esté inconnues, pour ce que je ne la voyois plus qu'en public, et bien souvent encore estant en ces lieux-là, je ne faisois pas semblant de la voir.[10]

We move steadily forward from one short clause to another and feel no obscurity arising from the length of the period. However, if we try to analyze the grammar, we discover that, beginning with the main verb and moving from one level of hypotaxis to another, we reach at

10. *Ibid.*, II, 158.

least six or seven degrees of subordination, from which we emerge through some sort of sleight of syntax after the word *autrement*. We find nothing so casually extreme in Amyot's dignified sentence structure, and, of course, such grammar is hardly Latinate. No better demonstration could be found of the essential Frenchness of elaborate hypotaxis. Interestingly enough, this style seemed elegant and simple in comparison with preceding fiction and its gaudy ornaments.[11]

The study of prose style has been, in the English-speaking world, focused on the emergence of new kinds of writing near the beginning of the seventeenth century. Attic, baroque, anti-Ciceronian, Stoic, and plain styles have been discerned; Seneca, Demosthenes, Tacitus, and the *genus humile* invoked. In France the new movement in vernacular prose is identified with a good part of Montaigne's essays, Book I in particular, and beyond Montaigne, a persistent admiration for Seneca runs on through the seventeenth century. For the moment, I shall simply observe some of the features of Seneca's prose and certain applications of them to French.

Seneca is usually spoken of as the first anti-Ciceronian, and his prose as the negation of all we identify with the grand oratorical style. In first place, of course, is his use of short cola in short periods.

> Ita fac, mi Lucili, vindica te tibi, et tempus, quod adhuc aut auferebatur aut subripiebatur aut excidebat, collige et serva. Persuade tibi hoc sic esse, ut scribo: quaedam tempora eripiuntur nobis, quaedam subducuntur, quaedam effluunt. Turpissima tamen est iactura, quae per neglegentiam fit. Et, si volueris attendere, maxima pars vitae elabitur male agentibus, magna nihil agentibus, tota vita aliud agentibus. Quem mihi dabis, qui aliquod pretium tempori ponat, qui diem aestimet, qui intellegat se cotidie mori? In hoc enim fallimur, quod mortem prospicimus: magna pars eius iam praeterit. Quicquid aetatis retro est, mors tenet.[12]

The maxim comes naturally to hand when subordination is confined to brief clauses; parallelism or antithesis of cola becomes prominent,

11. See pp. 145–47, herein. Also Adam, *Histoire*, I, 131–32.
12. Seneca, *Moral Epistles*, I, 1. "Exactly, dear Lucilius, insist on your rights to your own self. Up to this point, your time was being taken, being stolen, slipping away: gather it up and save it. Be assured that things are as I say: some instants are torn away from us, some are stealthily taken, others flow away. The worst loss is that which

and brilliant thoughts show off well, like the paradox of death being half-over because it is identical with a half-lived life. This much is opposed to the long Ciceronian period but not really to the patches of commata or brief cola Cicero uses intermittently and which we have seen imitated in Rabelais; nor is the idea of writing coruscant passages any more characteristic of Seneca than of Cicero; indeed they both have their Asianism, in the opprobrious term used by ancient defenders of a plain style. Croll, however, taking up the traditional distinction between figures of words or sound and those of thought, would assign the latter to Seneca and his imitators; but we see obviously from the homeoteleuthon, or rime, the anaphora, and the alliteration in the above passage that sound figures play an important role in Seneca's clipped periods as well.

There are interesting ambiguities about Senecan style. Although figures belong to all levels of style, generally they tend to be associated with the grand manner in classical times; the short colon is usually felt, when used exclusively, as belonging to the middle or low styles. Seneca's genre, furthermore, the diatribe, or informal philosophical essay, has behind it a tradition of *genus humile*, commonly thought most suitable for moral matters. Among Seneca's followers, one finds both a fairly elaborate manner and the plain style Croll would identify with Seneca; the latter occurs often, for example, in Montaigne. Of course, any style in which the highest philosophy is exposed deserves, in a sense, to be called high, whether figured or not, for what could be higher than truth; if Seneca attains it more surely than Cicero, then the system of styles is thrown out of balance. For a European, the Christianized stoicism of the sixteenth and seventeenth centuries, which retained Senecan stylistic features, is necessarily superior to Ciceronian pagan philosophy if he judges thought and style on religious grounds. Of course, Christianity also has behind it its own *genus humile*, the serious low style whose influ-

---

comes from carelessness. And if you look closely, the largest part of life is spent doing ill, a good part doing nothing, and all of it doing something other than one intended. Whom can you name who gives time its true value, a day its true price, who understands that he is dying a little every day? Our mistake is this: we see death ahead of us, but much of our existence already is given to death. All our past years belong to death."

ence Auerbach investigated in *Mimesis* and which reinforces the plain Senecan tendencies. In the course of the sixteenth century, both Ciceronian and Senecan philosophical style had their partisans, and within the Senecan domain, there are in theory at least two utterly conflicting manners, a plain one and a highly figured one, both capable of dealing with matters of the utmost elevation.

As an example of the French Christian Stoic style, I shall take Du Vair's *Traité de la constance et consolation ès calamitez publiques*, composed during the religious wars; despite its title, the work is an oratorical dialogue and is not in the least in treatise style.

> Nous sommes maintenant sur le retour, nostre fortune est sortie de chez nous comme d'une maison crevacee de tous cotez, nous sommes de- meurez attendans la cheute: les uns crient, les autres regardent, les autres s'enfuyent. Qu'y a-il tant à s'estonner? Un vieil homme meurt, une vieille maison tombe, que faut-il tant crier? Qu'y a-il en cela que ce que vous voyez tous les jours et par tout? Les fruits fleurissent, se nouent, se nour- rissent, se meurissent, se pourrissent; les herbes poindent, s'estendent, se fanent; les arbres croissent, s'entretiennent, se seichent, les animaux nais- sent, vivent, meurent; le temps mesme, qui enveloppe tout le monde, est enveloppé par sa ruine et se perd en se coulant.[13]

We see here a characteristic Senecan ambiguity: the thought is quite grand, and the examples, in part at least, are humble and homely. But it is almost impossible for the modern reader not to feel some presence other than a classical one in such writing—that of the Bible. Often in late sixteenth- and seventeenth-century literature, the commonplaces of Stoic thought are reinforced by reminiscences of the poetic books—Proverbs, Psalms, Job—or of Ecclesiastes, the Biblical example of an ancient diatribe or informal philosophical essay. The very syntax of Seneca's moral epistles finds correspondences in the paratactic Hebrew sentence. The common tendency to define the imagery of time and decay as baroque ignores the interesting question to what extent the baroque is Bible-inspired or the Bible, at least in part, a baroque work. In any case, Christian humanism should not be studied solely in terms of classical style.

In our passage from Seneca, as in the Du Vair, there were words

13. Guillaume du Vair, *Traité de la constance et consolation ès calamitez publiques*, ed. Jacques Flach and F. Funck-Brentano (Paris: Tenin, 1915), 108.

and phrases arranged in triplets with asyndeton; that is, *and* is omitted: *A, B, C.* Such a construction is normal in Latin, the alternative being polysyndeton: *A and B and C.* The imitation of the Latin arrangements in French, especially asyndeton, is a resource of elegant style. Rabelais, for example, almost never used it in *Pantagruel*, but it occurs a certain number of times in the more elaborate *Gargantua* and is frequent in the still more stylistically complex *Tiers Livre.* Generally, we observe that triplets, or larger numbers of parallel elements, suggest a more fastidious, thought-out approach to writing than does the often mechanical doublet. Obviously, in a style that avoids lengthy subordinate clauses, as do French imitations of Senecan style, even more than do Seneca's own sentences, patterning effects are greatly reduced in number, and considerable prominence is given the handling of double, triple, and multiple grammatical elements. This is especially the case when Seneca's sound repetitions are not present to tie together the sentences.

Beyond the handy opposition between a hypotactic Ciceronian period and a Senecan one, composed of largely paratactic clauses connected by semicolons, French evolved a synthesis of the two in the course of the seventeenth century, and we may see here, doubtless, the growing influence of punctuational typography. Individual hypotactic sentences are joined together in a massive period. In the 1665 *Avis au lecteur* in the *Réflexions ou Maximes morales*, La Rochefoucauld writes the following.

> Il est vrai que, comme ces Maximes sont remplies de ces sortes de vérités dont l'orgueil humain ne se peut accommoder, il est presque impossible qu'il ne se soulève contre elles et qu'elles ne s'attirent des censeurs. Aussi, est-ce pour eux que je mets ici une *Lettre* que l'on m'a donnée et qui a été faite depuis que le manuscrit a paru et dans le temps que chacun se mêloit d'en dire son avis; elle m'a semblé assez propre pour répondre aux principales difficultés que l'on peut opposer aux *Réflexions* et pour expliquer les sentiments de leur auteur: elle suffit pour faire voir que ce qu'elles contiennent n'est autre chose que l'abrégé d'une morale conforme aux pensées de plusieurs Pères de l'Eglise, et que celui qui les a écrites a eu beaucoup de raison de croire qu'il ne pouvoit s'égarer en suivant de si bons guides et qu'il lui étoit permis de parler de l'homme comme les Pères en ont parlé; mais, si le respect qui leur est dû n'est pas capable de retenir le chagrin des critiques, s'ils ne font point de scrupule de condamner

l'opinion de ces grands hommes en condamnant ce livre, je prie le lecteur de ne les pas imiter, de ne laisser point entraîner son esprit au premier mouvement de son cœur et de donner ordre, s'il est possible, que l'amour-propre ne se mêle point dans le jugement qu'il en fera: car, s'il le consulte, il ne faut pas s'attendre qu'il puisse être favorable à ces Maximes; comme elles traitent l'amour-propre de corrupteur de la raison, il ne manquera pas de prévenir l'esprit contre elles.

Here La Rochefoucauld shows the manner in which a writer sensitive to periodic structure can conceive of its unity: the movement is from *lettre* to the two *elle* clauses, then from the subordinate *celui* to *je*, and from the subordinate *amour-propre* to *il*; it is in the play of antecedents and personal pronouns that La Rochefoucauld finds the principle of periodic coherence. Sometimes it is said that a Latin period should have only one element serving as subject or object for all the verbs, as in our Latin quotation from Livy cited earlier; while this is an exaggeration, unsupported by practice, it is nevertheless true that the relation of verb subjects and personal pronouns is a significant aspect of period building. Like the paragraph-periods of Amyot, the quotation from La Rochefoucauld demonstrates a further development of the classical conception of the period as a complex of ideas and not merely a grammatical notion. Inseparable from this gathering together of sentences, hypotactic or simple, is the generalization of the use of paragraphing in seventeenth-century texts. Paragraphs, colons, and semicolons, as well as the occasional comma used to join closely two short independent clauses, combine to make a rhythm less of phonetic than of psychological value, a reading period rather than an oratorical one.

The period, it should by now be clear, can take more than one form. A minimal period, which consists of two cola, or sense phrases, might be made of two independent clauses joined by a coordinating conjunction (*and, but, or*) or by a mark of punctuation (the semicolon since the seventeenth century, or sometimes the older colon). A second and common form for a two-colon period would be a main clause and a subordinate one beginning with *if, when, although,* and so forth. Interspersed among periods, we commonly find, in Latin and in some French writers, simple sentences: Latin periodic writing especially is seldom so sustained as that in French often is. The ambiguity of independent and subordinate functions shows up in the transitional relative: *A quoi fut répondu que . . ., Ce qui fut fait.* We see why classical theorists preferred to think of meaningful wholes rather than details of grammar, especially since, reading aloud, one may alter such relations at will. In Latin the rhythmic ending, or clausula, helped define the period, but the details of this, besides being strictly inimitable, were not understood in the sixteenth century.

When I define not only Amyot's long sentences as periods but also La Rochefoucauld's constructions in which the unity in sense is marked by semicolons between several sentences, I am enlarging somewhat the classical idea of the period. With the cola (Latin: *membra*) of which the period is made, I shall attempt to be more precise than the classical treatises and suggest some notions of syntactic form. A noun and verb is a good general indication of typical colon material, whether the noun be subject or object and whether the verb be finite, participle, or infinitive. This provides the requirement of wholeness of sense, which one might define as susceptibility to being recast as a simple sentence. In La Rouchefoucauld's *je prie le lecteur de ne les pas imiter, de ne point laisser entraîner son esprit au premier mouvement de son cœur*, the first colon is *je . . . imiter*, with a finite verb complex; the second is an infinitive way of saying *ne laissez pas entraîner votre esprit*. These two cola fit the ample Ciceronian idea of the colon as about normal verse length—a hexameter in Latin, an alexandrine in French. However, from *au premier mouvement* to the end, we have a case other than the ones mentioned. Here *mouvement*, a verbal noun, corresponds to a Latin participle or gerund, and the whole to *votre cœur s'émeut*. Finally, the colon as a unit of meaning often corresponds to the phrase of French intonational patterns.

Classical works on rhetoric do not always make comprehensive or unambiguous statements about the period and its parts: the comma (Latin: *incisa*), a short unit, is often similar in length to a brief colon but tends to consist of an interjection, a vocative, or a connective adverbial expression, such as the *aussi*, *mais*, and *car* set off by punctuation in our quotation from La Rochefoucauld. The difference from the colon is that the comma has less of a rhythmic structure in itself. There is some variation as to whether the comma is counted as part of a colon; commata are normally included within the period. On the other hand, the Senecan or *style coupé* movement, illustrated by our quotation from Du Vair, has a new rhythmic element, which is the segmentation brought about by the multiplication of a syntactic component of the sentence: "Les fruits fleurissent, se nouent, se nourrissent, se meurissent, se pourissent." Such early examples as this and comparable sentences in Montaigne were the beginning of a genuinely new kind of prose.

3 Montaigne and Pascal

The origins of Montaigne's style lie in Seneca,[1] and the first book of the *Essais* especially shows the latter's influence; here is a passage near the end of "Que philosopher c'est apprendre à mourir": "Où que votre vie finisse, elle y est toute. L'utilité du vivre n'est pas en l'espace, elle est en l'usage: tel a vescu long temps, qui a peu vescu: attendez vous y pendant que vous y estes" (I, 20). The passage is written as a series of maxims like those in Seneca, which explains the absence of sentence links. A maxim is complete in itself, so there is less a forward movement in these lines than disjunction. Curiously enough, however, the passage has a pronounced feeling of unity in its tension, of conveying the concentrated essence of a situation and leaving out incidental, circumstantial material. The solemn apothegms, paradoxes, and antitheses suggest that such style borders on a most elevated form: the oracular utterance. Again, we see the ambiguous nature of the Senecan sentence as plain style or as an exalted kind of expression.

The effect of Montaigne's style derives, in part, from his reference to an earlier model of prose. Thus Guez de Balzac, attempting to characterize Montaigne's style, suggests that his most salient trait is the omission of connective adverbial or conjunctive material between sentences, with a consequent obscurity of sense at times; such is Montaigne's version of *style coupé*.[2] In other words, the notion that something was once part of normal prose and has been excised was

---

1. For general studies of Montaigne's style, see Floyd Gray, *Le Style de Montaigne* (Paris: Nizet, 1958), Zoe Samaras, *The Comic Element of Montaigne's Style* (Paris: Nizet, 1970), and Richard A. Sayce, *The Essays of Montaigne: A Critical Exploration* (London: Weidenfeld and Nicolson, 1972).
2. Jean-Louis Guez de Balzac, "De Montaigne et de ses escrits," in B. Beugnot (ed.), *Les Entretiens* (2 vols.; Paris: Didier, 1972), I, 283–87.

very apparent to Balzac. We who are accustomed to much implicitness in prose do not feel the obscurity as intensely as Balzac; but it is perfectly clear, when the connectives are supplied, as Auerbach attempted to do for a few sentences, how great a part of the sense we must bring to the text ourselves. This famous passage from the beginning of "Du repentir" is the one whose lacunae Auerbach experimentally filled: "Les autres forment l'homme; je le recite et en represente un particulier bien mal formé, et lequel, si j'avoy à façonner de nouveau, je ferois vrayement bien autre qu'il n'est. Mes-huy c'est fait. Or les traits de ma peinture ne forvoyent point, quoi qu'ils se changent et diversifient. Le monde n'est qu'une branloire perenne. Toutes choses y branlent sans cesse . . ." (III, 2). "*Whereas* others form man, I describe him, and, *furthermore*, I portray a particular one, *myself, who is, I know*, a very ill-made one, and *I assure you that* if I had to fashion him again, I would make him different from what he is now. *But unfortunately* . . ."[3] What is interesting here is that one can, with reflection, feel there is a lack; Montaigne is strengthening his style by what he does not say, by being concise in reference to a purely imaginary fuller form of expression and creating the impression that the speaker is consciously restraining himself through irony or excess of emotion. Only when a tradition of style has already been built up, as in France during the sixteenth century, is it possible to draw on such implied comparisons between the text at hand and another, hypothetical one.

We can observe between the first and the second passages a gradual internalization of Senecan stylistic devices. The aligned maxims give way to Montaigne's customary first person, and from moral qualities we move to the notion of individual perception against the background of nature's ceaseless change. At the same time, the tone is more relaxed; there is none of the violent tension of Seneca's hortatory manner. The earlier passage represents that kind of stoicism informing much of European tragedy around Montaigne's time, and which perhaps attracted Montaigne's wide audience, whereas in the later essays, as we see in the second quotation, Montaigne has abandoned Seneca's theatrical intensity.

3. Erich Auerbach, *Mimesis: The Representation of Reality in Western Literature,* trans. Willard Trask (Garden City: Doubleday, 1957), 253.

There is a further element of literary art in these passages, especially in the second one: much use is made of near isocolon or of phrases of similar if not the exact same length. This formal device has a distinctly unifying effect. Sometimes we find the same sort of recurrent arrangement of approximate phrase lengths that was to constitute an important resource for many neoclassical writers: "Le peuple reconvoye celuy-là [9], d'un acte public [5], avec estonnement [5], jusqu'à sa porte [4]: il laisse avec sa robe ce rolle [8], il en retombe d'autant plus bas [8] qu'il s'estoit plus haut monté [7]; au dedans [3], chez luy [2], tout est tumultuaire et vile [8]" ("Du repentir"). Montaigne's tendency toward isocolon is not always, we should note, a fully developed form of symmetry: the alternance of groups of about five and eight syllables is not strictly patterned. One finds in Montaigne both balanced constructions, such as isocolon with antithesis and *A* and *B* doublets, and pronounced irregularity. The symmetrical is certainly present, but it does not dominate long stretches of prose.

I note elements of polished technique in Montaigne because he has an opposite tendency as well: it is part of his design that we not merely classify him as another author who made this or that adjustment in the rhetorical tradition, but that, if necessary, we rather characterize him as being insouciant about all such matters. He likes at times to pretend to ineptitude where style is concerned: "Personne n'est exempt de dire des fadaises. Le malheur est de les dire curieusement. *Nae iste magno conatu magnas nugas dixerit* [he is surely going to make a great effort to tell me some monstrous piffle]. Cela ne me touche pas. Les miennes m'eschappent aussi nonchallament qu'elles le valent. D'où bien leur prend. Je les quitterois soudain, à peu de coust qu'il y eust. Et ne les achette, ny les vens que ce qu'elles poisent. Je parle au papier comme je parle au premier que je rencontre" ("De l'utile et de l'honneste" III, 1). This kind of sentence asyndeton and abrupt short phrase (which, however, is not completely devoid of a certain isocolon) is not *style coupé* in the normal sense, but *style heurté*, or *haché*—plain style almost to the point of the subliterary. It is part of the pervasive irony of the *Essais* that they contain an antidote to finished prose style as well as the thing itself.

The most characteristic type of longer sentence in Montaigne has a tacked-on final phrase, a form of the "descending" or "loose" sentence which we saw earlier in Rabelais and Amyot and which is sometimes associated, a bit hastily perhaps, with baroque style:[4] "Je ne fay point de doute qu'il ne m'advienne souvent de parler de choses qui sont mieux traictées chez les maistres du mestier, *et plus veritablement*. C'est icy purement l'essay de mes facultez naturelles, *et nullement des acquises*; et qui me surprendra d'ignorance, il ne fera rien contre moy, car à peine respondroy-je à autruy de mes discours, qui ne m'en responds point à moy; *ny n'en suis satisfaict*" (my italics; "Des livres" II, 10). The implication in the irregular or deliberately awkward passages in the *Essais* is that this is not literature but the authentic voice of a real man speaking; polished language belongs to the impersonal mode of rhetoric, uniform and codified in manuals, expressive of no one in particular. We especially notice in Montaigne's longer sentences the frequent absence of the clear, often balanced bipartite or tripartite periods employing clauses beginning with *car, de sorte que, bien que,* and so forth, which clearly articulate the divisions and stages of the argument. This is more a narrative account of opinions, eschewing to a surprising extent the overt logical-persuasive forms of reasoning. We observe here an automatic consequence of a change in method; according to classical theory, style necessarily corresponds to and follows genre.

When we try to penetrate the inner esthetic of Montaigne's essays, beyond the detail of wording and figures, we find that Montaigne, by juxtaposition, says a great deal about his style, more even than he at first seems to be saying. It is not too much to maintain that he employs covert strategies to win over the reader to his way of writing. Two of the best descriptions he gives of his own style—it is noteworthy how often he mentions it—are in "Consideration sur Ciceron" (I, 40) and "De l'institution des enfants" (I, 26). In the latter, Montaigne suddenly speaks of his own language, "succulent et nerveux, court et serré," just after warning against false, scholastic learning and vocabulary, but it is in the former essay that the subtle presentation of his own manner lies. The essay, like so many, has a

---

4. See Samaras, *The Comic Element*, 244, and Morris W. Croll, *"Attic" and Baroque Prose Style: The Anti-Ciceronian Movement*, ed. J. Max Patrick and Robert O. Evans (Princeton: Princeton University Press, 1969), 219–26.

somewhat devious movement, yielding its meaning most piquantly if we juxtapose widely separated passages. At first, Montaigne does not speak of his own style at all but expatiates on the vanity—unsuitable in a public figure, who should have better things to do—of Cicero's polishing and preserving his letters, even ones he never sent. Caesar comes next to mind, by contrast, for his writing is all the finer in that it is surpassed in importance by his deeds. (The antithesis with Cicero is not entirely logical.) The theme of letter writing comes and goes in the essay, in the course of which we learn of Montaigne's indifference to epistolary art and of the odd qualities of his style: "trop serré, desordonné, couppé, particulier." In the guise of deprecating any pretensions to letter writing one might perchance ascribe to him, he indirectly compares himself to Caesar, the figure who was initially Cicero's opposite; and the slightest acquaintance with Caesar's writings shows at least some distant kinship with Montaigne's clipped and dense language. Though Montaigne was only mayor of Bordeaux and not a public figure of the magnitude of Caesar, he has, nevertheless, the perspective and values proper to a statesman; a basis in reality lends authenticity to his style. The curious thing in all of this is not merely the roundabout parallel between Montaigne and Caesar, which is indeed very discreetly and fittingly made, but the obvious fact that nowhere are Cicero's speeches, the major expression of his eloquence and the record of an active life of public service, referred to. (In Montaigne's other substantial remarks on Cicero, in "Des livres," the orations are also ignored.) By his casual, desultory line of reasoning, Montaigne has omitted the principal piece of evidence against his denigration of Cicero. "De la vanité des paroles" (I, 51) is an attack on oratory as an institution *in the time of Cicero*: it develops the parallels of bad government and demagogy with rhetoric, and the mistaking of words, *copia verborum*, for things, *copia rerum*.

A further antithesis in Montaigne's thought, complementary to the contrast between words and deeds, is a distinction between the individuality of experience and generalization.

Il n'est desir plus naturel que le desir de conoissance. Nous essayons tous les moyens qui nous y peuvent mener. Quand la raison nous faut, nous y

> employons l'experience . . . qui est un moyen plus foible et moins digne;
> mais la verité est chose si grande, que nous ne devons desdaigner aucune
> entremise qui nous y conduise. La raison a tant de formes, que nous ne
> sçavons à laquelle nous prendre; l'experience n'en a pas moins. La conse-
> quence que nous voulons tirer de la ressemblance des evenemens est mal
> seure, d'autant qu'ils sont tousjours dissemblables: il n'est aucune qualité
> si universelle en cette image des choses que la diversité et varieté. ("De
> l'experience" III, 13)

We can derive from these statements the necessity of seeing all things
in their particular circumstances, which can modify superficial similarities. The opposite approach to experience is to synthesize general
laws, which would lead to a highly ordered logical structure with
"prefaces, definitions, partitions," to use the terms with which Montaigne, in "Des livres," characterizes Cicero's supposedly dreary and
unreadable writings. Although he does not name it, the work of
"moral philosophy" he refers to in that essay is doubtless *De Officiis*,
in which one sees a form of treatise style; for the whole direction of
Montaigne's thought is away from the classificatory method of Cicero's work and other edifices of systematic philosophy. (It is ironic that
Montaigne's admirer Pierre Charron was to recast his wisdom into a
treatise, *De la sagesse* [1601].)

Nowhere does one find profounder implications in Montaigne's
language than in his fondness for concrete words in situations where
elevated generality might be expected. One of the major assumptions
in French classicizing style is that abstract expressions or categories
belong to the highest decorum. Quite serious subjects in Montaigne,
on the other hand, may receive fine concrete definition, as in this
passage on behavior with the dying.

> S'il se tire quelque commodité de cette assistance, il s'en tire cent incom-
> moditez. J'ay veu plusieurs mourans bien piteusement assiegez de tout ce
> train: cette presse les estouffe. C'est contre le devoir et est tesmoignage de
> peu d'affection et de peu de soing de vous laisser mourir en repos: l'un
> tourmente vos yeux, l'autre vos oreilles, l'autre la bouche; il n'y a sens ni
> membre qu'on ne vous fracasse. Le cœur vous serre de pitié d'ouyr les
> plaintes des amis, et de despit à l'aventure d'ouyr d'autres plaintes feintes
> et masquées. Qui a tousjours eu le goust tendre, affoibly, il l'a encore plus.
> Il luy faut en une si grande necessité une main douce et accommodée à son
> sentiment, pour le grater justement où il luy cuit; ou qu'on n'y touche

point du tout. Si nous avons besoing de sage femme à nous mettre au monde, nous avons bien besoing d'un homme encore plus sage à nous en sortir. Tel, et amy, le faudroit-il achetter bien cherement, pour le service d'une telle occasion. ("De la vanité" III, 9)

The great number of those present, a sign of the importance and even grandeur of the dying man, becomes physically oppressive; the pathos of those who would cling to him turns into an irritant. From the dying man's point of view, which Montaigne is taking instead of that of the painter of domestic drama composing an eloquent tableau, all the ceremony has an unnecessarily painful quality, brought about by the adherence to an abstract decorum, according to which all the living are posturing and attempting perhaps to rise to elevated reflections. The whole irony comes from the contrast between particulars, the irreducible individuality of dying, and the generalized, edifying scene the survivors are enacting. The tableau is classicizing, the experience Montanian.

From his empirical notions of statesmanship, with its emphasis on deeds rather than theories, to a kind of moral-esthetic judgment on prose style, Montaigne is remarkably coherent in thought: he trusts the particular more than the general, the concrete more than the abstract, the personal more than the impersonal. The absence of normal notions of style is preferable to empty high style, reality to words. The basic antithesis, the most tangible form of Montaigne's thought, lies in the contrast between Cicero's style and his own. Montaigne goes very far at times in his insistence on his own traits as a writer: in a 1595 addition to "Consideration sur Ciceron" he defends his *matière* as infinitely "matérielle." The characterization of the essays at the beginning of "De la vanité" is famous: "Si ay-je veu un Gentilhomme qui ne communiquoit sa vie que par les operations de son ventre: vous voyez chez luy, en montre, un ordre de bassins de sept ou huict jours; c'estoit son estude, ses discours; tout autre propos luy puoit. Ce sont icy, un peu plus civilement, des excremens d'un vieil esprit, dur tantost, tantost lâche, et tousjours indigeste." The concrete is defended in its basest form, which, of course, symbolizes the antistyle, the jagged, subliterary sequences of sentences to be found here and there.

Montaigne's idea of style seems strikingly modern, comparable almost to some polemical stance of the twentieth century. We must be on guard, however, against anachronism: in the passage on the individuality of experience, which I quoted earlier, Montaigne only hesitantly rejects the findings of reason in favor of experiential knowledge; the former is nobler than empirical investigation, and Montaigne is reluctant to dislodge reason from the exalted place it customarily occupies in philosophy. His taste for the concrete is that of other writers of the late sixteenth century—d'Aubigné, Shakespeare—and is revolutionary only in the sense that they are.

The basic form of Montaigne's stylistic antithesis, the opposition between Cicero's work and his own, may surprise one in that it is a translingual notion: Montaigne is unconcerned by the fact that there is no real French Ciceronian style (beyond Rabelais' rather special use of it). Latin rhetoric is being compared with French; the two are put on the same plane, and the reader is expected to react as strongly to Latin style as to French. It is especially significant that Montaigne does not merely see himself as a follower of Seneca, the original anti-Ciceronian. Montaigne ceased to be a Senecan at a fairly early point, but he never stopped being an anti-Ciceronian; the end point of Montaigne's anti-Ciceronianism is not just Senecan style. He is also very different from Guez de Balzac; the latter considered himself a Senecan and defended his position on the grounds that his contemporaries were too mannered in their taste for the stronger Ciceronian rhetoric, which, however, he placed above all others. (Balzac, likewise, ignored the fact that one could not easily choose to be a Ciceronian in French for various linguistic reasons.) Montaigne's anti-Ciceronianism is, of course, more than a matter of vocabulary and sentence structure; the essay style in the larger sense, as opposed to the treatise with its "partitions" and definitions, is of equal concern to him.

The Senecan diatribe, the short, informal philosophical essay, is not the only classical genre with which Montaigne has affinities. His thematics have mediocre, realist origins. As Pascal put it, "La manière d'écrire d'Epictète, de Montaigne, et de Salomon de Tultie [Pascal himself] est la plus d'usage, qui s'insinue le mieux, qui demeure plus dans la mémoire, et qui se fait le plus citer, parce qu'elle est toute composée de pensées nées sur les entretiens ordinaires de la vie."[5] This puts one in mind of Roman satire, which is not a narrow kind of attack or mockery but a "mixed salad," the original sense of *satura*, in which various matters can find a place. The satire, like Montaigne's essay, has no rules, no form; its unity lies in the speaker or persona's cast of mind—his depiction of himself through his subjects and his attitude toward them. Various tones and levels of styles can be accommodated, exactly as in Montaigne's essay. The notion of form is, in general, quite different in Latin literature from that in European, quite relaxed and, at times, even difficult to perceive; and in characterizing the shape of the essays, it is fitting to recall at least this one Roman literary genre and its digressive aspects and elements of continuity.

Of the value of Montaigne's style there can hardly be any disputing, at least among those who have tried to read the lesser writers of his day; he was a strikingly original creator of prose. The nature of his style, however, is more difficult to define, first of all, perhaps, because of its composite character. As we have seen, his *style coupé* ranges from the formal to an almost subliterary *désinvolture*, the latter representing, in thoroughgoing fashion, the plain style ascribed by Croll to the baroque movement. The imagery likewise runs from the poetic vision of world change in the beginning of "Du repentir" to the equation of the *Essais* with excrement. There is an abundance of metaphor in Montaigne, but it is unevenly distributed, so that one hesitates to describe him as a consistent exponent of figurative language; many expressions are only slightly metaphoric, whereas others, like the *homme encore plus sage*, who will help one from the world as the *sage femme* helped one into it, are brilliant variations on set expressions, showing the most acute sense of figurative effect. Rhetorical analysis confirms what one might expect: that Montaigne used all the devices customary among sixteenth- and seventeenth-century writers; very little is illuminated by it, however, again because of the idiosyncratic distribution of figures.

Anti-Ciceronianism, baroque, and mannerism are the categories

5. 927 in the Lafuma numbering of the *Pensées*, which will hereinafter be used.

most frequently applied to Montaigne's style, and of the three, the first is the closest to Montaigne's own conscious notions about writing. By this term, however, we must not think that the consistent imitation of Seneca or anyone else is necessarily implied, or that the anti-Ciceronian sacrifices any ornament of style that Cicero might have used. Ciceronianism is actually the negative term, as used at least by those who, like Erasmus, did not approve of it as an ideal of style: it meant a narrow selection and combination of elements, whereas total freedom of choice was the anti-Ciceronian's privilege. Montaigne's remarks on Cicero, that is to say, on Cicero's overly polished letters and on his treatises, make it quite clear that in Montaigne's opinion, Ciceronianism was not even for its inventor an expression of the self but a web of rhetoric in the most negative sense. In the system of styles, there is a correspondence between subject and diction, and, as Christian reason and philosophy recognize man as a union of opposites, Montaigne's style expresses man's nature in a way that is both experientially and theoretically fitting; the low and the high are paradoxically related in man, as the Gospels remind the Christian, with their serious low style, and as do the liturgical and devotional images derived from it.

The description of Montaigne's work as baroque, or, more recently, mannerist, comes from the attempt to separate from the periodic, supposedly logical styles of the sixteenth century a phase of literature embodying the idea of instability both in thought and techniques of style. To this end the *Essais* have been compared with the poetry of inconstancy and change from Chassignet and Sponde on into the seventeenth century, but the form of Montaigne's images is as important as his themes. Here is one of Montaigne's similes: "Ainsi que ceux qui nous jugent et touchent au dedans, ne font pas grand'recette de la lueur de nos actions publiques, et voyent que ce ne sont que filets et pointes d'eau fine rejaillies d'un fond au demeurant limonneux et poisant." The fountain with its moving water is often thought of as a perfect image of baroque beauty and change; here Montaigne makes an unusual contrast between the attractive surface of the water and the mud beneath, representing the obscure world of motive. A certain ceremoniousness inherent in the simile form is counterbalanced by the familiar *faire grand'recette*, which, furthermore, in conjunction with the words *lueur* and *eau*, demonstrates Montaigne's almost Shakespearean indifference to mixing metaphors ("take arms against a sea of troubles"). If, however, we look at Montaigne's more classicizing contemporary Du Vair, we find this very different form of simile.

> Toutesfois, s'il y en a de si opiniastres, qui ne la [the soul] veulent voir que noyée dans la chair, et juger sa grandeur par l'ombre de ses effets, comme ils font la lune par l'ombre de la terre, si est-ce qu'au travers de cette sombre et pesante masse qui l'enveloppe, elle jette des étincelles, voire des flambees si vives de son immortalité qu'il faut que ceux qui la regardent, confessent, ou qu'ils la voyent ou qu'ils sont aveugles. Ils voyent que ce rayon de divinité, enveloppé dans ce petit nuage de chair, jette sa lumière d'un bout à l'autre du monde: après avoir mesuré ce qui est fini, passe jusques à l'infini, comprend les formes de toutes choses et s'y transforme, et reçoit les contraires, le feu et l'eau, le chaud et le froid, sans s'altérer ni corrompre.[6]

Du Vair is just as imagistic a writer as Montaigne in some ways, but he tends more to the formal, illustrative simile, the kind of image that since Aristotle has been considered as much a figure of reasoning as a decorative element and that has, furthermore, distinguished Ciceronian precedents. There is less abruptness, more completeness of detail than in Montaigne's image. When Du Vair is polemical and uses pejorative imagery, as in the traditional comparison of the state with a diseased body, the formal presentation of the simile, its ample development, dignify it: "Car comme la santé revient au corps . . . aussi, en une ville . . ." We do not find images that suggest, through their violent intrusion, the satiric low style—the *Essais* as excrement, for example—which is one of the distinctive features of Montaigne's language. Du Vair's style, in other words, is sustained, whereas Montaigne's embodies the mutability he speaks of in frequent variations of tones and levels of usage. If periodic categorizations of style are to be useful, we had best, I think, characterize Montaigne's fitful language as mannerist, as straining against the traditional, rhetorical

6. Guillaume du Vair, *Traité de la constance et consolation ès calamitez publiques*, ed. Jacques Flach and F. Funck-Brentano (Paris: Tenin, 1915), 222.

ideas of style. The elaborate, high-flown simile, worked out in much detail, has, on the other hand, both classical and baroque affinities; its ostentatiousness, its hyperrhetorical effect, makes it an especially important feature of baroque style.

Montaigne's style represents a self-conscious break with sixteenth-century habits of writing in both sentence structure and imagery, but its irreconcilable differences with the course of French prose in the seventeenth century are quite as great: the many passages in which Montaigne anticipates neoclassical *moralistes* are only moments in a style made up of contrasts. Neoclassicism was to share with Ciceronianism the characteristic of exclusionary and selective taste; it tended, furthermore, in less-gifted writers, to have the kind of impersonality Montaigne saw resulting from excessive stylistic care.

Pascal is often associated with Montaigne for his interest, sometimes in a spirit of contradiction, in the *Essais*. Even stylistic links exist, but Pascal's total conception of his *Apologie* was such that his borrowings from Montaigne retain very little of their original significance. He is often felt, nonetheless, to stand slightly outside the main currents of development of French neoclassical style.

Pascal's *Apologie* was to be a work of quite overt rhetoric in the original sense of eloquent persuasion.[7] Since his conception of rhetoric was an intentional one, its means could differ from the "fausses beautés" of Cicero (by which Pascal perhaps meant symmetry), and he is explicit in his preference for finding in books a man rather than an author or mere style and for ignoring commonplace principles of writing like the avoidance of word repetition (969). The filiation from Montaigne is here quite evident. Pascal, as well, specifically criticizes the false logic of the treatise style ("Pourquoi établirai-je plutôt la vertu en quatre, en deux, en un?" [46]) and considers his own method disordered but not confused or falsely urbane like Montaigne's leaping from subject to subject (44, 48). Certainly his rhetoric is immediately effective in a way treatise style could hardly hope to

---

7. For general studies of Pascal's style, see Patricia Topliss, *The Rhetoric of Pascal* (Leicester, England: Leicester University Press, 1966), and Michel Le Guern, *L'Image dans l'œuvre de Pascal* (Paris: Armand Colin, 1969).

be, and he has none of Montaigne's intermittent pretense of not trying to persuade anyone of anything.

The unfinished state in which Pascal left the *Apologie* gave a name
to the new genre of the *pensée*, related in its variety to the Montanian
essay and represented already in European literature by Jonson's *Tim-
ber, or Discoveries*, by the *réflexion* side of La Rochefoucauld's *Réflexions ou Sentences et Maximes morales*, and by Gracián's *Oráculo Manual*.
We know something of his general plan, of the recurrent system of
themes, but what we do not know is whether the whole would have
merely given the impression of brilliant passages connected by considerably less interesting prose. It has often been advanced that it was
a literary good fortune that Pascal never completed his *Apologie*, and
it has even been affirmed that, because paradox is Pascal's fundamental figure, the work never could have been put into any kind of recog-
nizably final form.[8] Pascal is, however, not the only seventeenth-century author whose final form turned out to be bits and pieces: Méré
and La Bruyère are fragmentary writers, and others, like Saint-
Evremond and Balzac, were given to the short essay. Montaigne, of
course, from many readers' point of view, is primarily a writer of extraordinary passages.

The Pascal we shall examine is the Christian pessimist occupied
with human *grandeur* and *misères*. This is not, we should note, the
definitive or final voice of Pascal, which is to be found in the later
parts of the *Pensées* (in both the Brunschvicg and Lafuma editions),
where salvation is seen more immediately. Indeed, the whole initial
presentation of man's plight could be said to issue from a fictitious
persona created for the needs of the argument. This tragic persona,
however, is the Pascal of most later literary allusions; he is also the
source of the most striking rhetoric in the *Pensées*. I shall, therefore,
quite consciously limit my discussion to the great vision of life as unresolvable paradox, which opens the work.

The habit of writing and perhaps thinking in fits and snatches is
related to an aspect of style: many fragments have one or two distinctive rhetorical devices, some of them quite idiosyncratic; it would

8. Lucien Goldmann, *Le Dieu caché* (Paris: Gallimard, 1959), 220.

seem that the thought and some particular features of its expression came together. In many ways, Pascal's use of rhetorical figures has the studied, brilliant character the devices have in Racine, more than their casual, fitful way of being introduced into Montaigne's prose. Here aposiopesis and polysyndeton join: "94. La vanité est si ancrée dans le cœur de l'homme, qu'un soldat, un goujat, un cuisinier, un crocheteur, se vante et peut avoir ses admirateurs; et les philosophes mêmes en veulent; et ceux qui écrivent contre veulent avoir la gloire d'avoir bien écrit; et ceux qui les lisent veulent avoir la gloire de les avoir lus; et moi qui écris ceci, ai peut-être cette envie; et peut-être que ceux qui le liront . . ." (The *pensée* drifts off with an incomplete sentence.) Polysyndeton is a rare figure in prose and is used here to convey the idea of an infinite series of absurd reactions. It is fundamental to Pascal's thought that in life there are no fixed points of reference, valid for everyone, that would allow it to be conducted rationally. The unending chain is indicated as well by the aposiopesis, or breaking off in *points de suspension*, which suggests that the reasoning might even form an indefinite spiral. Grammatical figures represent a logical pattern, which could have been perfectly well stated without them, though obviously not with the same stylistic reinforcement of the thought.

In one famous fragment, an unusual period is substituted for the standard sentence form, which would be "L'homme n'est que le plus faible roseau de la nature, mais . . .": "291. L'homme n'est qu'un roseau, le plus faible de la nature; mais c'est un roseau pensant. Il ne faut pas que l'univers entier s'arme pour l'écraser: une vapeur, une goutte d'eau suffit pour le tuer. Mais, quand l'univers l'écraserait, l'homme serait encore plus noble que ce qui le tue, puisqu'il sait qu'il meurt, et l'avantage que l'univers a sur lui, l'univers n'en sait rien." The sentence about the thinking reed has been called a baroque, loose period, such as we find in Montaigne, but despite the loose appositional use of the adjectival phrase, Pascal aims at and achieves a tight effect. The three cola, close in length, are arranged in graded, increasing intensity: the hyperbole of the second colon contrasts with the first, and the paradoxical third colon has both an antithetical relation to the second and a link, through its last word, to the first. The asyndeton with twos (*une vapeur, une goutte d'eau*) is distinctly uncommon in most renaissance and neoclassical styles: it represents the thought process more than *une vapeur ou une goutte d'eau*, which sounds logical and exhaustive rather than exploratory and progressive. Finally, the asymmetric construction with absolute noun (*l'avantage*) and reprise pronoun is one of the great expressive features of French style derived from speech and used most often by writers highly sensitive to syntax. The total impression this passage gives is one of irregularity, each sentence using a figure that differentiates it radically from normal syntactic structures. The series of antitheses is cast, not in a stable, conventional form, but in a dramatic, unfolding fashion, thanks to the unexpected grammatical turns.

Anacoluthon is in some ways the most difficult figure to use suitably, because the effect must outweigh the essentially undesirable faulty grammar: "69. Le plus grand philosophe du monde, sur une planche plus large qu'il ne faut, s'il y a au-dessous un précipice, quoique sa raison le convainque de sa sûreté, son imagination prévaudra." Anacoluthon is again, like polysyndeton and aposiopesis, primarily a poetic figure ("Je t'aimais inconstant, qu'aurais-je fait fidèle?") that is not normally felt to suit the middle language of prose. Nothing better illustrates Pascal's creation of a dramatic voice, as distinguished from mere exposition, than these devices. Here the circumstantial building up to the main clause makes the shift of subject from *philosophe* to *son imagination* all the more striking, yet not incoherent, thanks to the preparatory *sa raison*. Again, a simple antithesis is presented in an unfolding, heightening fashion.

In "Le plus grand philosophe du monde . . ." we see what starts out to be a classical suspension period with subject and verb widely separated. This periodic form, which we have observed to convey a primarily grammatical elegance in Latinizing sentences in Rabelais, Amyot, and Malherbe, is exploited by Pascal not only for surprise but also for tensional values as well: "269. L'homme, quelque plein de tristesse qu'il soit, si on peut gagner sur lui de le faire entrer en quelque divertissement, le voilà heureux pendant ce temps-là; et l'homme, quelque heureux qu'il soit, s'il n'est diverti et occupé par quelque passion ou quelque amusement qui empêche l'ennui de se répandre,

sera bientôt chagrin et malheureux." This period has unusually pronounced symmetries, which are all the more striking in that they, in
part, violate an unwritten rule of French style: two adverbial clauses
(such as *quelque . . . que . . .* and *si . . .*) are virtually never placed one
directly after the other; doubled, they give, with their prominent logical articulation, an intense feeling of the inevitability of man's condition. Moreover, when we look closely at the passage, we see that
the conclusion of the first part of the period is the beginning of the
second, and that the whole is a circular piece of reasoning: again Pascal emphasizes the infinitely regressive paradoxical character of life.
As a result, what seems at first to be conclusive and symmetrical
leads into the unstable and the logically indefinite.

Just as Pascal takes the classical suspension period and makes
something very much his own out of it, he develops a particular form
of the accretive French period in which subordinate clause after subordinate clause is added: "99. Ainsi, lorsqu'ils ne découvrent que des
imperfections et des vices que nous avons en effet, il est visible qu'ils
ne nous font point de tort, puisque ce ne sont pas eux qui en sont
cause et qu'ils nous font un bien, puisqu'ils nous aident à nous dé-
livrer d'un mal, qui est l'ignorance de ces imperfections. Nous ne de-
vons pas être fâchés qu'ils les connaissent, et qu'ils nous méprisent:
étant juste et qu'ils nous connaissent pour ce que nous sommes, et
qu'ils nous méprisent, si nous sommes méprisables." These sentences have the same general syntax characteristic of the additive period in Rabelais, Amyot, or d'Urfé, but they cannot be characterized
as "loose" or "descending" in sense, for the final clauses are logically
strong. Indeed, all the clauses have equal weight and similar mass:
the reasoning is dense, and the many short clauses insidiously moving from one level of subordination to another lead inexorably forward to the fact of man's ignorance and contemptibility. This closely
packed period with its overwhelming, incontrovertible logic is one of
Pascal's most characteristic rhetorical forms: an elaborate show of
ratiocination in the *Pensées*, when it does not point toward paradox,
customarily concludes with man's *misère*. We should observe that the
cliquetis of *qui* and *que*, even denser in Pascal than in other seventeenth-century prose writers, effectively ticks off the progression

from one injurious discovery to another; its effect here is less the frequent one of monotony than that of sinister concatenation.

Pascal is able to order his prose on a larger scale than what we have seen up to now. In the famous passage on imagination, one is struck by the rhythmic organization; there is a savant combination of short and long phrases, corresponding to simple sentences and sentences with a comparison or subordinate clause.

> 81. Cette superbe puissance,/ennemie de la raison,/qui se plaît à la contrôler et à la dominer,/pour montrer combien elle peut en toutes choses,/a établi dans l'homme une seconde nature./ Elle a ses riches,/ses pauvres;/ elle suspend les sens,/elle les fait sentir;/elle a ses fous et ses sages:/et rien ne nous dépite davantage que de voir qu'elle remplit ses hôtes d'une satisfaction bien autrement pleine et entière que la raison./ Les habiles par imagination se plaisent tout autrement à eux-mêmes que les prudents ne se peuvent raisonnablement plaire. Ils regardent les gens avec empire;/ils disputent avec hardiesse et confiance;/les autres/avec crainte et défiance; et cette gaieté de visage/leur donne souvent l'avantage/dans l'opinion des écoutants,/tant les sages imaginaires/ont de faveur/auprès des juges/de même nature./ Elle ne peut rendre sages les fous; mais elle les rend heureux, à l'envi de la raison,/qui ne peut rendre ses amis que misérables,/ l'une les couvrant de gloire,/l'autre de honte.

In the first sentence, the opening two phrases and the concluding two are symmetrical; the grand, balanced movement of the sentence emphasizes the haughty power of imagination. The short asymmetric sentences which follow are a contrasting development in *style coupé* for liveliness. Pascal alternates limping, short conclusions depicting reason (*les autres . . . , l'autre . . .*) with an affirmatively symmetrical sentence on imagination (*et cette gaieté . . .*). The more one examines such a passage, the more evident it becomes that Pascal had an extraordinary feeling for elements of prose rhythm and their possible correspondence with sense.

Semantically, this passage on imagination represents the full development of the *moraliste* manner, of which we saw a brief sample in the quotation from La Rochefoucauld in Chapter 2. A large antithesis, imagination and reason, informs the whole, and a kind of personification of imagination, half-queen, half-goddess, is the major figure, but it exists more at the grammatical level—the abstraction as subject of the verb—than as a realized image. The advantage of this technique lies in the way the world can be depicted under the sway of imagination without the undesirable complications of the visual. It is a very subtle compromise between full personification and the mere common noun. The theoretical basis for agents and forces like reason and imagination comes from the faculty psychology which developed as part of Christian philosophy from Augustine on. In the *moralistes*, we have a secularization of faculty psychology, which, however, does not cease to be basically in accord with strains of Christian thought. The finesse, the wit of the conflicts and strategies by which the *moralistes* represent inner life, is suggested by the enumeration here of imagination's subjects or devotees: this seems almost to be a brief theory of comic types, such as we find them in *Le Misanthrope*, *Les Femmes savantes*, and elsewhere. Indeed, the concluding three periods sketch the mechanism of a satiric plot. The sophistication of the *moralistes'* language is especially evident if we compare it to the earlier allegories of virtues or moral qualities that Christianity had given rise to. Such allegories always require of us some effort of historical adjustment, whereas the best seventeenth-century French maxims and *pensées* have hardly aged at all.

A critique of language, such as we have seen in Montaigne, is naturally a part of the *moraliste*'s concern.

> 192. *Justice, force.* Il est juste que ce qui est juste soit suivi, il est nécessaire que ce qui est le plus fort soit suivi. La justice sans la force est impuissante: la force sans la justice est tyrannique. La justice sans force est contredite, parce qu'il y a toujours des méchants: la force sans la justice est accusée. Il faut donc mettre ensemble la justice et la force; et pour cela faire que ce qui est juste soit fort, ou que ce qui est fort soit juste.
>
> La justice est sujette à dispute, la force est très reconnaissable et sans dispute. Ainsi on a pu donner la force à la justice, parce que la force a contredit la justice et a dit qu'elle était injuste, et a dit que c'était elle qui était juste. Et ainsi, ne pouvant faire que ce qui est juste fût fort, on a fait que ce qui est fort fût juste.

The whole *pensée* turns on the unstated difference between verbal, moral qualities (*juste, tyrannique, contredite, sujette à dispute, injuste*) and physical facts (*nécessaire, impuissante, fort, sans dispute*). Reconciling justice and power is impossible, because it is one of the paradoxes of life that the verbal and physical planes do not correspond: man is given a vocabulary of abstract values, which turns out to be idle in confrontation with his world. The form of this example is that of an elliptic series of syllogisms, a much-admired figure in traditional rhetoric, to which is given the name of enthymeme. The repetition of words inevitable in the syllogism becomes a figure in itself in Pascal: as the words recur, they seem to mean less and less, while the logical form they are embodied in becomes more and more insistent as it reaches its conclusion.

Definition is a traditional figure, as well as the enthymeme: "241. Les pères craignent que l'amour naturel des enfants ne s'efface. Quelle est donc cette nature, sujette à être effacée? La coutume est une seconde nature, qui détruit la première. Mais qu'est-ce que nature? Pourquoi la coutume n'est-elle pas naturelle? J'ai grand-peur que cette nature ne soit elle-même qu'une première coutume, comme la coutume est une seconde nature." The definition here is redundant. As we have seen, Pascal's figures either tend to be antitheses in one form or another or else lead to infinite, circular chains of reasoning. Fundamentally, of course, the unresolvable antithesis and the circle are both paradoxical, obviating any true logical progression.

Antithetical paradox characterizes Pascal's intermittent imagery. For him, there is no proof of God, no relation even to the divine in the physical world. The underlying assumption is that man is made for a moral life, not for the activities Pascal refers to as agitation: "269. Quand je m'y suis mis quelquefois à considérer les diverses agitations des hommes et les périls et les peines où ils s'exposent, dans la cour, dans la guerre, d'où naissent tant de querelles, de passions, d'entreprises hardies et souvent mauvaises, etc., j'ai dit souvent que tout le malheur des hommes vient d'une seule chose, qui est de ne savoir pas demeurer en repos, dans une chambre." Remaining at rest in a room has more than one interpretation: it is an ironic image in that it would be an attempt to remedy the physical with physical means, a recourse that would end in failure; on the other hand, remaining at rest is a symbol of the stark, bare soul refusing all traffic with the material. As Pascal strips man of human nature in fragment 241, he suggests here a radical rejection of the material on its own terms. Elsewhere his imagery conveys at once disproportion and similarity: "Les hommes s'occupent à suivre une balle et un lièvre; c'est le plaisir même des rois" (76). The exalted state of the king is not in keeping with the insignificance of a hare or ball, yet the royal condition and the amusements are material and therefore consonant, judged from the spiritual plane. The physical is the realm of absurd disparity: "La puissance des mouches: elles gagnent des batailles, empêchent notre âme d'agir, mangent notre corps" (59). Finally, we see Pascal's rhetoric strikingly at work, when he opposes the implicit spiritual value of life with death seen as a shovelful of earth: "Le dernier acte est sanglant, quelque belle que soit la comédie en tout le reste: on jette enfin de la terre sur la tête, et en voilà pour jamais" (341). Obviously Pascal did not absolutely consider life and death in this way; it is part of the tragic vision of the fictive author.

Pure sound figures, *schemata verborum*, are not characteristic of Pascal, but some elements of sound play a noticeable role. The asymmetrical sentence may have an unusual correspondence between intonation and syntax: "Le silence éternel/de ces espaces infinis/m'effraie." The repetition of *qui* and *que* in short, contentious cola is also a syntactico-phonetic device, and sometimes words are repeated in a pun: "Le cœur a ses raisons que la raison ne connaît point." Polyptoton, or repetition of word roots, is a very frequent figure: "43. Il n'y a rien sur la terre qui ne montre, ou la misère de l'homme, ou la miséricorde de Dieu; ou l'impuissance de l'homme sans Dieu, ou la puissance de l'homme avec Dieu." The figures joining sound and sense, like Pascal's other rhetorical devices, are doubtless to be found here and there in Montaigne and other earlier writers, but Pascal's deployment of them to color a certain *pensée* shows an especially acute sense of their value; they occur only when they will show off to a high degree. The comparison with Racine's exact use of figures has inevitably suggested itself.

Rhetorical figures are sometimes carelessly said to be characteristic of baroque literature, as if baroque and neoclassical styles did not spring from the same tradition and share the same arsenal of techniques. There is, however, one baroque feature to be found in Pascal: the *pensée neuve*, which Dominique Bouhours continuously emphasized in his seventeenth-century book on baroque and neoclassical styles.[9] Pascal's thinking reed, his wager, Cleopatra's hypothetical short nose, the wise and foolish subjects of imagination, and the philosopher standing on his board are all conceptual discoveries, and we perceive immediately the relation between Bouhours' term and *concetto, concepto,* and *conceit* in other literatures. This is "la manière de bien penser" in baroque style, whereas the use of figures is simply a general seventeenth-century trait. In other respects, the *Pensées* are rather ambiguously baroque and neoclassical at once: the tense, unresolved antitheses belong to the domain of effects commonly attributed to baroque style, whereas Pascal's vocabulary is circumscribed and neoclassical. There is a continuum of styles in the seventeenth century quite as real as any opposition between baroque and neoclassicism, and a work like the *Pensées* is situated at the point where we have difficulty ascribing it to one or the other movement.[10] We shall eventually encounter styles so pronouncedly baroque as to make Pascal's ways of writing seem remote from them. In any case, it is at least as important to examine Pascal's level of style as to give it a period qualification.

The *Pensées* belong to the thematic and stylistic domain which I would call tragic satire and which includes d'Aubigné's "style bas et tragique," the ironies of the voice from the whirlwind in Job, and the transformation of the satiric into tragedy, which Juvenal comments on and exemplifies in his sixth satire. There was actually, in the renaissance, a theory of tragedy as a vituperative genre, opposed to the laudatory one of epic. Pascal's tragic satire begins in blame, reproach, and despair: "99. La nature de l'amour-propre et de ce *moi* humain est de n'aimer que soi et de ne considérer que soi. Mais que fera-t-il? il ne saurait empêcher que cet objet qu'il aime ne soit plein de défauts et de misère; il veut être grand, il se voit petit; il veut être heureux, et il se voit misérable, il veut être parfait, et il se voit plein d'imperfections; il veut être l'objet de l'amour et de l'estime des hommes, et il

9. Dominique Bouhours, *La Manière de bien penser dans les ouvrages d'esprit* (Brighton, England: University of Sussex Library, 1971 [Paris: Brunet, 1715]). This later work is considerably richer in esthetic conceptions than *Les Entretiens d'Ariste et d'Eugène*.

10. We see this continuity in Bouhours' book, in which the interlocutors of his dialogues have, of course, no trenchant, *geistesgeschichtlich* notion of "baroque" and "neoclassical."

voit que ses défauts ne méritent que leur aversion et leur mépris."
The tragic paradoxes are cast in a largely paratactic style, with much
word repetition and a familiar use of *et* in the sense of *mais*; this is not
the *genus grande* but a demonstration of the way the most serious material can be treated below the highest level of diction. When the sentence structure is more sustained, we find the middle manner of
tragic satire: "237. *Grandeur et misères.* La misère se concluant de la
grandeur, et la grandeur de la misère, les uns ont conclu la misère
d'autant plus qu'ils en ont pris pour preuve la grandeur, et les autres
concluant la grandeur avec d'autant plus de force qu'ils l'ont conclue
de la misére même, tout ce que les uns ont pu dire pour montrer la
grandeur n'a servi que d'un argument aux autres pour conclure la
misére, puisque c'est être d'autant plus misérable qu'on est tombé de
plus haut; et les autres, au contraire." Counting participial constructions and elliptic ones, we find twelve clauses in these few lines;
the brevity of clauses, the density of the argument and the logical relations, and the word repetition, all differ from the sublime tone,
however elevated the matter of the "misères d'un roi dépossédé," as
Pascal calls man's state elsewhere. This peculiar combination of syntax and subject is unlike classical models of style and derives rather
from the Christian tradition. The Epistle to the Romans, the most
elaborate of Saint Paul's works, illustrates Christian rhetoric.

> What shall we say then? Is the law sinful? God forbid. Nay, I had not
> known sin but by the law: for I had not known lust, except the law had
> said, "Thou shalt not covet." But sin, taking occasion by the command-
> ment, wrought in me all manner of concupiscence. For without the law sin
> was dead. For I was alive without the law once: but when the command-
> ment came, sin revived, and I died. And the commandment, which was
> ordained to life, I found to be unto death. . . . Was then that which is good
> made death unto me? God forbid. (7:7–10, 13)

In these few lines, there are nineteen clauses. Antitheses can be
smooth and elegant or crabbed, when they are thick and hard to follow; this prose is remote from high style with its ample phrases
and graceful equilibrium. Pascal's serried reasoning obviously owes
much, directly or indirectly, to this source with its dense antitheses
and causal construction. Saint Paul's prose shows a pronounced taste

for short clauses and phrases, word repetition, paradox, gnomic statements, and questions. It is of course completely in keeping with the Christian paradox of the serious *genus humile* that Saint Paul sought grandeur—for there is a very subtle cultivation of effect in the Epistle to the Romans—in a style devoid of the usual signs of the elevated and that Pascal's *Apologie* was to a large extent conceived of in terms of tragic satire.

Nothing makes one feel more the technically lower range of style that Pascal uses in much of the *Pensées* than the one striking section in high style. Here is the *grand souffle,* as opposed to the narrower dimensions of the satiric colon: "390. Que l'homme contemple donc la nature entière/dans sa haute et pleine majesté;/qu'il éloigne sa vue des objets bas/qui l'environnent./ Qu'il regarde cette éclatante lumière,/mise comme une lampe éternelle/pour éclairer l'univers;/que la terre lui paraisse comme un point/au prix du vaste tour que cet astre décrit/et qu'il s'étonne de ce que ce vaste tour lui-même/n'est qu'une pointe délicate/à l'égard de celui que les astres/qui roulent dans le firmament/embrassent." Each grammatical unit opens with an ample phrase of nine to twelve syllables in the jussive subjunctive. The parallelism of these phrases creates the effect of high style as much as their length does. The poetic *astres* and *firmament,* the comparisons and antitheses are intensified by epitheton, a generally elevating figure: *éclatante lumière* and *lampe éternelle* alone are enough to raise the passage to the sublime. Although Pascal mocks poetic jargon, he is perfectly at home with its devices.

The character of Pascal's typical periods can be seen especially well in a contrast with Descartes'. The latter's solidly expository manner depends for much of its effect on syntactic doublings, as in the opening of the *Discours de la méthode.*

> Le bon sens est la chose du monde la mieux partagée: chacun pense en être si bien pourvu, que ceux même qui sont les plus difficiles à contenter en toute autre chose n'ont point coutume d'en désirer plus qu'ils en ont. En quoi il n'est pas vraisemblable que tous se trompent; mais plutôt cela témoigne que la puissance de bien juger et distinguer le vrai d'avec le faux, qui est proprement ce qu'on nomme le bon sens ou la raison, est naturellement égale en tous les hommes; et ainsi, que la diversité de nos opinions ne vient pas de ce que les uns sont plus raisonnables que les autres, mais

seulement de ce que nous conduisons nos pensées par diverses voies, et ne considérons pas les mêmes choses.

Like Pascal's period in fragments 99, 192, 43, or 237, Descartes' is nonoratorical; the subordinate clauses are weighty at the expense of the main one, and no attempt is made at variety in clause structure: the subject always comes first, followed as soon as possible by the verb. The complete lack of suspended sense or grammar, however, does not make for a "descending" structure or progressively weakened interest, since the thought itself is nicely articulated into major propositions supported by minor ones, all being conceived, furthermore, in binary, complementary patterns. But while Pascal's doublets tend to suggest paradox, to be a confutation of the powers of reason, the spirit of rational method prevails in Descartes' use of such movement: the basic intellectual process is to subdivide into twos. The tranquility of Descartes' bipartite manner contrasts with the nervous, desperate maneuvers of reason in Pascal; whereas the former writes relatively flowing, symmetrical prose, the latter's movement is too precipitous to give a real feeling of balance.

The *A and B* constructions, as we see, are of the utmost importance in analyzing Pascal and Descartes' expository styles. Neither author owes much, in this respect, to Latin. While Descartes' prose is sometimes called "close to Latin," it is not really Latinate in a high classical sense; nor for that matter is Descartes' written Latin, in the *Meditations*. The doublets both Pascal and Descartes use are often concealed in good Latin style, where the variety of *and*'s (*et, -que, ac, atque*) also prevents an effect of sameness. What would be an ordinary, even pedestrian doubling in French or English can be part of an interesting pattern of word order in Latin, as here: "Atque utinam res publica stetisset, quo coeperat, statu nec in homines non tam commutandarum quam evertendarum rerum cupidos incidisset!" (*De Officiis*, II, 1). "I wish that the government had stood as it was and not fallen into the hands of men who want not to reform it but to abolish it." The dull symmetries of the English correspond to an unusual arrangement in Latin: *-isset*—(accusative)—*ndarum*—*ndarum*—(accusative)—*isset*. This kind of *ABCCBA* design, with the added factor of varying spaces between the recurrent elements, is just one suggestion of all that Latin is capable of in the way of syntactico-phonetic structures. We see how profoundly different French neoclassical periodic structure is from Latin: as unlike as the doublings of Pascal and Descartes are, they both belong to a peculiarly modern kind of sentence formation. In both writers, bipartition seems to be the natural form taken by logical discourse, and the failure of logic in Pascal to solve matters belonging properly to faith does not diminish the significance of divisions into twos. In Descartes, on the other hand, where reason is operating in its proper sphere, the doublings proceed with calm order. The periods of neither author are always beautiful in the conventional sense of having elegant rhythm: it is the correspondence to prose style of the thought process and the attitude accompanying it that constitute their power.

4 Balzac and
      Bossuet

The early seventeenth century was characterized in literature by the appearance of a group of "modernists," who did not believe the future of French letters depended in any way upon direct imitation of the ancients: Descartes rejected the traditional body of philosophical writings; Vaugelas held that written language should not derive from previous models but should imitate speech and that women, because they knew no Latin or Greek, spoke the purest French; Théophile de Viau and Malherbe, each in his way, negated the sixteenth-century humanist notion of poetic style; and, finally, Balzac, while preserving a circumspect regard for Seneca and Cicero, based his prose on what his own ear perceived as the best French rhythmic patterns, with no concern for their exact conformity with Latin models of style.

Descartes' modernism is not always fully recognized because of the mistaken notion that his long sentences must somehow be an imitation of classical Latin. Actually, the innovation in his ideas on writing shows up perhaps most in his isolating and labeling the opposing methods of the essay ("analysis"), which follows the thought process, and of the treatise ("synthesis"), which is based on a rigorous arrangement in questions, axioms, definitions, and so forth.[1] In his own work, Descartes used both forms, and the distinction does not correspond to one of language: the *Discours de la méthode* in French and the Latin *Meditations* are essays; the replies to objections to the *Meditations* and the French *Des passions de l'âme* are treatises. Descartes, furthermore, did not simply make the distinction between treatise and essay but gave the latter a form well in advance of his

1. See Peter France, *Rhetoric and Truth in France: Descartes to Diderot* (Oxford: Clarendon, 1972), 51.

76

time: the autobiographical *Discours de la méthode* uses topic sentences for every paragraph (fifteen in Part I) and fastidious, unobtrusive links between them. The expository form, with its close relation of thought and style, is in every way like that which arose more generally in the wake of Buffon's remarks on form and style in the eighteenth century. Descartes established that the essay need not be disorganized, simply because it is informal and personal. The influence of Montaigne seems apparent in the very idea of basing a theory of knowledge on one's own life and experience, but Montaigne's essay is transformed into something more generally useful as a kind of exposition.

Despite his casual dismissal of literary studies in the *Discours de la méthode*, Descartes is a critic at times and, more specifically, an admirer of Balzac's. Descartes finds Balzac lucid, full of high flights of thought, harmonious, comparable to the classical orators, amazingly capable of saying everything in a style based on speech, ornamented but not so much so as to be weakened by it. The general drift of his remarks is modernist and seems almost extravagant, unless we reflect briefly on the general state of French prose in preceding decades— Montaigne excepted as an irregular, idiosyncratic writer. Most of what praise is given Du Vair, Du Perron, and Coeffeteau, the principal prose writers just prior to Balzac, tends to laud their grammar, the clarity of their sentence structure, or their happy choice in alternative expressions. Very little of it is literary in any higher sense, the major problem facing prose writers at the end of the sixteenth century being standardization of French and not individual expression. Their virtues were in a sense negative: they did not write *galimatias* or excessively long sentences. It is only with Balzac, if we follow the theorists of his century, that a truly new, creative idea in prose is formed.[2]

"L'unico eloquente," as Balzac was called, wrote primarily letters from his home near Angoulême and informal essays; his style, consequently, was generally less than sublime, and the modernist horror of *l'école* and humanist pedantry dictated the restriction of language that Descartes noted to words used at court. An important considera-

2. For a general study of Balzac's prose, see Gaston Guillaumie, *Guez de Balzac et la Prose française* (Paris: Picard, 1927).

tion in Balzac's writings was that all his work was destined to be read aloud, not quite as oratory, but with a certain ceremoniousness, as befitted the art of the writer. If one had to classify Balzac with regard to the authors of his day, he might best be called Senecan,[3] being given to asyndetic periods and apothegmatic utterances, but that hardly gives one an idea of his particular savor as a writer. The following passage consists of about two-thirds of a letter of condolence written to a lady who had lost her son. The principal colon divisions are marked by double slashes, additional intonational ones by a single slash.

> Si en l'estat où vous estes,//vous pouvez recevoir de la consolation,//Dieu seul vous en peut donner.//Pour ne rien perdre,//il faut luy offrir//tout ce qu'on perd.//C'est le moyen/de priver la Fortune/de ses droicts;//par là/on oste mesme à la Mort/la puissance de faire mourir.//Croyez-moy, Madame,/ faites une offrande du subjet de vostre douleur,//afin qu'il change de na-ture,//et qu'il devienne la matiere de vostre merite.//Si vous mettez sur les Autels/la chose que vous regrettez,//premierement,/vous en augmenterez le prix,//la faisant passer à un saint usage://Vous rendrez plus parfaite par cette consecration,//une creature que le temps n'avoit pas encore bien achevée;//mais outre cela,/vous la possederez en Dieu plus seurement//que vous ne la possediez en elle-mesme.//Dieu est fidele, Madame,/il vous gar-dera/ce que vous luy aurez donné://Vostre don sera un depost/que vous ne pourrez plus perdre,//l'ayant confié à Celuy chez lequel on trouve tout.//Ce sont des pensées de la Semaine Saincte,//et qui me viennent une fois l'an;// mais ce sont vos meditations de tous les jours://Et quoy que cette sorte de philosophie soit un peu eslevée et un peu abstraite,//elle ne l'est pas pour une ame de la hauteur de la vostre.[4]

This astonishing series of antitheses and conceits reminds us that the epigrammatic was not automatically associated with levity in the earlier seventeenth century. (By the 1670s and 80s, however, pious admiration for Balzac was tempered by the admonition not to imitate his flowery ways.) While the absence of sentence links intensifies the gnomic character of the sentences, the most artful device is the generalized isocolon or near isocolon, which is the greatest secret of Balzac's famous rhythm and harmony, his concinnity, in the classical expression. The cola are often ample, yet not unmanageably long for

3. See the preface to Jean-Louis Guez de Balzac, *Socrate chrestien*.
4. Letter of April 7, 1651, to Madame de Montausier.

reading aloud, and they are never "affectedly short," as one theorist said, voicing an early objection to some kinds of *style coupé*, among which we may often count Montaigne's. They may coincide with the intonational phrases or include more than one of them, constituting a larger rhythmic unit. Equally important, Balzac's cola are normally arranged by twos, threes, or fours, so as to lend great clarity of structure to the period: doublets and triplets are the basis of it, representing the symmetry of halves or of identical elements flanking a central section. The Ciceronian notions that the colon is about the length of a hexameter and that two to four of them is a good average length for a period are often realized in Balzac's prose. Occasionally, two cola will, instead of being nearly the same length, have a traditional unequal yet harmonious relation: one to three-fourths or one to two-thirds. Commata occupy a small place in Balzac's periods; hypotaxis is limited in complexity, adding clearly, when it occurs, to the logical outline of the whole period. Fluent sequentiality of syntax is essential to Balzac's style: there is no hyperbaton in it at all.

While Balzac passed for a Senecan, it is obvious that he is an entirely different kind of Senecan from Montaigne, who employed briefer cola and sometimes exaggerated plainness. It is clear that Balzac, complementing his Senecan affinities, also represents an adaptation, in a modern language, of Gorgian prose, the mannered style long predating the lengthily periodic one and appearing in one form, as we have seen, in Grandgousier's letter in *Gargantua*. Gorgian prose aimed at simultaneous isocolon, antithesis, and rimed colon endings. While the last, in Balzac's day, had completely fallen out of favor in France, the antithesis or *pointe* (Croll claims that in every *pointe* there is a concealed antithesis) and isocolon had not been so widely combined in French as to seem like a banal ornament. Indeed, however old the theory and influence of Gorgian prose was, Balzac's style had, for his contemporaries, an exquisite and entirely new movement.

If Balzac's *pointes* in his letter of condolence strike a modern reader as out of place or charmingly baroque, depending on one's taste, we must remember that rhythm and syntax are "regular," in the favorite seventeenth-century expression for wholeness and harmony; there is no eccentricity, and the general feeling was that such a letter needed the formality of figures. Balzac follows a decorum that is now un-

familiar, having been replaced by the convention of simplicity, with
its own artifices. Balzac had a keen sense of suitability in language.

> Vous dites vray, Monsieur,/on trouve partout de l'imposture./L'esclat ne
> presuppose pas/toujours la solidité;/et les paroles qui brillent le plus,/sont
> souvent celles qui pesent le moins./ Il y a une Faiseuse de bouquets,/et une
> Tourneuse de periodes,/je ne l'ose nommer Eloquence,/qui est toute peinte
> et toute dorée;/qui semble toujours sortir d'une boëte;/qui n'a soin que de
> s'ajuster,/et ne songe qu'à faire la belle:/qui par consequent/est plus propre
> pour les Festes/que pour les Combats,/et plaist davantage qu'elle ne sert;/
> quoy que neantmoins il y ait des Festes,/dont elle deshonoreroit la solem-
> nité;/et des personnes, à qui elle ne donneroit point de plaisir.[5]

(The last clauses demonstrate an important variant from isocolon:
progressive lengthening.) The background against which such comments should be understood needs a word. It was normal for people
of literary inclinations in the seventeenth century to include Spanish
and Italian literature in their reflections on vernacular style, and discussions of what we call the baroque especially involve references to
all three major romance literatures and to poetic and prose ornaments
indiscriminately treated. In Balzac's perspective, there are far more
exaggerated figures than the ones he uses, especially when one takes
Spanish and Italian styles into account. Descartes, who shared that
perspective, understood perfectly Balzac's relation to contemporary
literature when he praised Balzac for his savant simplicity. Certainly,
neither metaphor nor other figures of thought are allowed to impair
the perspicuity of Balzac's prose. The authority for the highly embellished middle style can be found in Cicero's *Orator*: in the middle
style, the most charming of all, ornaments follow one another in
dense succession, "illigantur lepores" (27:96).

The occurrence of descriptive passages in Balzac brings us to a further aspect of baroque rhetorical theory and practice.

> Il fit hier un de ces beaux jours sans soleil, que vous dites qui ressemblent à
> cette belle aveugle, dont Philippe second était amoureux. En vérité je n'eus
> jamais tant de plaisir à m'entretenir moi-même, et quoique je me pro-
> menasse en une campagne toute nue, et qui ne saurait servir à l'usage des
> hommes que pour être le champ d'une bataille, néanmoins l'ombre que le

5. Jean-Louis Guez de Balzac, "Discours cinquiesme, Paraphrase ou de la grande
éloquence," in *Oeuvres* (Paris: Lecoffre, 1854), 276–93.

ciel faisait de tous côtés m'empêchait de désirer celle des grottes et des forêts. La paix était générale depuis la plus haute région de l'air jusque sur la face de la terre; l'eau de la rivière paraissait aussi plate que celle d'un lac, et si en pleine mer un tel calme surprenait pour toujours les vaisseaux, ils ne pourraient jamais ni se sauver ni se perdre.[6]

These expressions could best be interpreted as hyperboles; for example, the shadow in the open field resembling the shade of a grotto, even though the day is not cold and gloomy but beautiful, is, to say the least, exceptional. The *pensées neuves* of baroque taste are excellently illustrated, and the guiding idea is that of a strange, special, *irregular* beauty. The eyes of the blind girl correspond to the sun, in a play on the Petrarchan eye-sun image, the empty sky being the first peculiarity of this landscape devoid of features—the sun and the eye are the major attractive elements in the sky and face. By the paradox we have already commented on, the empty field has the effect of a covered spot. Finally, even wind is absent, and the writer is happy without any exterior cause of pleasure. All this adds up to a kind of experience and beauty not in the rules. Of course, seventeenth-century esthetic thought included the idea of the irregular, the grace beyond the reach of art, the exceptional, in a sense, being foreseen and classified. It is characteristic of the relations between baroque and neoclassical taste that they are not based on genuinely different or heterogeneous conceptions of beauty but that their oppositions are a matter of adjustment involving the same sun, shade, and smooth waters. The whole baroqueness of effect depends on one's having some regular notion of beauty and referring to it.

The quality of the description, the comparisons, the vocabulary, the oxymora, and the moderate tone are not unrelated to descriptions in Théophile and Saint-Amant; that is to say, Balzac's passage is not remote from the lyric. But the stylistic features of the lyric are by no means the ones ascribed to it since romanticism. Lyric in renaissance theory was an embellished genre, indeed, perhaps the most embellished, but its pitch was in the middle-style range. In the seventeenth-century technical distinction, it was *agréable*, not sublime. Therefore, to find similarities between a prose passage and lyric of

6. Letter of September, 1622, to Monsieur de la Motte-Aignon.

that period is not to suggest that the prose reaches some rare point of elevation. Since every genre and tone has its own particular excellence, it is not a disparagement of lyric to situate it as one of the three facets of middle style, the others being satire and the didactic. It suggests the high value placed on each genre in itself; for example, one of Bouhours' learned participants in his dialogues considers Voiture to be among the most important of writers.

While we can speak of Balzac's description as baroque, we must recognize a number of factors and discriminations. If irregularity is held to be baroque, the sentence structure of Balzac is, on the contrary, striking in its approximation or realization of isocolon; certainly the deliberate asymmetries of Pascal's style have nothing in common with Balzac. The metaphoric *pensées neuves* we find in Pascal at first seem to be of another order than Balzac's comparisons and references to absent grottos, hypothetical battles, an exemplary *belle aveugle*, and becalmed ships; Balzac's style is florid and given to amplification. Pascal's images are based on unexpected logic, Balzac's on an exceptional and therefore surprising concept of beauty. It is perfectly in consonance with rhetorical theory, however, that a genre distinction be made.

If the idea of the baroque is to be useful, it has to be clear that there are baroque lyric and polemic-satiric styles (in verse, Saint-Amant and Sigogne, say) that resemble each other no more than neoclassical lyric and satiric styles have ever been supposed to; the imagistic, often somewhat grotesque passages in Pascal, like the picture of the philosopher on his board, can serve as an example of baroque satiric tendencies. While period styles exist at a certain degree of generality, genre and levels of style are often more germane to the actual conditions of writing, the esthetic choices, the relation of a work to what has gone before. The rhetorical order of styles seemed, in the renaissance and seventeenth century, a natural way art imitated the society of men and the idea of the universe, and it was not the negative thing it is sometimes imagined to have been. Not only did it provide a large number of models, it also absorbed and gave meaning to new kinds of writing like poetic prose or the informal essay.

I do not wish to imply, despite the foregoing, that the place a certain work or author occupied in the system of styles was totally unambiguous, and Balzac is a case in point. In the absence of any more imposing works of literature in the traditional high genres, Balzac's letters and essays, essentially middle-level genres, seemed formidably eloquent and even sublime to some contemporaries; and later on in the century, when readers began to feel that Balzac had deployed unduly grandiose means for the epistolary genre, his diction was sometimes supposed to have been an attempt at high style. By that time, however, there existed in fact a body of truly sublime prose writings in one of the highest of epideictic genres, Bossuet's *oraisons funèbres*, in which it is very easy to see the characteristics of true high style separating it from Balzac's prose: gravity, power, amplitude.

Bossuet did not arrive early at the *oraison funèbre* and a high neo-classical style. As elsewhere, religious literature is associated in France with baroque style, and Bouhours alludes to an abundance of sermons full of extraordinary *pointes*, which entertained the faithful for quite some time;[7] he even provides a sample of a *discours funèbre* for Louis XIII delivered in the candlelit Sainte Chapelle, whence a reference in it.

> Quoy donc, grand Soleil de nos Rois!/las, au milieu de nostre course,/ estes-vous déja au couchant,/et d'un si haut point de gloire,/estes-vous précipité/dans une éternelle défaillance?/Non, non, bel Astre,/vous montez en vous abbaissant,/et vous mesurez mesme/vos élévations par vos chutes./ Pompes funébres,/pourquoy me déguisez-vous ses triomphes?/Si ma Sainte Chapelle est ardente,/elle n'éclatera qu'en feux de joye;/ce sera dans les évidentes démonstrations/ou je reproduiray nostre Monarque tout auguste,/ parce qu'il a esté tout humble,/et hautement relevé dans Dieu/par une servitude couronnée,/pour n'avoir point eu de couronnes/qui ne luy fussent assujéties.
>
> Royale abstinence des plaisirs,/soleil naissant dans les abîmes,/plénitude dans le vuide,/manne dans les déserts,/toison trempée où tout est sec;/ corps desséché où les plaisirs le peuvent noyer,/corps trempé et tout imbu de consolations/où l'austérité le desséche!/Allez, grande âme,/digne hoste d'un si riche Palais.[8]

This is obviously the work of someone who had an ear for Balzacian rhythms, to judge by the exact or approximate isocolon I have indi-

7. Dominique Bouhours, *La Manière de bien penser dans les ouvrages d'esprit* (Brighton: University of Sussex Library, 1971 [Paris: Brunet, 1715]), 74.
8. *Ibid.*, 467–68.

cated with slashes. Moreover, it is not really the conception of the imagery that impairs the effect of this writing; indeed it builds up ingeniously to the final phrase *Ascendit super occasum*, alluding to the fact that Louis XIII died on Ascension Day—"He rose as he set." The reason for the somewhat grotesque impression the figures give is that the details of the diction are only imperfectly worked out. This is an abortive attempt to handle the highest laudatory material, the life of a king, in a baroque mode beyond the *agréable*, in the sublime tone; hence, we have the hyperbolic pomp, the vehement apostrophes. There exists, I believe, no fully realized example of baroque sublime style in French prose.

Bossuet's early sermons have the same Balzacian feeling for recurrent colon length as our *discours funèbre* for Louis XIII, but they are not in an epideictic so much as an admonitory genre. This is from a sermon on the Passion, preached in the 1650s before Bossuet came to Paris.

> O plaies, que je vous adore!/flétrissures sacrées,/que je vous baise!/ô sang qui découlez,/soit de la tête percée,/soit des yeux meurtris,/soit de tout le corps déchiré,/ô sang précieux, que je vous recueille!/Terre, terre, ne bois pas ce sang:/*Terra, ne operias/sanguinem meum:*/Terre, ne couvre pas mon sang,/disait Job./Mais qu'importe du sang de Job?/Mais ô terre,/ne bois pas/le sang de Jésus:/ce sang nous appartient/et c'est sur nos âmes/ qu'il doit tomber./J'entends les Juifs qui crient:/Son sang soit sur nous/et sur nos enfants./Il y sera,/race maudite:/tu ne seras que trop exaucée:/ce sang te poursuivra/jusqu'à tes derniers rejetons,/jusqu'à ce que le Seigneur,/se lassant enfin de ses vengeances,/se souviendra/à la fin des siècles/de tes misérables restes./Oh! que le sang de Jésus/ne soit point sur nous en cette sorte,/qu'il ne crie point vengeance/contre notre long endurcissement;/qu'il soit sur nous pour notre salut;/que je me lave de ce sang;/ que je sois tout couvert de ce sang;/que le vermeil de ce beau sang/empêche mes crimes de paraître/devant la justice divine![9]

We have spoken of the ultimate reality of the concrete and individual for Montaigne and of Pascal's tragic satire with its intermittent grotesque images: here in Bossuet we find a devotional Christian form taken by this same insistence on the bodily. It is not entirely possible to separate the patristic origins of this style from the pagan Silver

---

9. Jacques-Bénigne Bossuet, *Oeuvres complètes*, ed. F. Lachat (31 vols.; Paris: Louis Vivès, 1872), X, 15–16.

Latin rhetoric of horror and gruesome detail.[10] The concrete aspects of life that belonged to the satiric invade elevated discourse, dispelling the old conception of the sublime with a new kind of language that cannot be called high style in a classical-Ciceronian sense but that serves as the serious style replacing it. This is the other genre of baroque than the *agréable*; it is not the whole of baroque art, since no single style can ever serve all needs at any given time, but it is one that has received much attention because of its important place in European poetry. In this particular example, we see a prose counterpart to a typical form of that poetry: the baroque exercise of summoning up before the eyes a moment of sacred history, especially of the Passion, and an elaborate play on the figurative and literal sense of blood.

There is very little in the attempt at a baroque high style in the *discours* for Louis XIII, or in the convulsive monologue on the Passion, to suggest the way toward the neoclassical oration evolved by Bossuet and imitated by lesser figures. Essentially, it depended on a development of style in close parallel with worldly taste, coming about as Bossuet spent more and more time in contact with the court.[11] Other ecclesiastics went on writing in baroque style, but they had neither Bossuet's intimate knowledge of life in the royal entourage nor his responsibilities to the monarchy.

After a few years during which Bossuet delivered Lenten sermons in Paris and even before the court, he had the opportunity of undertaking a different genre, the first in which epideictic high or sublime style found appropriate prose expression; in the *oraison funèbre*, the neoclassical concern for the matching of style and genre achieved genuine fulfillment. Bossuet delivered twelve *oraisons funèbres*—not at the funeral ceremonies but much later—between 1665 and 1687; the one I shall take my examples from is the oration for Henriette of England, daughter of Charles I and wife of Louis XIV's brother. Chateaubriand thought it Bossuet's masterpiece because it did not banally treat the poetic theme of the contrast between beauty, grandeur, and

10. Erich Auerbach, *Mimesis: The Representation of Reality in Western Literature*, trans. Willard Trask (Garden City: Doubleday, 1957), 57–59.
11. For general studies of Bossuet and style, see J. A. Quillacq, *La Langue et la Syntaxe de Bossuet* (Tours: Cattier, 1903), and Thérèse Goyet, *L'Humanisme de Bossuet* (2 vols.; Paris: Klincksieck, 1965).

youth, on the one hand, and death, on the other. Bossuet succeeded in raising his commonplace material to the highest theological considerations, the wretchedness and greatness of mankind.

Chateaubriand, hurrying on to find melancholy, his measure of beauty, in Bossuet, passes a bit quickly over the particular problems facing the late seventeenth-century Christian writer addressing an aristocratic audience. Traditionally, Christianity had two principles for the imagery of grandeur: poverty on earth is associated with riches in heaven (or spiritual wealth on earth); the materially rich man will not easily enter the kingdom of heaven. The court of Bossuet's day, however, was organized around the worship of material wealth and presided over by Louis XIV, who, as deity, distributed bounty in a theological system of *pensions, charges*, and *bénéfices*, often in exchange for sacrifice in the form of gold. This society had its own noble or spiritual form of expression: neoclassical high style in literature and the fine arts, which had no relation to the traditional low serious style of Christianity, of which Balzac said, "Deux choses qui sont séparées partout ailleurs se rencontrent et s'unissent dans la Sainte Escriture: la simplicité [*i.e.*, plainness] et la majesté." This was a peculiarity of Christianity, whose triumph was, moreover, an "événement irrégulier."

Essentially, the system of the seventeenth-century court was self-contained and could have subsisted without Christianity, had it not been for quirks of tradition and individual psychology, which maintained Christianity as a separate, coexistent realm of values. The one point where the two structures met was the fact that, as Saint John Chrysostom observed, death, unlike the various theoretical Christian condemnations of vanity, actually makes one experience the emptiness of worldly ambitions. Courtiers could do without a redeemer, but they could not avoid death. The *oraison funèbre* was the highest expression of this meeting of courtly vanity and Christian contempt for the world.

There are many aspects of *éloquence* in Bossuet's orations that we need not examine in any detail, such as the rhetorical question or allusion and quotation; they are common to the preaching style in general and do not in themselves, despite superiority of handling, help isolate Bossuet's peculiar style. Isocolon is another matter, for it is treated in his mature style differently from the way Balzac used it.

> Considérez, Messieurs [6], ces grandes puissances [5] que nous regardons de si bas [8]. Pendant que nous tremblons sous leur main [9], Dieu les frappe pour nous avertir [8]. Leur élévation en est la cause [9]; et il les épargne si peu [8] qu'il ne craint pas de les sacrifier [9] à l'instruction du reste des hommes [9]. Chrétiens, ne murmurez pas [7] si Madame a été choisie [8] pour nous donner une telle instruction [9]. Il n'y a rien ici de rude pour elle [10], puisque, comme vous le verrez dans la suite [10], Dieu la sauve [3] par le même coup [4] qui nous instruit [4]. Nous devrions [4] être assez convaincus [6] de notre néant [5]; mais s'il faut des coups de surprise [8], à nos cœurs enchantés de l'amour du monde [11], celui-ci est assez grand et assez terrible [12]. O nuit désastreuse [5]! ô nuit effroyable [5], où retentit tout à coup [7], comme un éclat de tonnerre [7], cette étonnante nouvelle [7]: Madame se meurt [4], Madame est morte [4]![12]

The many isocolonic or near isocolonic phrases occur in twos, threes, and even fours. Although the eight- or nine-syllable length predominates toward the beginning, we see how varied the cola become later on; Balzac's art does not often show isocolon with this union of sameness and contrast. As important, however, is the fact that all but the first sentence finish with two isocolonic phrases or nearly so. There is something quite special here: the two phrases do not sound alike, since the second ends with the concluding intonational drop of all declarative French sentences. In other words, we have a special cadential unit, which cannot be matched by any other two isocolonic expressions earlier in the sentence. It is not surprising that Bossuet's two most famous phrases should be of this form: "Madame se meurt . . ." and at the end of his last oration, that for the Prince de Condé, "les restes d'une voix qui tombe, et d'une ardeur qui s'éteint." Bossuet is the first systematic user of this cadence, which, under his influence, at least to begin with, became an important resource of the grand style in French.

In our passage, it is notable that syntactic doublings do not occur; Bossuet often achieves grandeur without that handy formula for im-

---

12. It is unlikely that Bossuet actually counted syllables. Certain factors are, moreover, variables in calculating the number of syllables in the cola of writers like Bossuet, Rousseau, or Chateaubriand. There are optional mute *e*s pronounced in very formal

pressiveness. Generally, the hypotaxis draws no attention to itself, in keeping with Bossuet's frequent economy of means. The conclusion, however, borders on the realm of poetic syntax: a grammatically rather plain series of sentences leads to a dramatic final exclamation. Bossuet is often ingenious in the large-scale planning of his sentence structures, so that the unobtrusive alternates with the unusual.

Of the overall rhythmic patterns for periods, there exists, besides isocolon, the structure concluding with a longer phrase than what precedes: "Après que [2] par le dernier effort [5] de notre courage [5] nous avons [3], pour ainsi dire [4], surmonté la mort [5], elle éteint en nous [5] jusqu'à ce courage [5] par lequel nous semblions la défier [10]. La voilà [3], malgré ce grand cœur [5], cette princesse si admirée [7], et si chérie [4], la voilà telle que la mort nous l'a faite [10]." Here again sentence structure is highly planned; a period with clauses before and after the main verb yields to repetition and apposition. Bossuet's poetic syntax is juxtaposed to dissimilar sentence forms, and the latter are complexly embodied in various rhythmic patterns. The asymmetrical long phrases at the end of both sentences seem to constitute a final summing up of the effects of death. However, Bossuet has yet more. After these periods ending with a conclusive long colon, he proceeds directly to the opposite pattern, one of diminishing cola, to express the absolute nothingness of death: "Encore ce reste tel quel va-t-il disparaître [12]: cette ombre de gloire va s'évanouir [9], et nous l'allons voir dépouillée [8] même de cette triste décoration [9]. Elle va descendre à ces sombres lieux [9], à ces demeures souterraines [8], pour y dormir dans la poussière [8] avec les grands de la terre [7], comme parle Job [4], avec ces rois et ces princes anéantis [12], parmi lesquels à peine peut-on la placer [11], tant les rangs y sont pressés [7], tant la mort est prompte [5] à remplir ces places [5]!" There is a rhythmic enchainment from the long colon ending the preceding period to the long colon beginning *Encore ce reste*. This beginning is paratactic, only to lead into subordinate

---

delivery, just as there are optional liaisons. Obviously, all *es* will be pronounced to avoid the meeting of three consonants or of similar consonants (*Georg-e Sand*) and many *es* terminating adjectives before nouns (*ces grand-es puissances*). Often, the principle of isocolon serves as a guide to the most elegant choice of mute *es* to pronounce.

clauses toward the end, in keeping with Bossuet's large-scale plotting of varied sentence forms. Apposition, here, as often, a distinctly poetic device, occurs just as the sentence seems to have died out with *comme parle Job*; by a surprising reprise with *avec*, the sentence acquires new propulsion, only again to dwindle away in diminishing cola. Diminution of phrase length is a Latin pattern, not so common perhaps as augmenting cola, and a pattern that Bossuet made peculiarly his own. It may have great drama, as in *Madame se meurt* or be used, as here, to render nothingness and the realization of vanity.

The imagery in this passage is Bossuet's at its best: in his Christian humanist synthesis, the depiction of the return to dust is mingled with the Virgilian imagery of the clustered souls in Hades. The Biblical imagery he periodically uses is softened by its passage through the Latin Vulgate and blends easily with classical reminiscences.

Besides the diminishing pattern, there is also the abruptly short, unpaired final colon, as in this long period, which shows Bossuet playing with near isocolon interrupted by commata: "Notre princesse est persécutée avant que de naître [14], délaissée aussitôt que mise au monde [10], arrachée en naissant à la piété d'une mère catholique [15], captive dès le berceau des ennemis implacables de sa maison [17], et [1], ce qui était plus déplorable [8], captive des ennemis de l'Eglise [8], par conséquent [4], destinée premièrement par sa glorieuse naissance [12], et ensuite par sa malheureuse captivité [12], à l'erreur et à l'hérésie [8]." The parallel adjectival phrases, with their word repetitions, vary in length to compensate for syntactic sameness. However, following on *destinée*, we find Bossuet taking advantage of one of the few suspension devices left in neoclassical French: the long phrases with *par* widely separate the participle from its necessary *à* clause; *par* . . . is grammatically nonessential and intercalated. It is characteristic of the great writer to find some acceptable infringement of natural grammar and devise interesting sentence forms within the severe limitations of the stylistic standards of his day. This is a very subtle way of displacing stress of meaning to the end of the sentence, as is the sudden eight-syllable colon length. Of course, Bossuet achieves final emphasis by semantic means as well: the last word, *hérésie*, is one of tremendous emotional force for Bossuet, who devoted a good part of his energies to studying the religious deviations of the English and Germans in order to lead them back to sound doctrine. The period shows, in an especially intense form, the emphasis Bossuet tended to put on the end of his sentences; the final words are frequently essential and strong, to a greater extent than one feels them to be in earlier French prose writers.

Just as Bossuet uses the rhythmic device of diminution or abrupt shortening of cola to make a striking conclusion for his sentences, he also, as we have seen, employs syntax to the same end. Earlier, we observed that the classical construction in which the main verb, and sometimes the subject as well, is postponed until near the end of the period is impressively used by Rabelais, Amyot, Malherbe, and Pascal. Its contrast with normal word order has a perhaps even more dramatic effect in Bossuet, where it is judiciously used in what is largely a context of syntactically unexceptional sentences: "C'est pour cela que l'Ecclésiaste, le roi Salomon fils du roi David, car je suis bien aise de vous faire voir la succession de la même doctrine dans un même trône; c'est, dis-je, pour cela que l'Ecclésiaste, faisant le dénombrement des illusions qui travaillent les enfants des hommes, y comprend la sagesse même." The irony is created by the portentous opening and repetition of the opening of the period. In the following period there are two apodoses or conclusions, the first short and deflating, yet canceled out immediately by still another one: "De quelque superbe distinction que se flattent les hommes, ils ont tous une même origine; et cette origine est petite." One must admire the sure sense which led Bossuet to avoid the construction: *ils ont tous la même petite origine.*

Bossuet felt that Balzac was the only French writer who had influenced him; he read Latin far more than the vernacular and considered Cicero and the Bible his true sources. Certainly, he shares the habit of isocolon with Balzac, as well as with Latin prose, but the elaborate asymmetries of his style are characteristic of Cicero's constant variation in sentence form and of the general Latin formulas of increasing or decreasing length of cola. Cicero's art lies, to a large extent, in his range of sentence patterns, and Bossuet understood it far better than the preceding century of humanists, with the exception of

Rabelais. The constant yet often unobtrusive, unpointed parallelisms and antitheses Bossuet uses are, for example, characteristic of Cicero's refinement of detail. Bossuet's is a truly classical Latin concinnity, within the limits of French phonetic and syntactic possibilities.

The mention of Cicero suggests another question in analyzing Bossuet's style, that is, whether his art should be seen as baroque or neoclassical. To begin with, Bossuet suits more than Pascal the latter's notion that writing is a game of tennis in which one player handles more skillfully the ball that both play with: we see in the matter of Bossuet's prose some of the great devotional commonplaces and Biblical generalities, the repository of which are the poetic books from the prophets to Ecclesiastes. This would seem to suggest that Bossuet's place is among the neoclassical rather than the more baroque artists like Pascal, with their *pensées neuves*. However, it has become habitual to refer to the Biblical imagery of flux (life is a dream, dust, cloud, shadow, water in the night) as baroque, on the general grounds that neoclassical art avoids the idea of flux and is reluctant to use imagery. (Certainly, the imagery of flux is commonly said to constitute part of the baroque side of Montaigne and the poets contemporary with him.) Again, however, distinctions of genre rather than period are relevant: if the *langue noble* of neoclassical tragedy largely eschews metaphor and simile, the sublime can accommodate them. It had always been understood that stage language, dialogue and monologue, being a stylized representation of speech, could not generally aspire to the highest level of poetic figures but that all epideictic, laudatory rhetoric could and should. Bossuet's imagistic language, therefore, does not violate neoclassical decorum. Actually, these questions of baroqueness and neoclassicism are unnecessarily complicated, if one fails to understand that, as both kinds of style spring from the same rhetorical tradition, most of the elements of baroque literature can be found, to a lesser degree of density, in neoclassical writing, with the reverse being also true.

What, in any case, is the most important single aspect of the *oraison funèbre* is that it constitutes a prose genre corresponding to the ode to a royal or heroic figure, which, as a work of the highest style, was an object of special concern in the classical and renaissance teaching of epideictic rhetoric, witness Ronsard and Malherbe's odes to the royal family. No previously established prose genre in France—the panegyric does not have much of a history—inherited such a body of elevated rhetorical ways of expression, including, of course, the Longinian notion of sublime directness: "Madame se meurt." Thus we have, for the first time in seventeenth-century literature, abundant examples of how prose can reach the heights to which it came to aspire frequently in later centuries.

Seventeenth-century preachers other than Bossuet were much admired in their day, especially Bourdaloue, who began preaching after Bossuet's duties as supervisor of the dauphin's education and various commitments had taken him away from the Lenten and other sermons he had first become famous for. A passage from Bourdaloue can show, I think, why Bossuet is incomparably the greater writer.

> C'est de notre ferveur que dépend la sainteté de notre vie, mais c'est de la sainteté de notre vie que dépend la sainteté de notre mort. Voilà, dit Jean Chrysostome, l'ordre que la providence divine a établi entre ces trois choses, entre notre vie, entre notre ferveur et entre notre mort. Ce qui renverse cet ordre, c'est un certain fonds de lâcheté, qui fait d'abord une vie criminelle, et qui la fait terminer par une mort malheureuse; il s'agit donc ici de vaincre cette lâcheté pour remettre toutes choses dans leur ordre, puisque c'est cette lâcheté qui le pervertit et qui le change; et c'est ce qu'est venu faire principalement le Sauveur de nos âmes quand il a paru dans le monde. Qu'est-il venu faire ici-bas? *Ignem veni mittere in mundum*, je n'ai point eu d'autre dessein, dit cet adorable Sauveur de nos âmes, que de détruire la lâcheté des hommes et de ranimer leur ferveur: *Ignem veni mittere in mundum*.[13]

This talented, ingenious, circular rhetoric is reminiscent much more of Pascal than of Bossuet: the tight, almost contorted-seeming logic, with its abundant word repetitions, doubtless stems from the same Pauline and other stylistic sources. I should think that this showy display of dialectic would have dazzled the audience, like the baroque conceits of an earlier decade, rather than persuaded them. Bourdaloue uses also the violent, aggressive style, which Bossuet had cultivated at the beginning of his career; the images would be effective if they had not been used so very often.

13. Louis Bourdaloue, *Sermons choisis* (Paris: Garnier, 1936), 216–17.

Je n'ai qu'à dire à cet avare ce que Jésus-Christ dit dans l'Evangile: *veni et vide*, venez et voyez, venez à ce sépulcre, considérez-y ce cadavre. C'était un homme riche et opulent comme vous, qui avait un grand train comme vous, quantité de terres comme vous, quantité de rentes comme vous, il a eu la folie comme vous de vouloir laisser une famille grande et une postérité riche, venez et voyez: *veni et vide*; et qu'est-ce que cet homme? En est-il maintenant plus riche, son or et son argent l'ont-ils exempté de la pourriture, ses richesses l'ont-elles défendu contre les vers? Je n'ai qu'à dire à cet ambitieux: venez, idolâtre de la grandeur, venez, adorateur de la fortune, venez, esclave de la faveur, et voyez: *veni et vide*, ouvrez ce tombeau; tout superbe et tout magnifique qu'il est, qu'y remarquez-vous? ah! le dirai-je, chrétiens, et votre délicatesse le pourra-t-elle souffrir? vous y voyez un cadavre tout nu, tout décharné, tout rongé de vers, tout plein d'ordure et de pourriture. Hé bien! qu'en pensez-vous? C'était un homme comme vous.[14]

Bourdaloue is actually saying something of the same thing, at a different level, that Bossuet develops in the oration for Henriette of England: the emptiness of worldly vanities. Here, however, we encounter the old Christian polemic and satiric tone, the serious low style with its worms and dead bodies. Bossuet, in comparison, was not only *de bonne compagnie* in his funeral orations, his reliance on variation rather than monotonous repetition, passing for strength, is a much more difficult and effective kind of art. Bourdaloue gives the impression of being a narrow, single-minded ecclesiastic, shouting at his audience as his kind had done for centuries.

The genuine popularity that Bourdaloue enjoyed suggests the varied taste of readers and churchgoers of, say, Mme de Sévigné's generation. Traditional pulpit rhetoric—which may seem baroque to us but belongs to a longer tradition—persisted, with its admonitory images, and the newer neoclassicism of Bossuet did not entirely displace it, although Bossuet's manner left its mark on the more sober ecclesiastical productions such as Fléchier's noted *oraison funèbre* for Turenne. It would be too simple to imagine that the greater writers of Louis XIV's reign alone cultivated a neoclassical style and that the *minores* continued in the earlier baroque vein; what we find, actually, besides baroque, is a diversity of neoclassical styles, all adhering, in one way or another, to the traditions of rhetorical theory.

14. *Ibid.*, 208–209.

5 The Later Seventeenth Century, La Bruyère, and Saint-Simon

By the end of the 1660s, said La Bruyère in retrospect, French prose had become "regular," thrown off the yoke of Latinity, and recaptured the harmony and rhythm of Balzac's prose, which momentarily had been lost. Dominique Bouhours published in 1671 his series of dialogues between "Ariste" and "Eugène," which contained a radically neoclassical doctrine of style: all hyperbole and distorted word order and all avoidable metaphor were to be excised from French prose as foreign and unnatural. Genre is not discussed, but we sense Bouhours is speaking primarily of middle style. This is, of course, an extreme development of the anti-Latin, antihumanist principle put forth by Vaugelas decades before. Against these in some ways complacent views, we may set a passage from Fénelon's *Lettre à l'Académie* (1714), in which he interprets the same movement in French prose rather differently: "On a appauvri, desséché, et gêné notre langue. Elle n'ose jamais procéder que suivant la méthode la plus scrupuleuse et la plus uniforme de la grammaire. On voit toujours venir d'abord un nominatif substantif qui mène son adjectif comme par la main; son verbe ne manque pas de marcher derrière, suivi d'un adverbe qui ne souffre rien entre deux; et le régime appelle aussitôt un accusatif, qui ne peut jamais se déplacer. C'est ce qui exclut toute suspension de l'esprit, toute attention, toute surprise, toute variété, et souvent toute magnifique cadence."[1] Fénelon's typical sentence is not literally, of course, the sole syntactic pattern we find, but he is making the important point that style was in danger of becoming anonymously regular. As an illustration, we can use the preface to Charles

---

1. François de Salignac de la Mothe Fénelon, *Lettre à l'Académie*, ed. Ernesta Caldarini (Geneva: Droz, 1970), 71–72.

Perrault's *Parallèle des anciens et des modernes* (1688–1696); here, to reverse Pascal's *mot*, we find not a man but only an author.

> Rien n'est plus naturel ni plus vraisemblable que d'avoir beaucoup de vénération pour toutes les choses qui, ayant un vrai mérite en elles-mêmes, y joignent encore celui d'être anciennes. C'est ce sentiment si juste et si universel qui redouble l'amour et le respect que nous avons pour nos ancêtres et c'est par là que les lois et les coutumes se rendent encore plus authentiques et plus inviolables. Mais, comme ç'a toujours été le destin des meilleures choses de devenir mauvaises par leurs excès et de le devenir à proportion de leur excellence, souvent cette vénération si louable dans ses commencements s'est changé dans la suite en une superstition criminelle et a passé même quelquefois jusqu'â l'idolâtrie.

Every sentence is in strict natural word order; the deviations from the subject-verb-object sequence (such as *ayant* in the first sentence and the emphatic position of *par là* in the second) are themselves codified as allowable infringements. The many doublings have an interesting feature, if we compare them with those of Descartes, the model of functional expository prose; while every binary construction, on examination, is perfectly justifiable, the reader has not so much the impression of rational exploration, as in the *Discours de la méthode*, as that of a mold to which thought is made to conform. The regularity of doublets does not appear to represent the necessary processes of ratiocination.

It is not altogether true, however, that cadence and variety were everywhere excluded, as Fénelon claims. Such prose as Perrault's served for most uses, but neoclassical theory and sensibility recognized places where a distinctly higher style was needed, and, although much syntactic elaboration was out of the question, so strong was the adherence to natural word order, one could draw on a special vocabulary. Here are Racine and Boileau as *historiographes du Roi*, writing the *Précis historique des campagnes de Louis XIV*, which deserves an exceptional dignity of language: "Le Roi, instruit du dessein de ses ennemis, se met en état de les prévenir, et s'empare de la ville de Trèves. Alors l'Empereur crut qu'il était temps d'éclater; il ne se souvient plus des engagements qu'il avait faits avec le Roi, ni du traité qu'il avait signé. Il oublie que les Français, quelques années auparavant, sur les bords du Raab, avaient sauvé l'Empire de la fureur des infidèles. Il fait des plaintes et des manifestes remplis d'injures, et publie partout que le roi de France veut usurper la couronne impériale, et aspirer à la monarchie universelle."[2] The *langue noble* of tragedy is the model here, and we see the tendency toward those elevated synonyms of commoner words that, despite the narrowness of the literary vocabulary, nonetheless existed: *instruit du dessein* is superior to *ayant appris les intentions; se mettre en état de* has more syllables than *se préparer* and a vaster quality; *éclater* is at once strong and vague. *Manifestes* is a technical term of government which calls for *publier*, the latter being not only literal but also an elegant substitute for *faire savoir, faire croire. Sauver de la fureur des infidèles* is a stylish way of putting *sauver des infidèles furieux*, and *aspirer à la monarchie universelle* is a nice hyperbole, since even the imperium of Germany would not make Louis ruler of the world. The syntax, we note, corresponds in its doublets and word order to the model of the Perrault passage. Racine has no period particularly suited to his elevated subject matter.

On the stylistic plane, immediately beneath the theater of royal actions, the language of romance illustrates the elevated yet middle style, love being, however noble the lovers, on a less exalted plane than the epic of kingly military exploits. *La Princesse de Clèves* (1678) is written in a kind of idealized, moderately ceremonious colloquial idiom, free from self-conscious ornament or calculated *style coupé*: "Jamais cour n'a eu tant de belles personnes et d'hommes admirablement bien faits; et il sembloit que la nature eust pris plaisir à placer ce qu'elle donne de plus beau dans les plus grandes Princesses et dans les plus grands Princes. Mme Elizabeth de France, qui fut depuis Reine d'Espagne, commençoit à faire paraître un esprit surprenant et cette incomparable beauté qui luy a esté si funeste."[3] The hyperbolic expressions characteristic of Mme de Lafayette were approved by Vaugelas as part of the rapprochement between written and refined spoken usage. The repetition of *beau, bien fait, admirable*, and *grand* in the opening pages of *La Princesse de Clèves* goes, however, counter to

2. Jean Racine, *Oeuvres complètes*, Bibliothèque de la Pléiade (2 vols.; Paris: Gallimard, 1952), II, 213.
    3. Marie-Madeleine, comtesse de La Fayette, *La Princesse de Clèves*, ed. Emile Magne (Geneva: Droz, 1950), 7.

Vaugelas' principle of avoiding words recurring on the same page, but the effect is one of elegant carelessness. *L'honnête homme ne se pique de rien.*

There is one link between Racine's style in the *Précis* and Mme de Lafayette's studied negligence: the taste for abstract words, in many ways the key to French neoclassical literary vocabulary—and I emphasize the adjective French because we do not find in Italian or English, for example, anything quite like the density of distinctive uses found, even in prose, in French. Bouhours' *Eugène* takes care to note that French is far richer in abstractions than is high classical Latin, *ingratitude* being one of his examples of an abstraction that cannot be Latinized in one word. The semipersonifications of abstract qualities in the *moraliste* vocabulary we have seen in Pascal, and in regard to the general tendency to abstraction, *La Princesse de Clèves* contains a certain number of not uncharacteristic sentences such as "La singularité d'un pareil aveu dont elle ne trouvait point d'exemple, lui en faisoit voir tout le péril." In poetic or *précieux* language (*les commodités de la conversation*: chairs) both singulars and plurals of abstractions, used with a freedom unknown since Latin high style, make a kind of blur between the concrete and the abstract.[4] Such attenuation or *Dämpfung* is as proper to French neoclassicism as the softening figure of litotes (*ne pas haïr* for *aimer*).[5] Another, related grammatical and lexical device, which has received less attention, involves the special category of abstract words related to verbs. Besides their other uses, they tend to be joined to common, colorless verbs in many places where we would naturally use a more precise and dynamic verb; some of the most easily perceived and typical effects of neoclassicism come from this: "La passion de M. de Nemours pour Mme de Clèves

4. *Cf.*, "Atque hoc quidem omnes mortales sic habent, externas commoditates . . . ubertatem frugum et fructuum, omnem denique commoditatem prosperitatemque vitae a dis se habere." Cicero, *De Natura Deorum*, II, 36. "But mortals think that all external goods, abundant harvests and fruits, all the comfort and prosperity of their lives come from the gods." *Cf.* also, "celebrities" and "commodities market" and see Ferdinand Brunot, *Histoire de la langue française des origines à nos jours* (13 vols.; Paris: Armand Colin, 1966), III, 461–63.
5. See Leo Spitzer, "Die klassische Dämpfung in Racines Stil," in *Romanische Stil- und Literaturstudien* (2 vols.; Marburg: Elwert, 1931), I, 135–268. For further remarks on attenuation, see Donna Kuizenga, *Narrative Strategies in La Princesse de Clèves* (Lexington, Ky.: French Forum, 1976), 87–116.

fut d'abord si violente qu'elle lui *ôta le goust* et mesme *le souvenir* de toutes les personnes qu'il avait aimées et avec qui il avoit *conservé des commerces* pendant son absence. Il ne *prit* pas seulement *le soin* de chercher des prétextes pour rompre avec elles; il ne put *se donner la patience* d'ecouter leurs plaintes et de répondre à leurs reproches. Mme la Dauphine, pour qui il *avoit eu des sentiments* assez passionnez, ne put tenir dans son cœur contre Mme de Clèves."[6] *Oter le souvenir de*, *avoir des sentiments pour*, *conserver des commerces*, and the others are ways of saying *faire oublier*, *aimer*, *écrire*, and so forth.

In speaking of Mme de Lafayette's colloquial quality, we should be aware of different ways of interpreting Vaugelas' dictum: "La plus grande de toutes les erreurs en matière d'écrire est de croire, comme font plusieurs, qu'il ne faut pas écrire comme l'on parle. Ils s'imaginent que quand on se sert des phrases usitées, et qu'on a accoutumé d'entendre, le langage en est bas, et fort éloigné du bon style." Montaigne certainly used elements of speech, but his plain style was deliberately abrupt and irregular. Balzac, with his natural word order, comparatively limited hypotaxis, and restricted vocabulary, seemed exquisitely colloquial to his contemporaries; he represented, however, a kind of idealized speech, and the effect of it needed the background of contemporary prose with its ungainly ways. Mme de Lafayette certainly strikes one as artlessly conversational in some respects: her sentences regularly, monotonously begin with the subject and verb; the use of unsummarized reported speech is abundant and unvaried, her narrative technique being far less sophisticated in this respect than Rabelais'. The illusion of everyday speech persists until we try to imagine her style expressing other things and we become aware how narrowly tied it is to the subject matter. The writer who finally realized fully Vaugelas' idea of spoken style was Mme de Sévigné, and she is an essential part of our picture of the total system of styles in French neoclassicism: the quotidian and contingent are expressed with appropriate familiarity.

Sévigné's style often borders on the low, which, in the classical rhetorical sense, does not mean necessarily the usage of coarse per-

6. Mme de La Fayette, *Princesse de Clèves*, 46.

sons but a realistically conversational style, pitched at a perfectly po-
lite level.

> J'ai trouvé de la douceur dans la tristesse que j'ai eue ici: une grande soli-
> tude, un grand silence, un office triste, des ténèbres chantées avec dévo-
> tion (je n'avais jamais été à Livry la semaine sainte), un jeûne canonique, et
> une beauté dans ces jardins dont vous seriez charmée: tout cela m'a plu.
> Hélas! que je vous y ai souhaitée! Quelque difficile que vous soyez sur les
> solitudes, vous auriez été contente de celle-ci: mais je m'en retourne à Paris
> par nécessité; j'y trouverai de vos lettres, et je veux aller demain à la Pas-
> sion du P. Bourdaloue ou du P. Mascaron; j'ai toujours honoré les belles
> Passions.[7]

The mingling of the pious and *mondain*, the choice of solitudes (note
the *précieux*-high style plural of the abstract) and the humdrum necessities of life, is characteristic. Sévigné hit upon the sentence asyndeton and parataxis, which she uses regularly but not rigorously,
without fully realizing perhaps that her prose constituted an important new conception of style from the later seventeenth century on.
Her form of relaxed *style coupé* permitted very rapid changes in mood
from lyric to ironic to matter-of-fact, and so forth. Some realistic
styles of the eighteenth century are very reminiscent of the range of
Sévigné's letters; limitations in sentence structure are compensated
by tonal alterations. Sévigné's fanciful letters are famous; here is a
perhaps less well known aspect of her correspondence.

> Vous me demandez, ma chère enfant, si j'aime toujours la vie. Je vous
> avoue que j'y trouve des chagrins cuisants; mais je suis encore plus dé-
> goûtée de la mort: je me trouve si malheureuse d'avoir à finir tout ceci par
> elle, que si je pouvais retourner en arrière, je ne demanderais pas mieux. Je
> me trouve dans un engagement qui m'embarrasse: je suis embarquée dans
> la vie sans mon consentement; il faut que j'en sorte, cela m'assomme; et
> comment en sortirai-je? Par où? Par quelle porte? . . . Rien n'est si fou que
> de mettre son salut dans l'incertitude; mais rien n'est si naturel, et la sotte
> vie que je mène est la chose du monde la plus aisée à comprendre. Je
> m'abîme dans ces pensées.[8]

Sévigné moves nimbly from a lightly put query to a monologue,
bemused then serious, on metaphysical problems, with exactly the

---

7. Letter of March 26 (Holy Thursday), 1671, to Mme de Grignan from Livry.
8. Letter of March 16, 1672, to Mme de Grignan from Paris.

same questions Pascal insists the *libertin* must ask himself about the surpassing importance of the immortality of the soul and man's ultimate destination.

For La Bruyère the prose of Louis XIV's reign was, unlike that which preceded, purely French; Ariste and Eugène are more specific, identifying the major neoclassical prose movement as *style coupé* and belittling the Roman contribution to it as not being of the best Latinity. In Bouhours' dialogue, Balzac and Voiture are credited with the perfection of it. While we associate the sentence containing multiple pauses especially with La Bruyère, we have seen in Pascal's discussion of imagination that it occurs earlier, and Balzac even used it imitatively in his essay on Montaigne. The later version of *style coupé*, defined by its many breaks within the sentence, can be considered most peculiarly French, a notion borne out by comparison with other modern literatures; and it is possible to demonstrate why phonological reasons contributed to the place of honor the highly segmented *style coupé* came to occupy in French. With the dropping of unaccented final *e* sounds near the beginning of the seventeenth century, French became oxytonic, not only in words but also in phrases, where the individual word accents on the ultima are absorbed into the larger pattern of the end-position phrase accent. With the combination of the rising intonational movement and the final accent, a pause, such as a comma marks, becomes peculiarly sharp in definition. Books on phonetics represent it thus: ⎯⎯ , ⎯⎯ , ⎯⎯\ . Languages like English and Italian have no such acute divisions within the sentence ordinarily. Therefore the *coupes* of the *style coupé* can truthfully be said to play a special role in French. At the same time, however, as we see the Frenchness of *style coupé*, we must remember that a passage like the following was read by Frenchmen with the accent on the final syllable of words and phrases, so that it became phonologically almost French.

> Verba, selecta, propria, significantia: immo quae plus aliquid semper dicunt quam dicunt. Qui proprius quidam eius Genius videtur, ut in parcimonia verborum more energeia atque efficacia sit; in brevitate, claritas et splendor. Sunt allusiones, imagines, translationes, crebrae et paene con-

tinuae: quae delectant simul et docent; et in rem animum, atque extra rem mittunt. Est cura, non affectatio; decor, non comptus; tractata oratio, non torta. Est et compositio quaedam et viriles numeri: sed ut structuram agnoscas, mollitiem abnuas; et pugnae atque arenae omnia, non delectationi aut scaenae parata. Iam in ipsa brevitate, et stricto dicendi genere, apparet beata quaedam copia.[9]

This is Justus Lipsius (1547–1606), the great anti-Ciceronian humanist and abiding object of controversy for the seventeenth century, in his guide to Stoic philosophy, where he is describing and exemplifying, in his own fashion, the style of Seneca. Despite La Bruyère's contention that the prose of the later seventeenth century was finally, absolutely French, one could argue that highly segmented *style coupé* represents a re-Latinization of French prose along radical Senecan lines, and it would be unwise to discount such learned influences on French style, especially in the work of such a *grand lettré* as La Bruyère himself.

Style coupé is not without an interesting relationship to the general question of sentence structure as it was conceived of in the seventeenth century. Many of La Bruyère's *Caractères* can be read as miniature studies in style, based on the problem of finding interesting and expressive uses of natural word order. Within the limits of the subject-verb-complement pattern, and using the general formula of multisegmented *style coupé*, La Bruyère discovered a whole world of variations. For example, in the famous portrait of Giton, the rich man, the opening sentence contains seven nouns as complements of *avoir*: "*Giton* a le teint frais, le visage plein et les joues pendantes, l'œil fixe et assuré, les épaules larges, l'estomac haut, la démarche

9. Quoted in Basil Anderton, *Sketches from a Library Window* (New York: Appleton, 1923), 29. Here is Anderton's translation: "His words are choice, suitable, and significant; they always mean something more than they actually say. And this seems a special genius of his, that in an economy of words he has a wonderful force and efficacy; in brevity he has clearness and brilliance. Allusions, figures, metaphors, are frequent, almost continuous; and these both please and instruct, directing the mind to the subject and even beyond the subject. There is carefulness without affectation; ornament without finery (*comptus*); there is close arrangement in what he says, but nothing forced or crabbed. Style also is apparent, and virile harmony and rhythm, yet in such a way that, while you recognize artistic construction, you will admit no effeminate artificiality, and it is for fighting and the arena that the whole equipment is made, not for pleasure and scenic show."

ferme et délibérée." The fourth and the seventh nouns have two adjectives, the others one. Furthermore, there is an *et* between the second and third nouns; the others are in asyndeton. This *et*, moreover, belongs to a rhythmic, as distinguished from a syntactic, pattern; it joins with the *et*s connecting adjectives to make a series of double units as opposed to the single ones: *A, A and B, A and B, A, A, A and B*. In this rhythmic analysis we have six units, not the seven of syntactic divisions, and they are asymmetrically arranged. In the regular, natural sentence, by multiplication of one or more sentence elements and ingeniously varying the syndetic relation, La Bruyère finds a thitherto unsuspected range of verbal art. If we think merely of the ways two, then three elements can be varied in sequence, we see basic devices of his style:

A, B
A and B
A, B, and C
A and B, C
A, B, C
A and B and C

The stylistic value of such variation is extraordinary within the narrow system of natural word order, especially when the range of the latter is decreased further, as in La Bruyère, by largely eliminating subordinate clauses.

We have seen the effect of varying syndeton and asyndeton within the single sentence. The large-scale effects of paragraph structure are likewise arresting.

> *Giton* a le teint frais, le visage plein et les joues pendantes, l'œil fixe et assuré, les épaules larges, l'estomac haut, la démarche ferme et délibérée. Il parle avec confiance; il fait répéter celui qui l'entretient, et il ne goûte que médiocrement tout ce qu'il lui dit. Il déploie un ample mouchoir et se mouche avec grand bruit; il crache fort loin, et il éternue fort haut. Il dort le jour, il dort la nuit, et profondément; il ronfle en compagnie. Il occupe à table ou à la promenade plus de place qu'un autre. Il tient le milieu en se promenant avec ses égaux; il s'arrête, et l'on s'arrête; il continue de marcher, et l'on marche: tous se règlent sur lui. Il interrompt, il redresse ceux qui ont la parole: on ne l'interrompt pas, on l'écoute aussi longtemps qu'il veut parler; on est de son avis, on croit les nouvelles qu'il débite. S'il

s'assied, vous le voyez s'enfoncer dans un fauteuil, croiser les jambes l'une sur l'autre, froncer le sourcil, abaisser son chapeau sur ses yeux pour ne voir personne, ou le relever ensuite, et découvrir son front par fierté et par audace. Il est enjoué, grand rieur, impatient, présomptueux, colère, libertin, politique, mystérieux sur les affaires du temps; il se croit des talents et de l'esprit. Il est riche. ("Des biens de fortune," 83)

Perhaps the simplest way to elucidate the structure of the portrait is to consider separately the different elements of repetition and variation. First are the clause junctures. La Bruyère never uses a connective between the units constituting sentences from the punctuational standpoint. However, these may contain more than one independent clause combined in more than one way. The sentences are numbered:

1. (*Giton*): subj-verb-long complement.
2. (*Il parle*): subj-verb; subj-verb, *et* subj-verb.
3. (*Il déploie*): subj-verb *et* verb; subj-verb *et* subj-verb.
4. (*Il dort*): subj-verb; subj-verb; subj-verb.
5. (*Il occupe*): subj-verb.
6. (*Il tient*): subj-verb; subj-verb *et* subj-verb; subj-verb *et* subj-verb; subj-verb.
7. (*Il interrompt*): subj-verb, subj-verb: subj-verb, subj-verb, subj-verb; subj-verb, subj-verb.
8. (*S'il s'assied*): subordinate clause, subj-verb, verb, verb, verb, *ou* verb, *et* verb.
9. (*Il est*): subj-verb-long complement; subj-verb.
10. (*Il est*): subj-verb.

We note variations besides the number of clauses grouped and their length: clauses may be joined by a comma, semicolon, or colon; of the long complements, one is in nouns, the other adjectives; the long series of verbs is in the infinitive. The second sentence has augmenting clause length; the last two sentences form a diminishing clause pattern. When two adverbs occur in succession (*et profondément*; *en compagnie*) the first has a disjunctive, irregular relation to its verb. The contrast between sentences with *être* and complements and with other verbs is quite noticeable, as well as the variation among transitive, reflexive, and intransitive verbs. Finally, the repeated *il*, which ties together the whole, as in a Latinate period, is replaced, at the artistically asymmetric point of just over half-way through the paragraph, by *on* and *vous*, the *il* returning to close the paragraph. An examination of clause length would reveal subtle relations of the clauses with sentences and between sentences, but I have sufficiently pointed out, I hope, the extraordinary means deployed by La Bruyère.

While the same term, *style coupé*, is used for Montaigne and Balzac as for La Bruyère, it is obvious that this is a radically new kind of style: whereas the curt, the *coupé*, in Montaigne and Balzac, refers to sentence asyndeton, La Bruyère's prose is doubly cut, both between and within sentences. Balzac's prose is flowing and balanced, La Bruyère's clipped and asymmetrical. Parataxis is usual in the latter but not systematic in the earlier writer. Isocolon, above all, distinguishes the two, La Bruyère generally preferring irregular combinations. Finally, there is simply no comparable kind of syntactic imagination in Balzac, no sense of the interplay of syndeton and asyndeton and of other variations.

The minute segmentation of La Bruyère's prose in the portrait of Giton or elsewhere in the *Caractères* could be taken as a series of clues followed by the answer to the enigma, and that is probably the way his contemporaries generally read it, fascinated as they were by the idea of a book with keys. We, however, see it in the light of Voltaire's narrative *style coupé* and modern fictional technique. What impresses us is the external, imagistic, impersonal, and logically disconnected quality of La Bruyère's portraits, as well as the irony that results from the difference between what is said and what is implied. This is the exact opposite of the presentation of character in *L'Astrée* at the beginning of the seventeenth century: in d'Urfé's portraiture and narration, everything is tied together in what is almost a superfluity of logical and other relations—a profoundly rationalized method of telling. La Bruyère, on the other hand, anticipates the purely representational technique frequent in fiction from *Madame Bovary* on: it is not surprising that he is often mentioned and praised in Flaubert's correspondence or that imitations of him occur in *L'Education sentimentale*.[10]

10. Flaubert uses La Bruyère's portrait technique notably in describing Mme Dambreuse in *L'Education sentimentale*, Pt. III, Chap. 4. For general studies, see Jules Brody,

Moreover, we even find that for Flaubert as for La Bruyère, the interplay of syndeton and asyndeton, the habit of making them both optional and unpredictable, seems to be an important part of the scenic
method, in which every detail is meant to count fully. La Bruyère
and Flaubert often avoid regular formulas like *A, B, and C*, which,
through their automatic quality, permit us to pass inattentively over
the content of the series. Irregularity makes us fully aware of what we
are reading.

In the varied genres of *Les Caractères*—brief essays, epigrams,
speeches, enumerations, maxims, notes, and stories, as well as portraits—there are several stylistic tendencies. On one occasion ("Du
souverain" 7) La Bruyère uses the common seventeenth-century style
with doublets, and his voice becomes indistinguishable from that of
the Perrault passage we saw earlier. Elsewhere, we find the Latin and
Greek omission of the copula ("Verba, selecta, propria, significantia"): "Talent, goût, esprit, bon sens, choses différentes, non incom-
patibles" ("Des jugements" 56). Among other one-time grammatical
effects is this one: "Que de dons du ciel ne faut-il pas pour bien régner! Une naissance auguste, un air d'empire et d'autorité, un visage
qui remplisse la curiosité des peuples empressés de voir le prince, et
qui conserve le respect dans le courtisan; une parfaite égalité d'humeur; un grand éloignement pour la raillerie piquante, ou assez de
raison pour ne se la permettre point; ne faire jamais ni menaces ni
reproches; ne point céder à la colère, et être toujours obéi; l'esprit facile, insinuant; le cœur ouvert, sincère . . ." The syntactic device is
the apposition, but one is surprised to find infinitives mingled with
nouns, the model evidently being the Latin infinitive's use as a
gerund. The idea of a nominal style (or, more precisely, one avoiding
finite verbs in independent clauses) developed side by side with La
Bruyère's parataxis and in one form ("Talent, goût . . .") shares the
same rhythmic segmentation. On the other hand, the list of the sov-
ereign's requisite qualities tends toward the doublet and ample, oratorical phrasing. The nominal style has greater range than one might
think. It was used somewhat before La Bruyère by Bossuet in his *Discours sur l'histoire universelle*: "Là paraissent les mœurs contraires des

"Sur le style de La Bruyère," *L'Esprit Créateur*, XI, No. 2 (1970), 154–78, and Doris
Kirsch, *La Bruyère ou le style cruel* (Montreal: University of Montreal Press, 1977).

deux frères: l'innocence d'Abel, sa vie pastorale, et ses offrandes agréables; celles de Caïn rejetées, son avarice, son impiété, son parricide, et la jalousie mère des meurtres; le châtiment de ce crime, la conscience du parricide agitée de continuelles frayeurs; la première ville bâtie par ce méchant, qui se cherchait un asile contre la haine et l'horreur du genre humain . . ."[11] This is a highly concise narrative nominal style: clauses are represented by an adjective (*agréables*), a past participle (*rejetées*), an apposition (*mère*), a verbal noun (*châtiment*) with subjective genitive (*de ce crime*), and so forth. The Latin model is the elliptic infinitive clause with *esse*.

The most extraordinary developments of nominal style occur in passages of Saint-Simon. His portraits range from the unexceptional to extremely peculiar effects, both of sense and grammar.

> Régulièrement laide, les joues pendantes, le front trop avancé, un nez qui ne disait rien, de grosses lèvres mordantes, des cheveux et des sourcils châtain brun, fort bien plantés, des yeux les plus parlants et les plus beaux du monde, peu de dents et toutes pourries, dont elle parlait et se moquait la première, le plus beau teint et la plus belle peau, peu de gorge, mais admirable, le cou long, avec un soupçon de goitre qui ne lui seyait point mal, un port de tête galant, gracieux, majestueux, et le regard de même, le sourire le plus expressif, une taille longue, ronde, menue, aisée, parfaitement coupée, une marche de déesse sur les nuées, elle plaisait au dernier point.[12]

From adjectives and the regular kind of apposition with the article (*les joues pendantes*), Saint-Simon passes to nouns belonging to the descriptive appositional type that begins to be common in narration only in the nineteenth century (*un gros homme, cheveux roux, quarante ans*). The whole portrait is, moreover, syntactically curious in the placing of so many appositional elements before the subject of the verb.

Saint-Simon did not have behind him any tradition of physical description in prose suitable to the level of the subject. In the absence of a technique *toute faite* and obeying the general neoclassical desire for

---

11. Jacques-Bénigne Bossuet, *Discours sur l'histoire universelle*, Première Partie, "Première Epoque."

12. Louis de Rouvroy, duc de Saint-Simon, *Mémoires*, Bibliothèque de la Pléiade (7 vols.; Paris: Gallimard, 1953), III, 4.

concision, he evolved a nominal style, which may, as in the description of the duchesse de Bourgogne above, carry ordinary constructions to extreme lengths in order to convey the contrasts and odd details necessary in the depiction of such an important person as a probable future queen of France. In other cases, Saint-Simon uses ellipsis of the verb, as in the presentation of Monseigneur, Louis XIV's son, "absorbé dans sa graisse et dans ses ténèbres."

> De caractère, il n'en avait aucun; du sens assez, sans aucune sorte d'esprit; de la hauteur, de la dignité par nature, par prestance, par imitation du roi; de l'opiniâtreté sans mesure, et un tissu de petitesses arrangées, qui formaient tout le tissu de sa vie; doux par paresse et par une sorte de stupidité, dur au fond, avec un extérieur de bonté qui ne portait que sur des subalternes, et sur des valets, et qui ne s'exprimait que par des questions basses; il était avec eux d'une familiarité prodigieuse, d'ailleurs insensible à la misère et à la douleur des autres, en cela peut-être plutôt en proie à l'incurie et à l'imitation qu'à un mauvais naturel; silencieux jusqu'à l'incroyable, conséquemment fort secret.[13]

This period, largely paratactic and linear, is perfectly clear if we see the partitives all as a kind of accusative depending on the negative form of *avoir* or an understood positive form; the adjectives, on the other hand, *doux, dur, insensible, silencieux*, all must be felt as nominatives modifying *il*. The complicating factor is that both direct object nouns and the adjectives are modified by abundant prepositional phrases: the latter create a density in nominal style quite unlike our previous examples, and they are the major peculiarity of the more extreme French experiments in that style from Saint-Simon on through the late nineteenth-century revival of it. Saint-Simon concludes his period with adverbs customarily modifying whole phrases, *d'ailleurs, en cela, peut-être plutôt, conséquemment*, the effect of which is to emphasize ellipsis: each one makes us conscious of the absence of an *il était*. When we have absorbed these details and look again at the passage as a whole, we see how elegantly it is constructed: the absolute noun (*de caractère*) is balanced on the other side of the verb by *du sens assez*, the adverb *assez* sufficing to supply the positive *il avait* in our minds. *Sens, hauteur,* and *dignité* form an asyn-

13. *Ibid.*, III, 64.

detic triplet repeated by the triplet of *par* phrases: Saint-Simon, far
from being primarily colloquial and unrhetorical, is very fond of this
formal figure. Next comes the section with adjectives, the concision
of which is less elliptical, to be followed by the tightest passage of all
(*d'ailleurs* . . .). Saint-Simon concludes with his densest effect.

Because of his occasional familiar-sounding expressions ("elle
n'était pas mieux en belle-sœur"; that is, she was unfortunate in that
respect also), which often involve some more concise use of nouns
than modern idiom allows, Saint-Simon is sometimes taken to be
more an eccentric than a savant prose writer. On the contrary, his
style suggests the fruit of much Latin reading. When we encounter
Saint-Simon's syntactically irregular passages, we are dealing with
something more than the aphoristic omission of a form of the verb *to
be*, which we have seen in La Bruyère. Saint-Simon's most surprising
nominal sentences seem to have been suggested, at least in part, by
Tacitus, who, obscurer and more powerful than Seneca, was, for
many Latinists in the seventeenth century, the supremely eloquent
Roman *prosateur*. Tacitus commonly omits the copula or verbs of
speech: "Multus hinc ipso de Augusto sermo, plerisque vana miran-
tibus, 'quod idem dies accepti quodam imperii princeps et vitae su-
premus, quod Nolae in domo et cubiculo in quo pater eius Octavius
vitam finivisset. . . . Non regno tamen neque dictatura sed principis
nomine constitutam rem publicam; mari Oceano aut amnibus longin-
quis saeptum imperium; legiones, provincias, classes, cuncta inter se
conexa; ius apud cives, modestiam apud socios; urbem ipsam magni-
fico ornatu, parca admodum vi tractata, quo ceteris quies esset.'"[14]
The easiest and certainly the least imaginative way of looking at such
passages is rigorously to supply main verbs; it is also the way to destroy utterly the effect Tacitus aimed at. Saint-Simon, who was quite a
competent Latinist, seems to have been inspired by the *Annals* to em-

---

14. Tacitus, *Annals*, I, 9. "There was much talk of Augustus, and the people were
struck by idle coincidences. They noted that the prince had died the same day he had
once received the imperial power; that he died in Nola in the same house and room as
his father. . . . Neither kingship nor dictatorship but the title of prince had permitted
him to pacify the state. The Ocean or distant rivers had made a frontier for the Empire.
Legions, fleets, and provinces were joined by a common bond; legality was customary
in dealing with citizens; Rome itself had been magnificently embellished. Some little
show of power had confirmed the general quietude."

ploy a dense, even obscure syntax in which we have the same feeling of constriction, terse irony, and carefully chosen detail.

For one of his most remarkable descriptions, the passage rendering the tensions in the crowd of courtiers as Monseigneur lay dying, Saint-Simon resorts to a very Latinate effect, eliminating *il y avait* (*il n'y avait point de propos*), then *étaient* (*les simples curieux étaient presque nuls*): "Parmi ces diverses sortes d'affligés, point ou peu de propos, de conversation nulle, quelque exclamation parfois échappée à la douleur et parfois répondue par une douleur voisine, un mot en un quart d'heure, des yeux sombres ou hagards, des mouvements de mains moins rares qu'involontaires, immobilité du reste presque entière; les simples curieux et peu soucieux presque nuls, hors les sots qui avaient le caquet en partage, les questions, et le redoublement du désespoir des affligés, et l'importunité pour les autres." The most extraordinary effect is the depiction of disembodied words, eyes, gestures; these are abstracted from any person and, so to speak, are sketched in the air. Saint-Simon modulates into a verbal mode and then returns to nominal style.

> Ceux qui déjà regardaient cet événement comme favorable avaient beau pousser la gravité jusqu'au maintien chagrin et austère, le tout n'était qu'un voile clair, qui n'empêchait pas de bons yeux de remarquer et de distinguer tous leurs traits. Ceux-ci se tenaient aussi tenaces en place que les plus touchés, en garde contre leur satisfaction, contre leurs mouvements; mais leurs yeux suppléaient au peu d'agitation de leur corps. Des changements de posture, comme des gens peu assis ou mal debout; un certain soin de s'éviter les uns les autres, même de se rencontrer des yeux; les accidents momentanés qui arrivaient de ces rencontres; un je ne sais quoi de plus libre en toute la personne. A travers le soin de se tenir et de se composer, un vif, une sorte d'étincelant autour d'eux les distinguait malgré qu'ils en eussent.[15]

The abundance of verbal nouns, *satisfaction, mouvements, agitation, accidents, changements, soin, étincelant*, creates a kind of aura of excitement emanating from Monseigneur's enemies, but Saint-Simon is describing, rather than the look of any persons in particular, an atmosphere whose signs are almost invisible. The avoidance of personal subjects and the indeterminacy of the nominal constructions

15. See Saint-Simon, *Mémoires*, III, 48.

represent an extraordinary use of grammar in the service of a subtle depiction. It is difficult to imagine any other French prose writer before the nineteenth century able to convey ambiance in this way. Passages like this one are, I should add, infrequent in Saint-Simon; this nominal style is generally saved for moments and events of the highest importance like those touching the royal family and questions of succession. In our second chapter, we saw that the multiple subordinations of Amyot's style could be converted into nominal style, and it is clear that Saint-Simon's nominal passages could easily be rewritten with a normal accompaniment of verbs. It is important to see this convertibility in sixteenth- and seventeenth-century styles, for it makes evident the element of choice and taste. Nominal style, in particular, is not some casual adaptation of notes for one's private use or some other familiar and telegraphic manner of writing. It has a certain classical authority behind it, and its effects are calculated and brilliant.

The concrete in Saint-Simon provides an interesting example of the way the classicizing tendency to abstraction works. Saint-Simon usually moves in the realm of generality to praise a woman's pleasing physical aspect: *beauté régulière* and such are his terms. But imperfections are carefully described: "ce qui la déparait le plus étaient les places de ses sourcils, qui étaient comme pelées et rouges, avec fort peu de poils." Ideal beauty, uniform, eternal, tends to lead to the hyperbolic but colorless language of Mme de Lafayette: *tout ce qu'il y avait de plus beau à la Cour.* Ugliness has more detail than beauty, and so within a framework that is perfectly neoclassical, without invoking the baroque, we find physical descriptions of some exactness. This is, of course, related to Pascal's satiric imagery and La Bruyère's representation of Giton sleeping noisily or blowing his nose.

Rhetorical theory has an ahistorical conception of style in that variations are made to depend on genre and level of usage. At the same time, we must observe that ornament does not belong merely to one or another style in a simplistic fashion: Senecan style, as we have seen, is ambiguous in its level of dignity; progressive periods occur in the *agréable* manner of *L'Astrée* and in the polemical *Pensées.* Of course, we do not find some devices, like the long simile, in any style whatsoever; there were artistic discriminations at work, but these were not, by and large, of the mechanical character so commonly ascribed to neoclassical esthetics.

There is, to be sure, an historical, evolutionary factor to be considered in sixteenth- and seventeenth-century prose. We have, on the one hand, the *agréable* baroque period in Balzac's style and, on the other, the neoclassical equivalent of it in La Fontaine's *Psyché* or the descriptive parts of Fénelon's otherwise didactically middle-style *Télémaque*. The devotional didactic writings of Saint François de Sales and Fénelon constitute another pair of baroque and neoclassical opposites. In one case, there is no real historical equivalence of styles: no worthy high baroque style exists as a complement to the high neoclassical style of Bossuet. Largely, of course, the history of seventeenth-century prose is one of progressive invention in the domain of middle style: Pascal's satiric and polemic *moraliste* style, with its reliance on intermittent elaborate sentence structures, is followed by the segmented *style coupé* of La Bruyère; Mme de Lafayette's fictional manner is much more restrained in periodic movement than d'Urfé's. Bouhours' contention that the history of French prose can be summed up as the growth of *style coupé* is not entirely valid, however. Part of it is also the movement from hypotactic sentences with weak main verbs (as in Amyot and Pascal) and the substitution of colorless verbs with verbal noun complements for dynamic verbs (*avoir des sentiments pour* for *aimer*) toward constructions using perhaps dependent finite verbs but no main ones, as in La Bruyère and Saint-Simon.

The elaboration of asymmetry and antisymmetry after Balzac's equilibrated periods is also of considerable importance; it is sometimes asserted that neoclassical art favors symmetries, which is true to some extent, but we shall also see that European baroque prose style in general shows, like Balzac and Descartes, a pronounced taste for bipartite, balanced constructions. It is very wrong to imagine a baroque esthetic of the asymmetrical as opposed to a neoclassical penchant for bipartition. Much later, the *Encyclopédie* summed up a principle which had been judiciously observed by Pascal, Bossuet, La Bruyère, and Saint-Simon: "La *symmétrie*, qui est le fondement de la beauté en architecture, en est la ruine dans la plupart des autres beaux-arts. Rien n'est plus insipide qu'un discours oratoire sym-métrique, bien arrangé, bien distribué, bien compassé." The specific criticism here is of high style, which in Bossuet's hands, however, has an elaborate interplay between the balanced and the irregular. The middle-style *moralistes* and Saint-Simon did not write in large sym-metrical forms, and the detail of their styles often reflects a taste for the asymmetrical. Certainly, claims that balanced doublets predomi-nate in neoclassicism, in contrast to the more irregular triads of ro-mantic prose, involve ignoring too many important exceptions to be more than a generality of limited usefulness. We must be extremely circumspect in regard to ideas of neoclassicism that have relevance to a particular work or class of works but may not be indiscriminately extended, as if the whole diversified system of neoclassical genres and styles, with its careful distinctions, did not exist.

6 The Eighteenth Century and the End of Neoclassicism

In the eighteenth century, *style coupé* is found not only in its pure form, and that very frequently, but also as a model toward which much prose tends, even when more hypotaxis or sentence linkage occurs than we encounter in the prototype. Two new adaptations of it are notable: Montesquieu's expository *style coupé* and Voltaire's use of it in his *contes*.

The tendency of *style coupé* toward disjunction and brevity is reflected in the great number of short chapters in Montesquieu's *L'Esprit des lois* (1748), including, of course, the famous two-sentence one, "Idée du despotisme": "Quand les sauvages de la Louisiane veulent avoir du fruit, ils coupent l'arbre au pied, et cueillent le fruit. Voilà le gouvernement despotique." It is as if the brief chapters, juxtaposed more than articulated in their relation, were the correspondent of *style coupé* on the plane of book structure. And there is even an intermediate kind of disjunction between the dimensions of sentence and chapter, which is the short paragraph, sometimes reduced to as little as a sentence. Thumbing through its pages or glancing at its table of contents, one would gather that *L'Esprit des lois* is a work in treatise style, so numerous are the chapter and paragraph divisions and so specific the titles. There is a profound conflict in Montesquieu's work between the articulations of thought antecedent to the writing of the book and the suppression of such articulations on the explicit, formal level to produce brilliant effects. It is of considerable significance that the publication of *L'Esprit des lois* was followed shortly by Buffon's discourse to the Academy on style, in which the problems raised by just such a work as Montesquieu's are examined.

Narrative *style coupé* was tried once by La Bruyère in a short story ("Des femmes" 81) that closes a section of *Les Caractères*. La Bruyère's

113

little piece shows how monotonous pure *style coupé* can be in fiction, and we are not surprised that Voltaire modified it accordingly: he allows a modest number of sentence connectives and hypotactic structures while preserving the spirit of brevity. In fact, one of his major sources of effect is the interplay of causality, commonly expressed by sentence connectives (*donc, ainsi,* and so forth) or subordination (*parce que*), and abrupt juxtaposition of events. Causal relations are especially prominent in all their false coherence because of the general concision of style. At the same time, effects of absurdity come as well from a particular conception of his subject matter.

Micromégas (1752) in many ways supplies the theoretical grounding for the style of *Zadig* (1747) and *Candide* (1759), and other stories. Its principal allusion is to the great passage in high style in the *Pensées* headed "Disproportion de l'homme" and often called "les deux infinis," in which deity is intuited from the existence of the infinitely great and infinitely small. Man is the middle term between the extremes, between angels and beasts, as theology had usually seen him. In *Micromégas*, however, man is a mite, and the general point of view is that of a giant visitor from outer space. Earth is a "petit tas de boue," "notre petite fourmilière" (Chapter 1), "la taupinière" (Chapter 4); man and men "petites machines" (Chapter 5), "insectes invisibles," "cet atome" (Chapter 6), "petites mites" (Chapter 7). This imagery is anticipated in *Zadig*, when Zadig consoles himself by seeing life in its true perspective: "des insectes se dévorant les uns les autres, sur un petit atome de boue" ("La Femme battue"). As in the case of Pascal or La Bruyère, imagery is not so frequent in Voltaire that its effect is in any way diminished by context: these pictures of life stand out vividly. Essentially, Voltaire's version of *style coupé* is a language for insect narratives, for an account of small, almost mechanical creatures in the simplicity of their organisms, whose busy antlike movement is mindless and predictable ("Tout le monde fut pour lui, non pas parce qu'il était dans le bon chemin, non pas parce qu'il était raisonnable, non pas parce qu'il était aimable, mais parce qu'il était premier vizir" (*Zadig*, "Les Disputes et les Audiences") or ascribed by the creatures themselves to fantastic, insane metaphysical systems. The whole effect of Voltaire's *style coupé* narrative is that we unconsciously contrast it with some ideal, average narrative style, dignified in its movement and picturing man in his traditional place between angels and beasts.

Voltaire's use of imagery to make familiar things appear alien is very much in the line of *moraliste* prose, even though his genres are different. Bees are commonly compared to men in that they have an organized society; Voltaire finds something new in the old comparison: "Les abeilles peuvent paraître supérieures à la race humaine, en ce qu'elles produisent de leur substance une substance utile, et que de toutes nos sécrétions il n'y a pas une seule qui soit bonne à rien, pas une seule même qui ne rende le genre humain désagréable" (*Dictionnaire philosophique*, "Abeille"). This is what Remy de Gourmont called a dissociation of ideas, when the terms of a cliché are separated and recombined with new elements. Voltaire practices this constantly with the concept of causality as well, and even with grammar and idiom.

> La bonne compagnie ne se sert plus de tous ces vilains termes, and ne prononce même jamais le mot d'adultère. On ne dit point, madame la duchesse est en adultère avec monsieur le chevalier. Madame la marquise a un mauvais commerce avec monsieur l'abbé. On dit, monsieur l'abbé est cette semaine l'amant de madame la marquise. Quand les dames parlent à leurs amies de leurs adultères, elles disent: j'avoue que j'ai du goût pour lui. Elles avouaient autrefois qu'elles sentaient quelque estime; mais depuis qu'une bourgeoise s'accusa à son confesseur d'avoir de l'estime pour un conseiller, et que le confesseur lui dit: Madame, combien de fois vous a-t-il estimée? les dames de qualité n'ont plus estimé personne, et ne vont plus guère à confesse. (*Dictionnaire philosophique*, "Adultère")

We see, in *être en adultère avec*, Voltaire playing with the elegant attenuating construction of verb and noun complement plus preposition, as in *avoir du goût pour, avoir de l'estime pour*; the whole joke lies in the priest's converting the circumlocutious phrase, of the kind Mme de Lafayette was so fond, into the cognate verb, *estimer*, with a direct object.

Much of Voltaire's humor depends on the creation of a persona, a comic mask. In the famous lines (letter of August 30, 1755) thanking Rousseau for his *Discours sur l'inégalité*, we encounter an especially carefully constructed persona.

J'ai reçu, monsieur [5], votre nouveau livre [5] contre le genre humain [6], je vous en remercie [6]. Vous plairez aux hommes [5], à qui vous dites leurs vérités [8], mais vous ne les corrigerez pas [8]. On ne peut peindre avec des couleurs plus fortes [11] les horreurs de la société humaine [10], dont notre ignorance et notre faiblesse [10] se promettent tant de consolations [9]. On n'a jamais employé tant d'esprit [10] à vouloir nous rendre bêtes [7]; il prend envie [4] de marcher à quatre pattes [7] quand on lit votre ouvrage [6]. Cependant [3], comme il y a plus de soixante ans [8] que j'en ai perdu l'habitude [8], je sens malheureusement [6] qu'il m'est impossible de la reprendre [10], et je laisse cette allure naturelle [9] à ceux qui en sont plus dignes [7] que vous et moi [4].

The implied contrast here is between Rousseau, the man of nature, and Voltaire, the partisan of civilization; Voltaire therefore uses a number of prose artifices—symbols of a highly developed culture— to suggest his whole background of ideas. We are struck by the iso-colon, the antitheses, and the diminishing cola in the last sentence; the Ciceronian metonymies *notre ignorance* and *notre faiblesse* for *nous qui sommes ignorants* and *faibles* are highly elegant, and in *il prend envie de, se promettre des consolations, en perdre l'habitude,* and *il m'est impossible de,* we encounter refined verbal circumlocutions. The periphrasis *allure naturelle* juxtaposed to the unexpected *marcher à quatre pattes* are characteristic of the dual and opposite tactics of Voltaire's humor, which are attenuation, on the one hand, and abrupt translation into the concrete, on the other. A similar contrast can be felt between the direct, factual *nouveau livre contre le genre humain,* implying Rousseau is a crackpot writing book after book on the same foolish subject, and the compliments which follow.

Voltaire's fine feeling for the minutiae of style is conveyed in his various parodies and allusions; this Racinian passage from *Zadig* is especially successful, recalling *Phèdre* in particular.

Astarté était beaucoup plus belle que cette Sémire qui haïssait tant les borgnes, et que cette autre femme qui avait voulu couper le nez à son époux. La familiarité d'Astarté, ses *discours tendres,* dont elle *commençait à rougir, ses regards,* qu'elle voulait détourner, et qui se fixaient sur les siens, *allumèrent* dans le cœur de Zadig *un feu* dont il s'étonna. *Il combattit;* il appela à son secours la philosophie, qui l'avait toujours secouru; il n'en tira que des lumières, et n'en reçut aucun *soulagement.* Le devoir, la reconnaissance, *la majesté souveraine violée,* se présentaient à ses yeux comme des

dieux vengeurs; il combattait, il triomphait; mais cette victoire, qu'il fallait rem-
porter à tout moment, lui coûtait *des gémissements et des larmes.* Il n'osait
plus parler à la reine avec cette douce liberté qui avait eu tant de *charmes*
pour tous deux: *ses yeux se couvraient d'un nuage;* ses discours étaient con-
traints et sans suite: il baissait la vue; et quand, malgré lui, ses regards se
tournaient vers Astarté, ils rencontraient ceux de la reine mouillés de
pleurs, dont il partait des traits de flamme; ils semblaient se dire l'un à l'autre:
"Nous nous *adorons,* et nous craignons de nous aimer; *nous brûlons tous
deux d'un feu que nous condamnons."* (My italics)

As often in Voltaire, there are unstated contrasts and the effect of context: the mechanical ups and downs of Zadig's fortunes, the self-seek-
ing motives of most of the characters make Racine's language, with its
implication of a higher world of refined emotion and sentiments, especially grotesque. Voltaire's view of man as insect could easily lead
one to compare him with Pascal on the grounds that such a nasty
conception of life is as perverse as Pascal's fanatic inability to see life
as anything but a question of salvation. This would be short-sighted,
of course, and anachronistic. Voltaire believed in genres like any
eighteenth-century writer and reserved a higher view of life for his
tragedies, for Voltaire was an exceptionally complete writer, working
in the high styles of epic and tragedy as well as in middle and low
genres. If we do not read his high-style works much today, we risk
falsifying our view of his career as a writer and of the true character of
eighteenth-century literature.

Our modern taste is generally for middle- and low-style works, and
this is best exemplified by the great interest in the twentieth century
for Diderot. Not one of the giants for the public of his day, he is a
quintessentially middle- and low-style writer, with a taste for middle-
class drama, novels—including the buffooneries of *Jacques le Fata-
liste*—the letter, and the dialogue, the last two genres looming large
in his *œuvre.* It has been claimed that Diderot left his imprint on
middle-style writing,[1] something not easily accomplished; vast areas
of Voltaire's *œuvre,* for example, letters, much of the *Dictionnaire philosophique,* and *Le Siècle de Louis XIV,* cannot always be distinguished

---

1. See Leo Spitzer, "The Style of Diderot," in *Linguistics and Literary History: Essays in
Stylistics* (Princeton: Princeton University Press, 1948), 135–69.

from the work of any capable late seventeenth- or eighteenth-century writer. Indeed, confronted with passages from *Le Siècle de Louis XIV* and Racine's *Abrégé de l'histoire de Port-Royal*, one could not easily identify or differentiate the authors save on grounds of content. However, the idea of literary glory, *aere perennior*, was not attached so much to middle style as to the works we feel Voltaire and his contemporaries had less talent for. To understand their notion of high style and to suggest the full significance of Rousseau's contribution to the formation of a new notion of high style, some look at less-often-read eighteenth-century works is useful.

There was a good deal of discussion in the earlier eighteenth century about the essential characteristics of prose and poetry, such elements as description and poetic vocabulary being isolated as transferable from verse to the *poème en prose*.[2] The role of *vers blancs*, or units of twelve, ten, eight, and seven syllables in prose rhythm, was of particular concern, although the whole question was put badly from the start. There was an old humanist notion that prose should not contain lines of verse; this was an adaptation of the good Latin rule of not ending a period with a dactyl and spondee, for fear of its sounding like a hexameter closing out of place. Of course, Latin patterns of long and short syllables have only a limited influence on the total number of syllables in a line, whereas in French the number of syllables alone determines verse. The Greeks and Romans, as a matter of fact, like sequences of phrases of the same number of syllables in prose: this is the *prosaic* figure of isocolon, which, however, is a *verse* determinant in French. In any case, French writers like Bossuet had used isocolon because they were inspired by Latin prose, and they did not worry about whether the figure belonged to prose or verse. In the early eighteenth century, theorists like Batteux and Marmontel came up with the notion that isocolon, which they called, and thought of as, *vers blancs*, would produce in prose a poetic feeling, by which they meant an elevated lyric tone, that of the ode. Of course,

<hr/>

2. See Alexis François, *Les Origines lyriques de la phrase moderne* (Paris: Presses Universitaires de France, 1929), and Vista Clayton, *The Prose Poem in French Literature of the Eighteenth Century* (New York: Columbia University Press, 1936).

we have just seen that isocolon, as in Voltaire's letter of thanks for Rousseau's *Discours sur l'inégalité*, need not be lyric in the slightest; like other figures, it may appear as witty and intellectual, violent and bombastic, or delicately lyric. In any case, a renewed consciousness of isocolon came from the theoretical discussions, and there is one example of its application, Vauvenargues' posthumously published prose poem, "Eloge de Paul-Hippolyte-Emmanuel de Seytres," which, in its rigorous use of *vers blancs*, is especially suggestive of the theorists' idea of poetic prose.

> O Dieu! vous l'avez fait paraître [8]. Vous avez dissipé nos armées innombrables [12], vous avez moissonné l'espoir de nos maisons [12]. Hélas! de quels coups [5] vous frappez les têtes [5] les plus innocentes [5]! Aimable Hippolyte, aucun vice [8] n'infectait encore ta jeunesse [8]. Tes années croissaient sans reproche [8] et l'aurore de ta vertu [7] jetait un éclat ravissant [8]. La candeur et la vérité [8] régnaient dans tes sages discours [8] avec l'enjouement et les grâces [8]. La tristesse déconcertée [7] s'enfuyait au son de ta voix [8]; les désirs inquiets s'apaisaient [8].
>
> Ouvrez-vous, tombeaux redoutables [8]. Mânes solitaires, parlez, parlez [8]. Quel silence indomptable [6]! O triste abandon [5]! ô terreur [3]! Quelle main tient donc sous son joug [7] toute la nature interdite [7]? O Etre éternel et caché [7], daigne dissiper les alarmes [8] où mon âme infirme est plongée [8]. Le secret de tes jugements [7] glace mes timides esprits [7]. Voilé dans le fond de ton être [8], tu fais les destins et les temps [8], et la vie et la mort [6], et la crainte et la joie [6], et l'espoir trompeur et crédule [8]. Tu règnes sur les éléments [8] et sur les enfers révoltés [8]; l'air frappé frémit à ta voix [8]: redoutable juge des morts [8], prends pitié de mon désespoir [8].

There is a certain difference here from the practice of isocolon in Balzac or Bossuet, aside from the strictness of syllable count: the phrases are mostly short, and the grammar is the elementary grammar of much great poetry, employing vocatives, exclamations, imperatives, questions, plain statements, and a nice touch of polysyndeton. Such syntax allows considerable freedom of effect to sound devices. The poetry of the prose poem lies also in metaphor, simile, personification, and epithet. If the whole seems negligible as a poem, one should ideally read it in conjunction with some of Jean-Baptiste Rousseau's almost contemporary odes (1723): there is a distinct kinship of style, and Vauvenargues' poem seems less frigid in such a context.

The increasing number of works employing high style could be seen as a symptom of the decline of the seventeenth-century neo-classical system of styles, wherein it appeared in little more than the *oraison funèbre* or sermon. Aside from prose poems, prose epics, and idylls, one very famous example of it, Buffon's *Histoire naturelle* (1749–1804), seemed destined to live forever, for Buffon was to the late eighteenth century one of the four giants of his era, along with Montesquieu, Voltaire, and Rousseau. Buffon had even formulated his principle of style, which was to choose always the more general and therefore more noble terms. Here is man after a comparison of him with the lion.

> Tout annonce dans tous deux les maîtres de la terre; tout marque dans l'homme, même à l'extérieur, sa supériorité sur tous les êtres vivants: il se soutient droit et élevé; son attitude est celle du commandement; sa tête re-garde le ciel, et présente une face auguste sur laquelle est imprimé le carac-tère de sa dignité; l'image de l'âme y est peinte par la physionomie; l'excellence de sa nature perce à travers les organes matériels, et anime d'un feu divin les traits de son visage; son port majestueux, sa démarche ferme et hardie, annoncent sa noblesse et son rang; il ne touche à la terre que par ses extrémités les plus éloignées; il ne la voit que de loin, et semble la dédaigner. Les bras ne lui sont pas donnés pour servir de piliers d'appui à la masse de son corps; sa main ne doit pas fouler la terre, et perdre par des frottements réitérés la finesse du toucher dont elle est le principal organe; le bras et la main sont faits pour servir à des usages plus nobles, pour exécuter les ordres de la volonté, pour saisir les choses éloignées, pour écarter les obstacles, pour prévenir les rencontres et le choc de ce qui pourroit nuire, pour embrasser et retenir ce qui peut plaire, pour le mettre à portée des autres sens.

This could almost be a commentary on Racine's anatomical language: the head, hand, and arm, being noble parts of the body, can be named directly; feet, since they touch the base ground, are best de-scribed as "distant extremities." In general, the periphrases moralize and allegorize in the fashion of the old symbolic, theological science and view of the world we find in medieval and renaissance texts. This form of high style is obviously at its very end, to be replaced by an entirely new conception of the elevated.

Buffon, interestingly enough, in the *Discours* on style he made to the Academy (1753), rejected in one place the rhetorical notion of style as choice of word, ornament, and *pensées fines*, to insist that style grew out of an individual and consistent elaboration of a harmonious structure of ideas. He is out of sympathy with the fitfully scintillating manner of Montesquieu and Voltaire. "Le style est l'homme même" is the famous formula and seems, far more than Buffon's own style, to anticipate romantic conceptions of the unity of a work of literature. Even the notion of prose exposition organized around a few guiding ideas makes much of the literature of ideas before Rousseau look artificial or disconnected: the letters, dialogues, maxims, dictionaries, *réflexions*, miscellanies, seem almost as remote as treatises, to say nothing of the desultory composition of *L'Esprit des lois* or the *pensées* in imitation of Pascal's fragmented book.

Buffon's insistence on what we call composition provides a convenient occasion to reflect on a general fact in the history of literary genres in France: almost the only works of renaissance and seventeenth-century literature that could be said to be stylistically organized fall into the categories of tragedy, epic, and the ode—all verse genres. There are a very few distinguished prose exceptions: *Gargantua*, *Pantagruel*, and the *Tiers Livre* in imaginative literature and the *Discours de la méthode* in the literature of ideas stand out quite clearly for their proportions and coherence of detail. Otherwise, fragmentary brilliance tends to be the rule in prose. In classical literature, of course, the oration is the one organized prose form, but it has limited significance for European prose, having primarily influenced verse argument. Even Bossuet's *Oraisons funèbres* have only a general plan rather than a feeling of necessary rightness in every individual part. The attempt to organize a varied style into a distinct pattern will largely be the work of the nineteenth century and will be found in a very specialized strain of narrative, although some effort in that direction is perceptible already in some eighteenth-century novels.

Rousseau said he wrote with great difficulty and endlessly corrected and refined his sentences. The result is prose of extreme polish, both in shades of word choice and in rhythmic structure. *La Nouvelle Héloïse*, in particular, tiring as we may find reading very much of it at once, has many delicate nuances and shifts of style, which, like those of eighteenth-century poetry, we may not always perceive clearly, through general unfamiliarity with the minutiae of neoclassical principles of diction. As with Racine's work, there is a paradox in the critical appreciation of *La Nouvelle Héloïse*. Considered from one point of view, the book is an intricate example of style; from another, as Julie says (I, 32), "nos lettres étaient faciles et charmantes; le sentiment qui les dictait coulait avec une élégante simplicité: il n'avait besoin ni d'art ni de coloris, et sa pureté faisait toute sa parure." It is the rhetoric of simplicity, so characteristic of French neoclassicism, that accounts for the double character of art and naturalness in the novel. Human beings are reduced to a small number of faculties, such as *âme* and *esprit*, and the actors in the moral drama are few in number, as are the abstract nouns, typically almost personified, in this passage (Julie is writing to Saint-Preux about a period she will spend at her cousin's).

> Tu comprends quelle facilité nous aurons à nous voir durant une quinzaine de jours; mais c'est ici que la discrétion doit suppléer à la contrainte, et qu'il faut nous imposer volontairement la même réserve à laquelle nous sommes forcés dans d'autres temps. Non seulement tu ne dois pas, quand je serai chez ma cousine, y venir plus souvent qu'auparavent, de peur de la compromettre; j'espère même qu'il ne faudra te parler ni des égards qu'exige son sexe, ni des droits sacrés de l'hospitalité, et qu'un honnête homme n'aura pas besoin qu'on l'instruise du respect dû par l'amour à l'amitié qui lui donne asile. (I, 36)

This world of *discrétion, contrainte, réserve, droits, amour,* and *amitié* is not one of varied moral choice or diversified individual psyches. We observe how the terms fall into the limited pattern of love against duty and friendship, discretion being its mode of expression. The ethico-psychological language of French neoclassicism achieves much of its strength from the limited number of its elements and from the reduction of dilemmas to antithetical situations. The metonymic substitution of *amour* and *amitié* for the persons in love and showing friendship is a figure that emphasizes seeing characters primarily in terms of one quality. The basic traits stressed may be different: one may prefer La Rochefoucauld to Rousseau on the grounds that the former is truer, profounder, but the rhetorical structure of the *moraliste* language is the same—a few basic conflicts expressed often with semipersonifications.

In the changing shades of style in *La Nouvelle Héloïse*, we also encounter yet higher pitches of language than the *moraliste* mode. Tragic diction occurs, as in this letter of Saint-Preux's, wherein the figures of many of the letters, rhetorical questions, apostrophes, and exclamations are combined with varied isocolon and dramatic diminution of colon length.

> Il n'y a pas une ligne dans votre lettre [11] qui ne me fasse glacer le sang [8], et j'ai peine à croire [5], après l'avoir relue vingt fois [8], que ce soit à moi [5] qu'elle est adressée [5]. Qui? moi? moi? J'aurais offensé Julie [7]? J'aurais profané ses attraits [8]? Celle à qui chaque instant de ma vie [9] j'offre des adorations [7] eût été en butte [5] à mes outrages [4]? Non, je me serais percé le cœur mille fois [11] avant qu'un projet si barbare [8] en eût approché [5]! Ah! que tu le connais mal [7], ce cœur qui t'idolâtre [6], ce cœur qui vole et se prosterne [8] sous chacun de tes pas [6], ce cœur qui voudrait inventer pour toi [10] de nouveaux hommages inconnus aux mortels [11] . . . (I, 51)

The syntax of the last sentence might be termed passionate apposition, the latter tending to have strong emotive value in prose. The metonymy of the prostrate heart marks the height of increasing use of metaphor and figures of thought. All in all, this is tragic rhetoric, reaching the poetic level of the many quotations from Petrarch, Tasso, and Metastasio scattered through the novel and constituting a system of comparisons. It is important to observe that this poetic prose is less monotonous in syntax than that devised by the theorists of the early eighteenth century and that we have seen in Vauvenargues' prose poem on Hippolyte de Seytres. The latter seems in comparison to occupy some awkward intermediary place between prose and verse, while Rousseau's poetic style is firmly grounded in distinctly prosaic rhythms and syntax.

Such elevated style in a novel dealing with contemporary characters obviously violates the decorum of neoclassical levels of diction, which each correspond to a kind of subject matter. This is an innovation, a new conception of high style that could be said to mark the decadence of neoclassicism, the disintegration of the theory behind its verbal figures. Rousseau, however, was too refined an artist idly to upset the conventions on which his style was based. He attempts in *La Nouvelle Héloïse*, beginning with its title, to infuse his story with a special poetic color. Switzerland, with its "sérénité du climat," is a remote pastoral world, and Rousseau devotes significant pages to Saint-Preux's feelings as he draws near this paradisiacal spot (IV, 6), which is compared with a South Pacific island (IV, 10). The wine harvest and the wise exploitation of the land are described (V, 7), suggesting a Golden Age, and, in contrast to the glimpse of the outside world in the novel, Switzerland is governed by a natural association of men rather than by the artificial and nefarious society, instinct with hostility beneath its false and superficial gregariousness, which characterizes France. Rousseau therefore creates an image of Switzerland which it is not exaggerated to call poetic. Its people provide the rustic element of bucolic tradition, and the noble figures—Julie, Saint-Preux, and the others—act out the tragic pastoral, the elevated form of the idyllic convention worked out in the sixteenth century.

The sublime is far from being Rousseau's only manner. *Style coupé* is used frequently for narration or such effects as the opening of the *Confessions* or *Contrat social*. However, Rousseau's influence on subsequent prose is most closely associated with another new, unornamented lyric style found at times in the *Confessions* (as in the famous *nuit à la belle étoile* in Book IV) and especially in the *Rêveries d'un promeneur solitaire*, the title of which suggests, in its first and last words, the peculiarly new quality of this prose. The *Rêveries* are a kind of meditation, with only the vaguest suggestion of the rhetorical situation of speaker and audience.

> J'ai remarqué [5] dans les vicissitudes d'une longue vie [10] que les époques des plus douces jouissances [10] et des plaisirs les plus vifs [6] ne sont pourtant pas celles [6] dont le souvenir m'attire [6] et me touche le plus [5]. Ces courts moments [4] de délire et de passion [7], quelque vifs qu'ils puissent être [6], ne sont cependant [5], et par leur vivacité même [8], que des points bien clairsemés [7] dans la ligne de la vie [7]. Ils sont trop rares et trop rapides [8] pour constituer un état [8]; et le bonheur que mon cœur regrette [9] n'est point composé d'instants fugitifs [10], mais un état simple et permanent [9], qui n'a rien de vif en lui-même [9], mais dont la durée accroît le charme [9], au point d'y trouver enfin [7] la suprême félicité [7].

The rhetorical means—isocolon and doublets—are relatively modest; the thought is everything. We can see in this prose the shift in the conception of the sublime from the embellished manner of much of *La Nouvelle Héloïse* to a more modern lyric conception. Rousseau's art consists here in sustaining the mood and spinning out his poetic commonplaces without our being conscious of "amplification" of the old kind.

> Tout est dans un flux [5] continuel [4] sur la terre [3]. Rien n'y garde une forme [6] constante et arrêtée [6], et nos affections [5] qui s'attachent aux choses extérieures [9] passent et changent nécessairement comme elles [9]. Toujours en avant [5] ou en arrière de nous [6], elles rappellent le passé [6], qui n'est plus [3], ou préviennent l'avenir [6], qui souvent ne doit point être [7]: il n'y a rien là de solide [7] à quoi le cœur se puisse attacher [9]. Aussi n'a-t-on guère ici-bas [8] que du plaisir qui passe [6]; pour le bonheur qui dure [6], je doute qu'il y soit connu [7]. A peine est-il [4], dans nos plus vives jouissances [6], un instant où le cœur [6] puisse véritablement nous dire [8]: *Je voudrais* [3] *que cet instant* [4] *durât toujours* [4]. Et comment peut-on appeler bonheur [9] un état fugitif [6] qui nous laisse encore [5] le cœur inquiet et vide [6], qui nous fait regretter [6] quelque chose avant [5], ou désirer encore [6] quelque chose après [5]?

It is a momentous step in the history of style for meditative movement to replace vehement figures in representing an inner train of thought. Instead of the voice being louder, so to speak, the isocolon here has an effect of lulling moderation. There is no real analogy to this style in the classical conceptions of the speech or the neoclassical ones of theatrical language, which is to say that here fundamentals of rhetoric are abandoned. Without the example of Rousseau's subdued lyricism, it is difficult to imagine the last and greatest prose poem of the neoclassical movement, Maurice de Guérin's "Le Centaure" (written *ca.* 1835): "Pour moi, ô Mélampe! je décline dans la vieillesse, calme comme le coucher des constellations. Je garde encore assez de hardiesse pour gagner le haut des rochers où je m'attarde, soit à considérer les nuages sauvages et inquiets, soit à voir venir de l'horizon les hyades pluvieuses, les pléiades ou le grand Orion; mais je reconnais que je me réduis et me perds rapidement comme une neige flottant sur les eaux, et que prochainement j'irai me mêler aux fleuves qui coulent dans le vaste sein de le terre." The thematic distinctions often made about "preromanticism" in the eighteenth century are not nearly so important as the technical achievement of sustaining lyricism while discarding the vehement figures of rhetoric. If we look back at Vauvenargues' prose poem on the death of De Seytres, we immediately see the profound shift in artistic means.

The variety of styles used by Rousseau suggests the gradual increase and diversification of conceptions of literature in the later eighteenth century. One of the most interesting books of the period from this point of view is Laclos' *Les Liaisons dangereuses* (1782). Taken as a whole, the work is a kind of *drame* and reflects middle-level character types and values in the letters of the *présidente*, Cécile, Mme de Volanges, and Mme de Rosemonde. This new realism differs not only from seventeenth-century literature, where there was no place for it in the system of styles and genres, but from nineteenth-century realism as well, by its element of mimicry. The letters of Cécile or the *présidente* must be just as long as they would be in reality, the language of politeness and convention unabridged. While no one ever confused the type of language in a story by Balzac with that of actual people, the line was not so clearly drawn with epistolary novels like *Les Liaisons dangereuses* in the preceding century. We touch here on a radical kind of mimesis, inconceivable in high neoclassicism, whose exponents believed in and practiced a doctrine of selective and stylized imitation.

The documentlike character of many of the letters and our willingness completely to identify the style of a letter with personality, perhaps even with a real personality, creates the necessary factual background for Valmont and Mme de Merteuil's activities in the novel. We see them using words as disguises and even, up to the final moments of a seduction, as actions. It is not surprising that they are stunning rhetoricians, especially Mme de Merteuil.

> Revenez, mon cher vicomte, revenez: que faites-vous, que pouvez-vous faire chez une vieille tante dont tous les biens vous sont substitués? Partez sur-le-champ! j'ai besoin de vous. Il m'est venu une excellente idée, et je veux bien vous en confier l'exécution. Ce peu de mots devrait suffire; et, trop honoré de mon choix, vous devriez venir, avec empressement, prendre mes ordres à genoux: mais vous abusez de mes bontés, même depuis que vous n'en usez plus; et dans l'alternative d'une haine éternelle ou d'une excessive indulgence, votre bonheur veut que ma bonté l'emporte. (II)

The elements of relatively elevated style are numerous: the *confier l'exécution*, with its verbal noun, the elegant inversion of *il m'est venu*, the polyptoton of *user* and *abuser*, the Racinian hyperbole *éternelle*, and the metonymic *votre bonheur* and *ma bonté*. The dominant metaphor of all the exchanges between Valmont and Mme de Merteuil is the war for love equivalence frequent in Ovid, Horace, and the French tragic poets: "Comme je doutais encore d'un si heureux succès, je feignis un grand effroi; mais tout en m'effrayant, je la conduisais, ou la portais vers le lieu précédemment désigné pour le champ de ma gloire; et en effet elle ne revint à elle que soumise et déjà livrée à son heureux vainqueur" (CXXV). Literature, especially dramatic literature, supplies quite naturally various expressions that are not entirely metaphoric. Mme de Merteuil reads a little Crébillon and a letter from *La Nouvelle Héloïse* to prepare her tone for a seduction scene. Valmont sees himself surrounded by figures from a *drame*. He animates a *scène languissante* with a skillful *transition*, avoids letting a *scène de désespoir* go too far, and refers to the *pureté de méthode* in his verbal tactics. The theater metaphor is also found in Mme de Merteuil's letters: she had planned to train Cécile to *jouer les seconds* under her direction. The final estrangement is preceded by Mme de Merteuil's finding Valmont's phraseology confused and self-deluding.

From one point of view *Les Liaisons dangereuses* is a very unbalanced work in that the documentary, sometimes verbose letters of the *drame* characters cannot compare in interest to the great verbal invention of Valmont and Mme de Merteuil. From another, it is only by the presence of the less-brilliant letters that the pyrotechnic ones and the characters who write them can fully be appreciated. The novel is, of course, anything but a classical work in the sense that unity of style—the most important of the unities—is impaired by the very qualities that make it most interesting.

While it owes much to the *drame*, mock-heroic is the genre from which *Les Liaisons dangereuses* derives its greatest verbal power, just as the impassioned oration and pastoral description lie behind *La Nouvelle Héloïse*. The last great novel quite strictly indebted to a neoclassical genre is *Adolphe* (1816); in the opening analysis of Adolphe and his world the *moralistes'* language is prominent: "Je ne veux point ici me justifier . . . je veux simplement dire . . . qu'il faut du temps pour s'accoutumer à l'espèce humaine, telle que l'intérêt, l'affectation, la vanité, la peur nous l'ont faite." Asyndeton abounds in this *moraliste* middle style, as does polyptoton: "tout en ne m'intéressant qu'à moi, je m'intéressais faiblement à moi-même." Paradox and antithesis mark the analysis of conscious into unconscious motives, the *procédé* of La Rochefoucauld: "Je portais au fond de mon cœur un besoin de sensibilité dont je ne m'apercevais pas, mais qui, ne trouvant point à me satisfaire, me détachait successivement de tous les objets qui tour à tour attiraient ma curiosité." We notice several terms that belong more to the eighteenth-century psychological vocabulary than to the high *moraliste* mode of the seventeenth; *sensibilité, solitude,* and *nature* are the opposite of society: "L'étonnement de la première jeunesse, à l'aspect d'une société si factice et si travaillée, annonce plutôt un cœur naturel qu'un esprit méchant."

The simple system of antitheses between an egotistical society, painted in the terms and figures of La Rochefoucauld, and nature, conceived as a beneficent norm, breaks down as the novel progresses: "J'ai toujours été dirigé par des sentiments vrais et naturels. Comment se fait-il qu'avec ces sentiments je n'aie fait si longtemps que mon malheur et celui des autres?" (Chapter 8). Even the classical analysis of a motive into its opposite, *amour-propre,* proves unsatisfactory: "Il n'y a point d'unité complète dans l'homme, et presque jamais personne n'est tout à fait sincère ni tout à fait de mauvaise foi" (Chapter 2). At the end of the process of paradox heaped on paradox, we find that the maxims tend to destroy one another: "Les sentiments de l'homme sont confus et mélangés . . . et la parole, toujours trop grossière et trop générale, peut bien servir à les désigner, mais ne sert jamais à les définir" (Chapter 2). The *moraliste* system of analysis seems to move in circles.

The destructive *moraliste* style does not impair the coherence of the novel, because intercalated passages of high style provide displays of emotional energy contrasting with the analytical movement. These contain elevated rhetorical resources.

> Je m'arrête; je marche à pas lents: je retarde l'instant du *bonheur,* de ce *bonheur* que tout menace, que je me crois toujours sur le point de perdre; *bonheur* imparfait et troublé, contre lequel conspirent peut-être à chaque

minute *et* les événements funestes *et* les regards jaloux, *et* les caprices ty-
ranniques *et* votre propre volonté! *Quand* je touche au seuil de votre porte,
quand je l'entrouvre, une nouvelle terreur me saisit: je m'avance comme un
coupable, demandant grâce à tous les objets qui frappent ma vue, *comme si*
tous étaient ennemis, *comme si* tous m'enviaient l'heure de félicité dont je
vais encore jouir. (Chapter 3)

The repetitions of *bonheur*, leading into an opposition and a polysyndetic (*et . . . et . . . et*) enumeration, are a first example of heightened
figures. Apposition is used sparingly but grandly in neoclassical
prose, and polysyndeton is customarily restricted to verse high style.
Second comes the oratorical kind of asyndeton with twos, in which
for ringing emphasis a construction is doubled (*quand . . . quand . . .
comme si . . . comme si*); this asyndeton of clauses or long phrases is
not at all the understated kind used with words or short phrases, and
the examples one finds of it are very much in the vein of high style.
Finally, in the remainder of the passage, which I have not quoted,
there are further examples of repetition and asyndeton. Much the
same sort of repetition, together with other kinds, characterizes the
following lines.

Cette sensibilité que l'on méconnaît parce qu'elle est souffrante et froissée,
cette sensibilité dont on exige impérieusement des témoignages que mon
cœur refuse à l'emportement et à la menace, qu'il me serait doux de m'y
livrer avec l'être chéri, compagnon d'une vie régulière et respectée! Que
n'ai-je pas fait *pour* Ellénore? *Pour elle* j'ai quitté mon pays et ma famille; j'ai
pour elle affligé *le cœur d'un vieux père* qui gémit encore loin de moi; *pour elle*
j'habite ces lieux où ma jeunesse s'enfuit solitaire, *sans* gloire, *sans* honneur
et *sans* plaisir: tant de sacrifices faits *sans devoir* et *sans amour* ne prouvent-
ils pas ce que *l'amour* et *le devoir* me rendraient capable de faire? (Chapter 7)

Here a notable sign of high style is the deictic or objectifying expression: *cette sensibilité* for *ma sensibilité*, *un vieux père* for *mon vieux père*.
Even if these expressions were, so to speak, brought down to the
level of *ma sensibilité*, there remains the characteristic high style
metonymy of the emotion for the person, as in *l'emportement* and *la
menace*, which mean *Ellénore furieuse et menaçante*. We have seen this
Latinate figure a number of times, and it plays a notable role in the
oratorical style, having, at the same time, an obvious kinship with the
personified psychological forces of *moraliste* middle style. Finally, in

the last sentence above, there is an elliptical syllogism, or enthymeme, one of the high ornaments of rhetoric, in which repetition acquires a brilliant logical-persuasive force.

Yet another style occurs in *Adolphe*, which is that of the prose poem. Adolphe and Ellénore read together the English nature poets of the eighteenth century, and in the following passage Adolphe's meditation follows the formula, evolved in England toward the middle of the century, of sublime thoughts springing from a contemplation of the landscape.

> Le jour s'affaiblissait: le ciel était serein; la campagne devenait déserte; les travaux des hommes avaient cessé, ils abandonnaient la nature à elle-même. Mes pensées prirent graduellement une teinte plus grave et plus imposante. Les ombres de la nuit qui s'épaississaient à chaque instant, le vaste silence qui m'environnait et qui n'était interrompu que par des bruits rares et lointains firent succéder à mon imagination un sentiment plus calme, plus solennel. Je promenais mes regards sur l'horizon grisâtre dont je n'apercevais plus les limites, et qui, par là même, me donnait, en quelque sorte, la sensation de l'immensité. (Chapter 7)

We recognize the opening commonplaces of Gray's "Elegy Written in a Country Churchyard." The sublime thought of immensity introduces, of course, an emotive note quite different from the *moraliste* range of experience and provides Adolphe with an escape from psychological paradoxes. The scene near the end of the novel, where Adolphe and Ellénore walk on the frozen grass, begins with the special kind of heightened personification known as pathetic fallacy: "C'était une de ces journées d'hiver où le soleil semble éclairer tristement la campagne grisâtre, comme s'il regardait en pitié la terre qu'il a cessé de réchauffer." The passage concludes with the thought of harmony between man and nature: "Comme tout est calme! me dit Ellénore; comme la nature se résigne! Le cœur aussi ne doit-il pas apprendre à se résigner?"

Adolphe is not only one of the most fastidiously written books in French, it is also an extraordinary anthology of seventeenth- and eighteenth-century style, from the middle-level *moraliste* manner to the high dramatic oratorical mode and the poetic prose genre of late neoclassicism. The novel stands at the very end of neoclassical tradition; of the important works of that tradition only Maurice de Gué-rin's version of poetic prose follows it. *Adolphe* is a synthesis of neo-classical forms of expression just before the dissolution, as far as major literature goes, of the sensibility and esthetic which produced them.

7 The European Context: The Legacy of Boccaccio

The full significance of Boccaccio for European literature is not generally understood outside Italian studies. Aside from his place as a writer of fiction, he is the creator of the first highly developed prose style in the vernacular. There is no prose of comparable artistry in French before Rabelais, nor in English till even later. The whole Italian tradition of prose, following Boccaccio, reached a high degree of rhetorical self-consciousness when French prose was just beginning to be formed, and, although I am not concerned with narrow questions of influences, the significance of Italian styles for French will shortly, I think, be evident. Boccaccio's major invention I shall consider first: a narrative style in which actions are elaborately linked.

The early romance narrative style, which has many representatives in Old French especially, tends toward a series of independent sentences (with intermittent *when* clauses), whose linkage is brought about, insofar as there really is any linkage, by the particle *si* (Latin *sic*) in French and Italian. The peculiar effect of this narrative manner is that all actions seem put more or less on the same plane. Boccaccio is the first to use, in a thoroughgoing fashion, a system of varied sentence connectives and subordination in which relative clauses, appositions, adverbial clauses, participles, adverbs, gerunds, infinitives used as gerunds, and infinitive clauses order and join the actions presented, to a degree that is as extraordinary in retrospect as it was in relation to the earlier narrative technique.

> Nella nostra città, la qual sempre di varie maniere e di nuove genti è stata abbondevole, fu, ancora non è gran tempo, un dipintore chiamato Calandrino, uom semplice e di nuovi costumi, il quale il più del tempo con due altri dipintori usava, chiamati l'un Bruno e l'altro Buffalmacco, uomini sol-

lazzevoli molto, ma per altro avveduti e sagaci, i quali con Calandrino usavan per ciò che de' modi suoi e della sua simplicità sovente gran festa prendevano. Era similmente allora in Firenze un giovane di maravigliosa piacevolezza, in ciascuna cosa che far voleva astuto ed avvenevole, chiamato Maso del Saggio, il quale, udendo alcune cose della simplicità di Calandrino, propose di voler prender diletto de' fatti suoi col fargli alcuna beffa o fargli credere alcuna nuova cosa: e per ventura trovandolo un dì nella chiesa di San Giovanni e veggendolo star attento a riguardare le dipinture e gl'intagli del tabernaculo il quale è sopra l'altare della detta chiesa, non molto tempo davanti postovi, pensò essergli dato luogo e tempo alla sua intenzione.[1]

Although the first sentence has its main verb early, the effect is not that of a descending, accretive period, such as we see in Amyot and sometimes in Rabelais, for the thought contained in the last clause is essential to the whole. The hyperbaton of closing clauses with a verb creates a certain grammatical tension, reinforcing the strong forward movement of the sense. In the long, double second period, there is an elaborate suspension between *e per ventura* and *pensò*, the latter forming part of still another clause which has no adequate meaning until the last word is reached. This passage embodies the strongest kind of vernacular periodic syntax: both sense and grammar make the structure cohesive, with no trailing off effect at the end. It is a rhetorical model for the other modern languages. Boccaccio did not arrive at this stylistic ease without some effort; his early works betray less expert handling of the period. With reference to French narration we should note that certain concise participial constructions were developed in Italian, which were never to have a real French counter-

1. Giovanni Boccaccio, *Il Decamerone*, "Giornata ottava," III. "In our city, where there have always been many strange people and distinctive ways of living, there was, not long ago, a painter named Calandrino, a simple man with odd habits, who most of the time associated with two other painters, named Bruno and Buffalmacco, amusing men but also sharp and wise, who associated with Calandrino in order often to make great fun of his simple-mindedness and habits. There was likewise in Florence a marvelously delightful young man, charming and astute in everything he set out to do, named Maso del Saggio, who, hearing examples of Calandrino's simple-mindedness, undertook to make a joke of him by playing a trick on him or making him believe some outlandish thing; and by chance, finding him one day in the church of San Giovanni and seeing him looking attentively at the paintings and carvings of the tabernacle over the altar of the said church, the tabernacle which had been installed there not long before, he realized the time and place had come for his purpose."

part. Their absence has perhaps something to do with the less impressive effect periodic style often has in French compared with
Italian, and they include an absolute impersonal construction (*biso-
gnandogli qualcosa*); a past participle with a pronoun object (*levatosi in
piè, un accidente sopravenutogli*), which makes an imposing *parola sdruc-
ciola*; and a kind of Latinate indication of part of body (*a' quali ragiona-
menti Calandrino posto orecchie . . .*).

Comparisons between Boccaccio and the French authors of *nouvelles* in the immediately following centuries are never flattering to
the latter, who seem generally to lack fluency and verve in linking
sentences and subordinating some actions to others, to say nothing
of their more limited grammatical means; however, the basic syntactic
tendencies are the same and represent a break with the earlier, more
paratactic kinds of narrative. Boccaccio, in other words, represents
the ideal type of the elaborately connected *nouvelle* style and the
proof it is a viable one and not some aberration of minor French writers. Rabelais' is the first use of elaborate style in French fiction which
is comparable in polish to Boccaccio's, and the study of the two in
conjunction is a remarkable demonstration of the effects possible
with this now-remote kind of hypotactic narrative movement.

Boccaccio's narrative style in the *Decameron* is of such originality as
to excite interest quite abstracted from the tales themselves. It is indeed in the creation of forms of literary expression that a good part of
his greatness lies. His secondary works, while they seem at times flat
or turgid, also demonstrate his capacities for linguistic invention, and
their more involved periods lie as well at the origin of the characteristic cinquecento style first represented by Pietro Bembo.

Bembo was the chief exponent in the early sixteenth century of
Ciceronianism in Latin style and imitation of Petrarch and Boccaccio
in Italian. It is to him that renewed interest in the trecento masters is
ascribed. His joint concern with Cicero and Boccaccio led him to a
kind of Italian prose in which the latter's tendency toward the use of
end-position verbs and other hyperbatic constructions is intensified.
Theoretically at least, if there is such a thing as Ciceronianism in vernacular prose, it should be found in Bembo's work. Here is a period
from the *Prose della Volgar Lingua* (1525), a work devoted to the ennobling of Italian style.

Questa città, la quale per le sue molte e riverende reliquie, infino a questo dì a noi dalla ingiuria delle nemiche nazioni e del tempo, non legger nemico, lasciate, più che per li sette colli, sopra i quali ancor siede, sé Roma essere subitamente dimostra a chi la mira, vede tutto il giorno a sé venire molti artefici di vicine e di lontane parti, i quali le belle antiche figure di marmo e talor di rame, che o sparse per tutta lei qua e là giacciono, o sono publicamente e privatamente guardate e tenute care, e gli archi e le terme e i teatri e gli altri diversi edificii, che in alcuna loro parte sono in piè, con istudio cercando, nel picciolo spazio delle loro carte o cere la forma di quelli rapportano; e poscia, quando a fare essi alcuna nuova opera intendono, mirano in quegli essempi, e di rassomigliarli col loro artificio procacciando, tanto più sé dovere essere della loro fatica lodati si credono, quanto essi più alle antiche cose fanno per somiglianza ravicinare le loro nuove; per ciò che sanno e veggono che quelle antiche più alla perfezion dell'arte s'accostano, che le fatte da indi innanzi.[2]

The opening lines contain a past participle functioning as a relative clause (*lasciate*), with its modifiers of temporal indication, indirect object, and agent; this goes much further in the direction of condensed syntax than what we normally find in sixteenth-century French prose. From *nemiche . . . nemico* on, we also observe a use of balancing or parallel constructions, syntactic or rhythmic (*più che per . . . , sopra i quali . . .*), which give shape to the period. We have a strong sense of construction by unitary figures, as when polysyndeton suddenly dominates (*figure . . . e gli archi e . . .*); elsewhere we find a subtly tripartite construction in *sé Roma subitamente dimostra a chi la mira*. The latter exemplifies the possibilities of giving a free hand to varied accentual patterns in hyperbaton ($-$ $-$ x / $-$ x x $-$ x x $-$ x / $-$ x $-$ x),

2. Pietro Bembo, *Prose della Volgar Lingua*, III, 1. "This city, which—as much or more because of its many and reverend ancient remains, which to this day have been preserved for us from the attacks of enemy nations and time, no less an enemy, as from the seven hills it still rests on—is immediately recognized as Rome by whoever sees it; this city, I repeat, sees everyday the arrival of artists, from near or distant lands, who seek out eagerly the beautiful ancient statues of marble or sometimes of copper, which either lie scattered here and there throughout the city or else are publicly and privately preserved and held dear; nor do such artists fail to seek out also the arches and baths and theaters and other public buildings that partly still stand, copying, as with the statues, their form in small sketches or wax models to take back home with them. These foreign sculptors and architects, when the time comes then that they wish to make new works, look to their copies, and, attempting to make a likeness by their skill, consider themselves all the more to be praised insofar as their new works have been made to resemble old ones, for they know and see that the ancient ones more closely approach artistic perfection than any made since."

an important structural element French can less often avail itself of. This division of the period into a number of well-defined and differently shaped subunits is something we might well call Ciceronian and has little resemblance to the haphazardly arranged and shapeless hypotaxis so often misnamed "Ciceronian" in discussions of French prose of the sixteenth century.

In regard to the intricate period above, one might venture the criticism that the four main verbs tend to be confused with the subordinate ones, which are also in the indicative mood. This problem can, however, be avoided in elaborate Italian periodic prose; the following opening clause of a sentence contains only two finite verbs, one of which is in the subjunctive: "Per la qual cosa avisando io, da quello che si vede avenire tutto dì, pochissimi essere quegli uomini, a' quali nel peregrinaggio di questa nostra vita mortale, ora dalla turba delle passioni soffiato e ora dalle tante e così al vero somiglianti apparenze d'oppenioni fatto incerto, quasi per lo continuo e di calamita e di scorta non faccia mestiero, ho sempre giudicato . . ."[3] The -*ndo* form, called a gerund in Italian, is equivalent to a clause with *since* or *as*; an infinitive clause is governed by the gerund, on which, in turn, depends the subjunctive *a' quali . . . faccia*. The parallel participles *soffiato* and *fatto incerto* have complements of agent different in length and complexity, the second one illustrating the true Italian present participle. The coexistence of the latter (-*nte*) with the -*ndo* form of the verb provides Italian syntax with some distinctions unknown to French.

The road-of-life metaphor upon which the above-quoted passage is based is not untypical of the tendency in Bembo toward laboriously stated banalities, and the contempt in which someone like Leopardi held the cinquecento style is grounded not entirely on the disregard for normal Italian grammar but also on the often negligible content of Bembo and his followers. Bembo created a vernacular Ciceronianism

3. Pietro Bembo, *Gli Asolani*, I, 1. "For which purpose, as I have observed from everyday examples, that very few men can continuously be without compass and escort in this pilgrimage of our mortal life, a road which sometimes is buffeted by the whirlwind of passions, sometimes is darkened by the simulacra of private thoughts having the semblance of reality, for which purpose, I say, it has always seemed to me desirable that . . ."

in a very real sense; his manipulation of Italian, in the achieving of elegance reminiscent of Latin, is, at times, awesome indeed, but in the sense of capturing high moments of history, of eloquence as distinguished from orotundity, there is less to be said for him.

We must distinguish clearly between Ciceronianism as an elegant—or perverse—syntactic ideal, based essentially on various forms of hyperbatic suspension, and Ciceronianism as high style in the true classical sense, joining to grammatical dexterity the highest matter, such as the destiny of the state and the order of the universe. It is also of the utmost importance in studying the evolution of European styles not to debase the nobler sense of Ciceronianism merely because of the Neo-Latin quarrels between Erasmus and the Bembists over whether one should admit into one's prose a phrase not attested in Cicero.[4] The creation of a vernacular Ciceronian high style is quite unrelated to such anecdotica and constitutes not so much a close imitation as a free reinventing of the Latin *genus grande*.

A genuinely Ciceronian sense of grandeur is perhaps first revealed in Francesco Guicciardini's *Storia d'Italia* (written 1538–1540), along with not inconsiderable powers of periodic refinement. Here is the great opening section of the *Storia d'Italia*: "Io ho deliberato di scrivere le cose accadute alla memoria nostra in Italia, da poi che l'arme de' Franzesi, chiamate da' nostri Principi medesimi, cominciorono con grandissimo movimento a perturbarla: materia per la varietà e grandezza loro molto memorabile e piena di atrocissimi accidenti, avendo patito tanti anni Italia tutte quelle calamità con le quali sogliono i miseri mortali, ora per l'ira giusta di Iddio, ora per l'empietà e sceleratezze degli altri uomini, essere vessati."[5] The lengthy apposition (*materia . . .*) is often a very high-flown construction in prose, as we have seen in Bossuet's evocations of the vicissitudes of fortune. Prolonging the apposition is a gerund clause, the particular value of which we

4. The famous document is Erasmus' polemical dialogue *Ciceronianus* (1528).
5. Francesco Guicciardini, *Storia d'Italia*. "I have, on deliberation, chosen to write the things which have happened in our memory in Italy, since the time that the French armies, summoned by our very leaders, began, with great activity, to perturb the land: a matter which, for the variety and importance of the occurrences, is quite worthy of memory and full of horrible incidents, for Italy has suffered for many years all those calamities by which mortal men are tormented, sometimes through the just wrath of God, sometimes through the impiety and wickedness of other men."

may see by comparing it with the French equivalent (*l'Italie ayant souf-fert*), which is stiff, and with an Italian finite form (*perchè l'Italia a pa-tito*), which is less dignified; the *avendo* with postposed subject is at once sonorous and concise; it avoids excess multiplication of finite verbs. A peculiar combination of a balanced closing (*ora . . . ora . . .*) and a suspended construction concludes the period with both breadth and point—a period generally striking for the clarity of its outlines.

The development of a period is often dependent on doublings, triplings, and even further multiplication of individual sentence elements. Simple doublings with *and* may be mechanical if overly frequent. The following period, again from the introductory section of the *Storia d'Italia*, demonstrates Guicciardini's great sophistication in handling such matters.

> Tale era lo stato delle cose, tali erano i fondamenti della tranquillità d'Italia, disposti e contrapesati in modo che non solo di alterazione presente non si temeva, ma nè si poteva facilmente congetturare da quali consigli, o per quali casi, o con quali arme si avesse a muovere tanta quiete; quando nel mese d'aprile dell'anno mille quattrocento novantadue sopravenne la morte di Lorenzo de' Medici: morte acerba a lui per l'età (perchè morì non finiti ancora quarantaquattro anni); acerba alla patria, la quale per la reputazione e prudenza sua, e per l'ingegno attissimo a tutte le cose onorate ed eccellenti, fioriva maravigliosamente di ricchezze e di tutti quei beni ed ornamenti da' quali suole essere nelle cose umane la lunga pace accompagnata; ma fu morte incomodissima ancora al resto d'Italia, così per le altre operazioni, le quali da lui per la sicurtà commune continuamente si facevano; come perchè era mezzo a moderare e quasi un freno ne' dispareri e ne' sospetti, i quali per diverse cagioni tra Ferdinando e Lodovico Sforza, principi di ambizione e di potenza quasi pari, spesse volte nascevano.[6]

The *tale* clauses are juxtaposed without *and*; the participles *disposti* and *contrapesati* are linked by *and*, on the other hand; the two clauses that follow not only lack *and* but have an ABBA arrangement in re-

6. *Ibid.* "Such was the state of things, such were the bases of Italy's peacefulness, disposed and counterbalanced in such a way that for the moment no turn for the worse was to be feared, nor could anyone guess by whose plans or by what contingencies or by which nation's armies such peace could be destroyed; when, in the April of the year 1492, occurred the death of Lorenzo de' Medici: a bitter death for him at his age (be-

spect to verbs and their complements. *Da quali, per quali,* and *con quali* are not only a triplet but use *or*. The dramatic center of the period occupies, interestingly enough, a subordinate *quando* clause, which has the notable distinction of having no reduplication. In the concluding clauses, there is a kind of varied triplet: *morte acerba, acerba,* and *ma fu morte,* the expressions being semantically a threesome but grammatically asymmetrical. The element of variation is also noteworthy in the way doublings are interconnected, so that, for example, *di richezze* and *di tutti* are parallel, but the latter forms, in turn, the doublet *beni* and *ornamenti.* This very complicated structure also draws, like the previous quotation, on the resources of apposition and on a combination of balanced elements and syntactic suspension in the conclusion. Ciceronian is certainly an appropriate term for such complexly planned prose. All the intricacy is not, of course, confined to the syntactic level; as in the other period quoted from the *Storia d'Italia,* the dramatic and logical structure of the material is such as to achieve resolution only with the grandiose cadential pattern: *i quali* [3] *per diverse cagioni* [7] *tra Ferdinando e Lodovico Sforza* [11] *principi di ambizione e di potenza quasi pari* [15] *spesse volte* [4] *nascevano* [4].

In comparison with French and English, Italian is notable for its easy inversions, its long words (many common ones have as many as five or six syllables), and its traditional reliance on verb forms rather than nouns (*e.g., stabilirono d'incontrarsi*: they arranged a meeting; his book is a reflection of: *nel suo libro si rispecchia*). The gerund, in particular, gives Italian a fine supplement or substitute for adverbial conjunctions (*lo farò potendo*: I shall do it if I am able). In the following, the gerund is first combined with an adverbial clause to create a kind of interlocking expression difficult to obtain otherwise. The object precedes the verb in the opening words.

---

cause he died before the age of forty-four), a bitter blow for Florence, which, through his reputation and prudence and his mind active in all things excellent and honored, was flourishing marvelously in wealth and all benefits which long periods of peace customarily bring; but his death was even most ill-timed for the rest of Italy, because of his other activities, in which he continuously engaged for common security, since he was a medium for moderating and almost a restraining element in the differences and suspicions which, for various reasons, often arose between Ferdinando of Naples and Lodovico Sforza of Milan, leaders almost equals in their authority and power."

Il principio dell'anno nuovo fece molto memorabile una cosa inaspettata e inaudita per tutti i secoli; perchè parendo al Pontefice che la oppugnazione della Mirandola procedesse lentamente, e attribuendo parte alla imperizia, parte alla perfidia dei capitani, e specialmente del nipote, quel che procedeva maggiormente da molte difficoltà, deliberò di accelerare le cose con la presenza sua, anteponendo l'impeto e l'ardore dell'animo a tutti gli altri rispetti; nè lo ritenendo il considerare quanto fosse indegno della maestà di tanto grado che il Pontefice romano andasse personalmente negli eserciti contro alle terre dei Cristiani; nè quanto fosse pericoloso, disprezzando la fama e il giudizio che appresso a tutto il mondo si farebbe di lui, dare apparente colore e quasi giustificazione a coloro, che, sotto titolo principalmente di essere pernicioso alla Chiesa il reggimento suo, e scandalosi e incorreggibili i suoi difetti, procuravano di convocare il Concilio e suscitare i principi contro a lui. Risonavano queste parole per tutta la Corte.[7]

Here we see the phonetically weighty gerund used to articulate much of the period. The typical punctuation, the semicolon before *nè lo ritenendo*, shows to what extent the gerund is assimilated to a full clause. One of its advantages is flexibility in construction: *parendo* has no subject, *attribuendo* an implied *he*; the later gerunds differ similarly in regard to subject. The construction *ritenendo il considerare quanto fosse* is a characteristically Italian multiplication of verb forms, in preference to the undynamic use of nouns, and it is paralleled by the further infinitive *dare colore*. Like the periods of Guicciardini we have previously seen, this one can be analyzed into parallel but varied elements; in this case, as we see from the *queste parole* in the concluding sentence, it represents a great piece of deliberative rhetoric, a summary and heightening of real speech.

7. *Ibid.*, IX. "The beginning of the year was made memorable by something unexpected and unheard-of throughout the centuries; since the Pope thought the siege of La Mirandola was going slowly and since he attributed to inexperience in part, and to the treachery of his captains in part, and especially that of his nephew, the slow progress due above all to great material difficulties, he decided to hasten matters with his own presence, as he considered his strong desire and burning courage valuable more than anything else, and he was not restrained by the consideration of the great unsuitability of the Pope, in all the majesty of his rank, going in person amid an army attacking Christian states; nor did he, despising the reputation and opinion everyone would have of him, consider how perilous it was to give fair semblance and justification to those who, mainly on the grounds that his stewardship was dangerous for the Church and his defects scandalous and incorrigible, were attempting to summon a Church Council and incite leaders against him. These words resounded throughout the court."

After seeing in Guicciardini the marriage of oratorical strength and complex periodicity, which we can call true vernacular Ciceronianism, it becomes evident that the term is most often used in a very approximate or trivial sense in the discussion of renaissance literature. Even Boccaccio shows, in his sentence linkage, doublings, and end-position verbs, traits that are not much more than medievally Latinate; indeed, Christine de Pisan's French, while considerably less elegant than Boccaccio at his best, exhibits very similar features, and no one would think of calling her a Ciceronian. One should note also that the Bembist-Ciceronian manner never resulted in anything more than philological curiosities. *Gli Asolani* never had the popularity of Castiglione's *Cortegiano* on the same subject of ideal love; indeed, Castiglione's book, like Machiavelli's *Principe*, Cellini's autobiography, and other classics of the cinquecento, is far removed in style from the involved syntax of Bembo and the *boccaccevoli*, as they have been called. Castiglione, for example, wrote in long but relaxed periods not unlike those of *L'Astrée* later on, and satisfied the same kind of courtly audience.[8]

When we leave the realm of Italian, it is clear that there do not even exist quite such hyperbatic, would-be Ciceronian styles as Bembo's, the other modern languages having proved too inflexible or their writers too timid. Rabelais occupies a very special position in regard to Ciceronian high style; his adaptation of it to French is stunning in its effects, but of course Ciceronianism is only a very intermittent part, if an important part, of his elaborate system of styles. Ciceronianism is a symbol of high moral value in Rabelais' complicated quest romance, but the books were conceived or grew in such a way that we cannot simply equate classical magnanimity, conveyed in the *genus grande*, with the one supreme value, any more than we can the message of the evangelicals or the wine of the spirit.

Aside from Rabelais, the French prose writers of the sixteenth century offer little that could seriously be termed Ciceronian, and a basically unclassical way of using doublings and subordinate clauses is also evident in English writers who are sometimes called Cicero-

8. *Cf.* Bembo's famous speech in *Il Cortegiano*, Book IV.

nian. Roger Ascham believed in Cicero's central importance in education, but neither his English nor his Latin owes much to Cicero. Sir
Thomas Elyot is likewise untouched by genuine classical influences
in his artful prose, which stands in the same relation to Latin as
Christine de Pisan's; that is to say, its Latinity is as much medieval as
anything else. But Richard Hooker's *Of the Laws of Ecclesiastical Polity*
(1593) stands out, like Guicciardini's works, as the prose of someone
who had the exact sense of high Ciceronian seriousness coupled with
extraordinary dexterity in arranging the elements of a modern language so as to suggest Latin periodicity.

> The stateliness of houses, the goodliness of trees, when we behold them
> delighteth the eye; but that foundation which beareth up the one, that root
> which ministereth unto the other nourishment and life, is in the bosom of
> the earth concealed; and if there be at any time occasion to search into it,
> such labour is then more necessary than pleasant, both to them which un-
> dertake it and for the lookers-on. In like manner, the use and benefit of
> good laws all that live under them may enjoy with delight and comfort,
> albeit the grounds and first original causes from whence they have sprung
> be unknown, as to the greatest part of men they are. (I,1,ii)

This complexly composed passage represents the high-style simile in
its intricate pairings; it exemplifies the surprising variety we find in
Hooker, who, following the treatise pattern necessarily, has much
that is Latinate only in a routine fashion, just as we discover in
Cicero's treatises substantial passages in less than the grand manner,
yet rises with frequency to considerable eloquence. The solid basis of
clarity and skill is a Ciceronian virtue on which the greater virtues, by
no means commonly or easily achieved in English prose at the end of
the sixteenth century, are founded. The narrow historical situation of
Hooker's work—a justification of the legal and theological grounding
of the Anglican church against Puritans and Presbyterians—does not
prevent its often being of compelling pleasure to read: "Though for
no other cause, yet for this; that posterity may know we have not
loosely through silence permitted things to pass away as in a dream,
there shall be for men's information extant thus much concerning the
present state of the Church of God established amongst us, and their
careful endeavour who would have upheld the same" (Preface, 1).
    We see from the few writers who have seemed to us genuinely

touched by the Roman *genus grande* in its spirit and techniques that we cannot loosely speak of the Ciceronianism of the renaissance when we merely mean long and not especially well formed subordinate clauses. We may even question, as when we found Amyot making three Greek sentences into one great paragraph of a sentence in French, whether there is anything very classical at all about such syntax; certainly the leisurely, additive hypotaxis of Castiglione or d'Urfé is remote from Latin tradition. That writers had examples of hypotaxis before their eyes in Latin when none yet existed, of any complexity, in the vernacular, is not in question, but whether the vernacular *génie de la langue*, certainly in the case of French, evolved its own tendencies, partly at least as an internal matter, is what one may ask.

If Boccaccio's contribution to the rise of some kind of Ciceronian prose seems slimmer than is suggested sometimes by literary histories, it is not altogether to be gainsaid, nor is another experiment of his without some consequence: Jacobo Sannazaro, writing in a Latinate manner and drawing some of his inspiration from Boccaccio's pastoral episodes, especially the *Ameto*, wrote the *Arcadia* (1504), a mixture of verse and prose, the first European pastoral novel, in a sense, and, perhaps more important, the archetype of one strain of poetic prose.

> Ove, se io non mi inganno, son forse dodici o quindici alberi di tanto strana ed eccessiva bellezza, che chiunque li vedesse, giudicarebbe che la maestra natura vi si fusse con sommo diletto studiata in formarli. Li quali alquanto distanti, ed in ordine non artificioso disposti, con la loro rarità la naturale bellezza del luogo oltra misura annobiliscono. Quivi senza nodo veruno si vede il drittissimo abete, nato a sustinere i pericoli del mare; e con più aperti rami la robusta quercia, e l'alto frassino, e lo amenissimo platano vi si distendono, con le loro ombre non picciola parte del bello e copioso prato occupando. Ed èvi con più breve fronda l'albero, di che Ercule coronar si solea, nel cui pedale le misere figliuole di Climene furono trasformate.[9]

9. Jacobo Sannazaro, *Arcadia*, "Prosa I." "There, if I am not mistaken, are ten or fifteen trees of such strange and excessive beauty that whoever should see them would be of the opinion that Mother Nature had with the greatest pleasure worked out their shape. They, somewhat distant from one another, and placed in a natural, not artistic

The end-position verbs provide an element of refined syntax, but it is the epithets that are the most characteristic device of style: they ennoble the prose as the trees do the spot. The arresting thing about Sannazaro's epithets is that they anticipate neoclassical habits of diction; the *épithète de nature* adds only what we already know: the oak is strong, the poplar has a short leafy branch. The redundancy gives rhythmic fullness yet semantic evenness to the style, with no element standing out as surprising or taking undue attention from the whole. Now if this were merely a borrowing from customary vernacular poetic diction, it would have less significance; as it happens, there is little, save Petrarch, in previous Italian poetry to provide the pastoral model. Sannazaro's work stands at the beginning of the great age of Italian renaissance poetry with its prefiguration of much of the neoclassical diction of other languages. Prose is not in this case inferior to or behind poetry. As the mixture of verse and prose in the *Arcadia* suggests, there is no great difference for Sannazaro between the dictional systems of the two, and in this degree of equality we find the key to a significant body of sixteenth-century prose.

The stability and persistence of Sannazaro's poetic conception of prose is also of note; here is Fénelon's pastoral poetry in the *Télémaque* some two hundred years later.

> On arriva à la porte de la grotte de Calypso, où Télémaque fut surpris de voir, avec une apparence de simplicité rustique, tout ce qui peut charmer les yeux. On n'y voyoit ni or, ni argent, ni marbre, ni colonnes, ni tableaux, ni statues: cette grotte étoit tapissée d'une jeune vigne qui étendoit ses branches souples également de tous côtés. Les doux zéphyrs conservoient en ce lieu, malgré les ardeurs du soleil, une délicieuse fraîcheur. Des fontaines, coulant avec un doux murmure sur des prés semés d'amarantes et de violettes, formoient en divers lieux des bains aussi purs et aussi clairs que le cristal; mille fleurs naissantes émailloient les tapis verts dont la grotte étoit environnée.

---

fashion, ennobled beyond measure the natural beauty of the spot with their scattered arrangement. Here one can see knotless the arrow-straight pine, born to bear the perils of the sea; and with wider branches the strong oak and the high ash and the lovely sycamore spread themselves in that spot, covering, with their not inconsiderable shadows, no little part of the beautiful and thick grass. And there is the tree with shorter leafy branches with which Hercules would crown himself, into the trunk of which the weeping daughters of Clymene and sisters of Phaeton were transformed."

The continuity of the style lies also in the important descriptive topos, which is a kind of paradox or hyperbole: nature surpasses art in forming a scene of esthetic beauty by means of the *je ne sais quoi*, or grace beyond the reach of art. All the elements of the scene are described with that generality Buffon recommended to the would-be writer of sublime style and which, like other elements of neoclassical poetic diction, have not only early renaissance but even Boccaccian antecedents.

The third kind of prose for which Boccaccio provided a model—and here a demonstrably quite influential one—was the novel of passion. His *Fiammetta*, translated and imitated, illustrates the often involved style of his minor works.

> E qual succisa rosa negli aperti campi fra le verdi fronde sentendo i solari raggi cade perdendo il suo colore, cotal semiviva caddi nelle braccia della mia serva, e dopo non picciolo spazio, aiutata da lei fedelissima, con freddi liquori rivocata al tristo mondo mi risentii; e sperando ancora che egli alla mia porta fosse, quale il furioso toro ricevuto il mortal colpo furibondo si leva saltellando, cotale io stordita levandomi, appena ancora veggendo, corsi, e con le braccia aperte la mia serva abbracciai credendo prendere il mio signore, e con fioca voce e rotta dal pianto in mille parti dissi: "O anima mia, addio."
>
> . . . .
>
> Il giorno era già chiaro in ogni parte, onde io nella mia camera senza il mio Pànfilo veggendomi, ed attorno mirandomi, e per ispazio lunghissimo, come ciò avvenuto si fosse ignorando, la serva dimandai che di lui fosse, ed ella piangendo rispose: "Già è gran pezza che egli nelle sue braccia qui recatavi, da voi il sopravegnente giorno con lagrime infinite a forza il divise."[10]

10. Giovanni Boccaccio, *Fiammetta*, Chap. II. "And as a cut rose in open fields amid the green trees, feeling the sun's rays, falls and loses its color, so half-alive, I fell into the arms of my maid, and, after no little time, aided by her, the faithful one, I came to my senses, summoned back into this mournful world by cold liquids; and hoping yet that he was at my door, as a furious bull mortally wounded takes little leaps, so, stunned, I rose, still barely able to see, and ran and with open arms embraced my maid, thinking to seize my love, and, with a weak voice broken by tears into a thousand pieces, said, 'Farewell, O my soul.' The day already filled the sky, and, thus seeing myself in my room without my Pamphilus and gazing around me and for a long time ignorant of how all that could have come about, I asked my maid what had become of him, and she replied, weeping, 'It is a long while since he, having brought you here in his arms, was, with infinite tears, separated perforce from you by the coming light of day.'"

The grammatical structure is a series of sentences, most with subordinate clauses, which are loosely strung together with *and* in such a way as to render the flood of emotion and make the exact syntactic form not immediately clear at all moments. The similes, the periphrasis *freddi liquori*, the almost mysteriously concise *egli . . . qui recatavi*, the many inversions in word order, make of this an intensely poetic kind of prose, quite different from the equally poetic pastoral style. There is a whole strain of violently imagistic language stemming from the *Fiammetta*, as in *Illustrations de Gaule et Singularitez de Troye*, written by Jean Lemaire des Belges (1473–before 1525).

> Lequel [Paris] tout embrasé de feu venerien dont encores navoit esté si vivement attaint, tenoit ses yeux inseparablement fichez en elle. Mais les pupilles errans et vagabondes en leur circonference, estincelloient de desirs amoureux, comme font les rayz du soleil matutin, reverberez en la clere fontaine. Et son gentil cœur alteré de chaleur vehemente, buvoit à grands traits la fervente liqueur de cupidineux appetit. Laquelle non pouvant digerer, tout ainsi que les flambes dune fournaise, dont le feu est trop vehement, pressent lune lautre à lentree du souspirail, ainsi du noble estomach de lenfant Paris vuydoient souspirs en si grand multitude, que lun ne donnoit lieu à lautre. (I, 25)

This is a mythological account of the connection between Troy and Gaul, which in other passages could exemplify the pastoral style. The characteristic, perhaps, of the novel of passion is that there appears to be a disparity between the concrete, real situation, Fiammetta's being brought home or Paris' sighing amorously, and the extremes of figurative language used in describing it. Expressions of the kind usually associated with baroque literature are not difficult to find. Often an ordinary passage will be juxtaposed to unexpectedly and momentarily ornamented style, as here the alliterative and assonantal clause is juxtaposed to the exclamation (the source is "Hélisenne de Crenne"'s *Les Angoysses douloureuses qui procedent d'amours* [1538], usually called the first novel of passion in French): "Au temps que la déesse Cibele despouilla son glacial et gelide habit et vestit sa verdoyante robbe tapissée de diverses couleurs, je fuz procreée de noblesse, et fuz cause à ma naissance de reduyre en grand joye et lyesse mes plus prochains parens, qui sont pere et mere, par ce qu'ilz estoient hors d'esperance de jamais avoir generation. O qu'à juste

cause je doibs mauldire l'heure que je nasquis!" It is highly instruc-
tive to do some reading in the more elaborately written fiction from
Fiammetta on, if we want to understand precisely why *L'Astrée* was so
greatly admired by its contemporaries. What may seem to us loose or
monotonous in it appeared then as elegantly understated, sustained
in tone, and truly courtly, so great was the difference between the
bombast of amorous anguish and d'Urfé's careful prose. On the other
hand, the novel of passion, although none of its embodiments are
major literature, must be counted as an important genre in that it uses
abundant simile and metaphor and thereby forms the first current in
European literature of what is felt to be poetic prose. The notion that
prose can be as ornamented as verse is not negligible for the creation
of styles from the high humanist period through the baroque.

8 *European Ornamented Prose from 1500 to 1660 and the Neoclassical Aftermath*

We must beware, in studying the evolution of renaissance and seventeenth-century prose, of imagining there are neat historical sequences such as a "Ciceronian" prose followed by more elaborately wrought baroque styles, or a period when sound figures were in fashion yielding to one when metaphor and other figures of thought predominated. We find in the beginnings of highly ornamented prose such diverse strains as Boccaccio's and Jean Lemaire des Belges' similes, pastoral epitheton, and Jean Molinet's inner rime with alliteration. The common quality of such varied writing can be characterized with the old English term *aureation*, the use of "golden," Latinate words, and we must first of all understand in what sense aureation can be applied to Italian figured prose.

Unlike Boccaccio, very few of the eminent prose writers of the cinquecento were Italian speakers by birth. Bembo, Sannazaro, Tasso, Castiglione, and others came from the north or the south, and Venetian, Neapolitan, and so forth were their native forms of speech. Italian they learned as a related language, and it always maintained something of the character of an artificial, purely literary creation; this was true, in fact, even for Tuscans, on whose dialect the greater language was based. Italian was therefore very much a golden tongue, full of alternative forms to permit the phonetically most brilliant choice of words, but the first choice, that of Italian itself, was of an idiom which was already an ornament in itself.

> Appena avea otto anni forniti, che le forze di Amore a sentire incominciai; e de la vaghezza di una picciola fanciulla, ma bella e leggiadra più che altra che vedere mi paresse già mai, e da alto sangue discesa, inamorato, con più diligenzia, che ai puerili anni non si conviene, questo mio de-

siderio teneva occulto. Per la qual cosa colei, senza punto di ciò avvedersi, fanciullescamente meco giocando, di giorno in giorno, di ora in ora più con le sue eccessive bellezze le mie tenere medolle accendeva; intanto che con gli anni crescendo lo amore, in più adulta età ed a li caldi desii più inclinata pervenimmo.[1]

In this passage from the *Arcadia*, we see the characteristic element of choice of *medolle* over the alternative *midolle*, for some nuance of harmony; the practically superfluous but literarily precious double forms *ed* and *e*, *desiderio* and *desio*; and *picciola* chosen over *piccola*. *Fanciullescamente* is, with its seven syllables, one of those rare words of great eloquence when appropriate, and *meco* better suits the rhythm than the regular *con me*. *Avea* and *aveva* were both Italian; *ai* and *a li* were both used. I say nothing of the word order, which is elegantly classicizing to a degree impossible in French.

Almost every Latin word of some dimension could be brought easily into Italian. Such was the sense of aureation for English, and French as well went through a period when something like the Italian free importation of Latin words was attempted in prose. Few writers were involved, but the results are worth observing. In the following passage by François Habert (*ca.* 1520–*ca.* 1560), we find the fanciful image of a winter Flora who scatters snow lilies; there are also sound effects of a sort we have not found in Italian.

> Un jour après longue fatigation d'entendement [õ, t, ã] obnubilé de la continuelle [o, u, l] assuéfaction aux Muses, voulant icelluy par intermission solacier, délibérant [l, s, i] de commigrer en quelque beau et illustre lieu rural [l, r], pour ainsi ennuys et vie contristée et mélencolique [i] donner prompt allefement, jestimai que ceste rurale commigration estoit à mes esprits [è] utile et salutaire [u, t, i, l] prévoyant que la belle Flora de blancheir [b, l] eminente sur la neige avoit desvestu tous [é, è] arbrisseauts de leur hyemal et automnal [l] habit pour iceux décorer et revestir de leur

---

1. Jacobo Sannazaro, *Arcadia*, "Prosa VII." "I was fully eight when I began to feel the powers of love, and, in love with the beauty of a little girl of noble birth, little but beautiful and graceful more than any it seemed to me I had ever seen, in love with more eagerness than is fitting for a still small boy, I kept my desire hidden. For which reason, without realizing it, childishly playing with me, she from day to day ever more inflamed my tender marrow with her extreme beauty; while, in the meantime, love growing with our increasing years, we arrived at an age more adult and more inclined to hot desires."

robbe lilialle [r, l], dont mise soubz les pieds m'a tristesse. L'âme de laquelle [whence my soul] se transporta au fleuve de Léthé [l] pour se munir
d'obliance, je parviens après longue itinération en une florissante et nayve
prairie circonvoysine d'ung odoriferant [i] et souef verbocage, où desja par
prevention de son doulx amy Titan la belle Aurora sea clère et irradiante
lumière [r, l, è] avoit espandue.[2]

Here the sounds, indicated after each distinctive series of repetitions,
occur in patterns independent of sense. This is a much more subtle
form of art, and perhaps a more difficult one as well, than the homeoteleuthon, polyptoton, and alliteration of initial consonants we saw in
connection with the medieval background to Rabelais. It is made possible to a large extent by the polysyllabic and Latinate vocabulary,
with the great range of sound combinations it offers over the purely
native word forms. At the same time, there is not so limited a sound
system as to produce the constant accidental repetitions of Italian.

Elaborate patterns of sound found their greatest exponent in England: John Lyly's novel *Euphues* is, of course, the famous exemplar,
but other prose like Thomas Lodge's novel *Rosalynde*, George Pettie's
A Petite Pallace, or certain nonverse interludes in Shakespeare's plays,
are equally worthy of note.[3] Lyly's prose is said to follow the bipartite
antithetical period of Gorgian prose, but some grammatical analysis
will show this to be not entirely exact: "An old gentleman in Naples
seeing his pregnant wit, his eloquent tongue somewhat taunting, yet
with delight; his mirth without measure, yet not without wit; his say-
ings vainglorious yet pithy: began to bewail his nurture and to muse
at his nature, being incensed against the one as most pernicious, and
inflamed with the other as most precious." The strict Gorgian model
can be exemplified in this sentence from Seneca (the Gorgian effect
not being confined to Greek): in the end of the Golden Age, "avaritia
paupertatem intulit [r, p, t, i] et multa concupiscendo omnia amisit [u,
m, n, a, s]." The series of antithetical words rather than clauses is not
identical with the Gorgian ideal. In any case, we find elements of eu-
phuism already present in earlier European prose; sound plays occur

2. Quoted in René Sturel, "La Prose poétique au seizième siècle," in *Mélanges offerts
par ses amis et ses élèves à M. Gustave Lanson* (Paris: Hachette, 1922), 47.
3. For all aspects of Lyly's prose, see Albert Feuillerat, *John Lyly: Contribution à
l'histoire de la renaissance en Angleterre* (Cambridge: Cambridge University Press, 1910).

in Molinet and Habert; parallel phrases or balanced word groups are
to be observed in Habert and Sannazaro. Lyly's prose does not have
behind it solely the authority of one special strain of Greco-Roman
prose, but its rhythmic and alliterative tendencies seem to mark European ornamented prose less ostentatiously fashioned. The euphuistic
series, however, has so strong an effect that one loses the sense of
prose structure at times and is tempted to break his sentences into
lists of pairs; this multiplication of the elements of the sentence is
Lyly's peculiar form of bipartition.

> The freshest colors soonest fade, the teenest razor soonest turneth his
> edge, the finest cloth is soonest eaten with moths, and the cambric sooner
> stained than the coarse canvas: which appeared well in this Euphues,
> whose wit, being like wax, apt to receive any impression, and bearing the
> head in his own hand, either to use the rein or the spur, disdaining coun-
> sel, leaving his country, loathing his old acquaintances, thought either by
> wit to obtain some conquest, or by shame to abide some conflict; who, pre-
> ferring fancy before friends and his present humor before honor to come,
> laid reason in water, being too salt for his taste, and followed unbridled
> affection, most pleasant for his tooth.

Lyly's sound patterns depend very much on the resources of English:
a large vocabulary of monosyllables makes alliterations or rimes
rather than homeoteleutha; the lexicon is, in general, very considerable by French or Italian standards, even without recourse to the aureate; strong impure initial consonants have great effect (such as the
series *pri-*, *pr-*, *pl-*, *st-*, *str-*, *spi-*, *sk-*, and so forth). We observe here
that kind of doubling motivated by decorative amplification, unlike
Descartes' sober divisions into twos: as often happens in rhetoric,
one form serves two different ends.

Generally, the bipartite sentence would seem to have some superior frequency in the ornamented language of the seventeenth century, and aureate language less of a role; bipartition, however, need
not mean that every period contains merely two clauses in any strict
fashion, even though that tendency is important.

> ¡Oh vida, no *habías de comenzar*, pero ya que *comenza*ste no *habías de* acab*ar*!
> No hay cosa más deseada ni más frágil que tú *e*res, y el que una vez te
> pi*er*de, ta*rde* te recup*era*: desde hoy te estimar*ía* como a perd*ida*. M*ad*ras*ta*
> se mon*str*ó la naturale*za* con el hombre, pues lo que le quitó de con-

ocimiento al nace*r*, le restituye al mori*r*: all*í porque se* perc*iban* los bienes que *se* rec*iben*, y aqu*í porque se* sient*an* los males que se conjur*an*. ¡Oh tir*ano* mil veces de todo el ser hum*ano*, aquel primero, que con escandalosa temeridad fio su vida en un frágil leño al inconstante elemento! *Vestido di*cen que tuvo el pecho de ac*eros*, mas yo *di*go que re*vestido* de y*erros*.[4]

Gracián uses fairly loose but nonetheless perceptible means of creating balance; the repeated endings are often not full rimes: *eres/recupera, pierde/tarde, estimaría/perdida*. We see here approximate homeoteleuthon, the Latin and especially Senecan tradition being closer to this style than what we find in Lyly or Habert. Italian prose, which in its earlier ornamented forms—epithetic, metaphoric, aureate, or Ciceronian—had shown itself surprisingly independent of the Latin heritage in regard to sound repetitions, acquired in Daniello Bartoli, one of the very few representatives of anything one might call baroque prose in Italian, a version of assonantal and alliterative style: "Gli amici suoi, mentre vollero esser*gli* pietos*i*, *gli* furono, senza saperlo, crudel*i*, perchè, rimettendo*gli* a forza d'elleboro il senno in *capo, gli* tolsero l'allegrezza dal *cuore*; onde quegli che non avrebbe dato la sua *pazzia* per tutta la *saviezza* del mondo, risanato, *si piangeva savio e s'invidiava pazzo*; a gli amici, perchè ritogliendolo da una innocente allegrezza l'avean renduto alle noie de' suoi primi fastidi, e di *finto uditore* l'aveano fatto *vero attore* di tragedie, tutto dolente, 'Me *occidistis*, amici, non *servastis*,' ait."[5] Italian prose is by this point much

4. Baltasar Gracián, *El Criticón*, Part I, "Crisi Primera." "Oh life, you should not have begun, but once begun, you should not end! There is nothing more fragile or desired than you, and he who loses you once will not soon recover you; from this moment on, I should consider you lost. Nature has shown herself to be a wicked stepmother to man, since the knowledge taken away from him at birth is returned only at death: first so he may perceive the blessings he is receiving, second so he may feel the ills being exorcised. Oh thousandfold tyrant of human beings, he who with shocking boldness first entrusted his life to the changing waters in a fragile wooden boat! They say his breast became stout with courage, but I say it was armed with error."

5. Daniello Bartoli and Paolo Segneri, *Prose scelte* (Turin: Unione Tipografico-Editrice, 1967), 86. From *L'Uomo di lettere*. "His friends, while they wanted to take pity on him, were, without knowing it, cruel, for with hellebore restoring sense to his head, they took joy from his heart; whence he, who would not have given his madness for all the wisdom in the world, cured, wept for being wise and envied his mad state. To his friends, because, taking him from an innocent happiness, they had restored him to the wretchedness of his earlier troubles and made him, the feigned hearer of tragedies, into the true actor of a real one, he sorrowfully said, 'You killed me, not benefited me, my friends.'"

more standardized and unlikely to deploy alternative forms. An entirely new conception of ornamented prose has taken over, and we find another new, half-phonetic, half-witty resource in puns, or the play on concrete and figurative meanings.

> Zeusi, quel sole de' *pittori* che fece non tanto lume alla *pittura illustrandola*, quanto ombra a' *pittori* suoi emuli *oscurandoli*, ritrasse in tela il *volto* d'un'Elena di si nobile *lavorio*, che *vinto* rimase dalla copia l'esemplare, e parve ch'Elena vera *cedesse* a sé stessa *dipinta*, perchè se *vera trasse* da Troia un Paride a *rapirla*, *dipinto trasse* tutta la Grecia per *ammirarla*. Quale ella fosse sia vostra pensiero *d'immaginarvelo*; mio certo non sarà di *descriverla*, sì perchè io stimo che un'Elena non possa acconciamente ritrarsi con altro pennello, che con un *fumante tizzone tolto* dall'incendio di *Troia*; nè lumeggiar con *altro chiaro*, che col fuoco che incenerò una città e distrusse un regno; nè ombreggiare con *altro oscuro*, che con quello d'un perpetua infamia.[6]

This and our previous examples point to an at least partial definition of baroque in terms of exuberance and ludism.

It is clear that prose styles like Habert's, Lyly's, or any other ornamented one should be seen as part of a large movement in European prose, whose individual embodiments differ somewhat as this or that figure appeals, but which has an essential unity. This movement is not entirely poetic, for the sound figures all have some classical prose authority, and the tropes can be exemplified in Cicero and others. When we draw near to the period of neoclassical prose, we encounter in English and French some distinctive kinds of ornamentation. Sir Thomas Browne, while favoring sound repetitions and more or less regularly segmented sentences, tends toward an aureate diction we have previously seen in French prose. Especially in *Hydriotaphia* (urn burial), Browne's prose moves in a series of thoughts neither detached nor tightly related through logical indications.

---

6. *Ibid.*, 76–77. "Zeuxis, that sun of painters, who cast not so much light on painting when he made it illustrious, as he did darkness on his rival painters when he put them in the shadow, drew on canvas the face of a Helen of such noble workmanship that the copy outshone the original, and it seemed that the true Helen yielded to her painted image, because if the real one drew from Troy a Paris to ravish her, the painted one drew all Greece to admire her. What she was like, you may occupy yourself with imagining; my occupation will not be to describe her, since I judge that a Helen cannot be fittingly drawn with any pen save a smoking firebrand from the burning of Troy, nor highlighted save with the fire that burned a city and destroyed a kingdom, nor shadowed with any darkness other than that of perpetual infamy."

Pyramids, arches, obelisks, were but the irregular*ities* of vainglor*y*, and wild enorm*ities* of ancient *magna*nimity. But the *most magna*nimous *reso*lution *rests* in the Chri*st*ian *r*eligion, which tram*p*leth u*p*on *p*ride, and sets on the *n*eck of ambitio*n*, humbly *p*ursuing that infallible *p*er*p*etuity unto which all others must *di*minish their *dia*meters, and be poorly seen in angles of contingency.

*P*ious s*p*irits who *p*assed their days in *r*aptures of futurity made little more of this world than the world that was befo*r*e it—while they lay obscu*r*e in the chaos of p*r*eordination, and night of their fo*r*e-beings. And if any have been so happy as truly to underst*an*d Christi*an an*nihila*tion*, ex-tasis, *e*xolu*tion*, transforma*tion*, the ki*ss* of the *S*pouse, *g*usta*tion* of God, and *ingr*e*ssion in*to the divi*n*e s*h*adow—they *h*ave already *had an h*and*s*ome *an*ticipatio*n* of *h*eaven: the gl*or*y of the *w*orld is surely *over*, and the earth in ashes unto them.

The use of a varied vocabulary, the exploitation of the characteristic English juxtaposition of the classical and the Germanic (*chaos of preordination, night of fore-beings*), the cultivation of sound repetition—all these features were to contribute to subsequent heightened styles in English and characterize them in contrast to French. The bifurcation in style of the two languages is not yet complete, however, in the early seventeenth century, and we find one case of a French style still drawing on ornament in the general European manner. Saint François de Sales' prose in the *Introduction à la vie dévote* (1609) is the work of a humanist who drew on the epic or Ciceronian simile, like Boccaccio or Hooker, and pursued, within the limits of a somewhat aureate French, the poetic plays of sound earlier attempted. While one may incline to talk of ecclesiastical baroque, it would be unwise to forget the relations of Saint François' devotional prose to earlier efforts at suaviloquence.

Mon intention est d'instruire ceux [ē, t, s] qui vivent ès villes [v, i], ès ménages, en la court, et qui par leur condition sont obligés de faire une vie commune quant à l'extérieur; lesquels bien souvent, sous le prétexte d'une prétendue impossibilité [p, t, é], ne veulent seulement [eul] pas penser à l'entreprise [p] de la vie dévote [d], leur étant avis que, comme aucun autre animal [au, n, m, a] n'ose goûter de la graine de l'herbe [g, r, è] nommée *palma Christi*, aussi nul homme ne doit prétendre à la palme de la piété chrétienne [m, p, t, é] tandis qu'il vit emmi la presse des affaires temporelles [r, è]. Et je leur montre que comme les mères perles vivent emmi la mer [l, m, r, è] sans prendre aucune goutte d'eau marine, et que vers les

> îles Chélidoines il [l] y a des fontaines d'eau bien douce au milieu de la mer [m], et que les piraustes volent dedans les flammes sans brûler les ailes [l], ainsi peut une âme vigoureuse et constante vivre au monde [v, m] sans recevoir aucune humeur mondaine [m], trouver des sources d'une douce [ou, s] piété au milieu des ondes amères de ce siècle [m, l], et voler entre les flammes des convoitises [v-f, l] terrestres [t, r] sans brûler les ailes [l] des sacrés désirs de la vie dévote [r, d, i, é, v].[7]

The use of *ès* and *emmi*, already archaic, the allusions to *palma Christi*, *piraustes* (or firebirds), and *les îles Chélidoines* (or Swallow Islands) give Saint François' prose a distinct air of lexical *recherche*. Of the tropes, aureate diction, and sound plays of European ornamented prose in the sixteenth and seventeenth centuries, French was subsequently to reject everything save the continuous metaphor, allusion, and pun in the *précieux* convention. We may conclude the examination of ornamented prose with Vincent Voiture, since his prose leads us back toward the mainstream of French middle style in the seventeenth century.

Précieux literature has often been mentioned in connection with baroque, although it is generally felt some distinction must be made. Voiture's prose adheres in most ways to the neoclassical tendencies of its day but allows the *métaphore filée*, the one case in which the figure was felt to be appropriate by French purists. Sound play exists only in the form of the homonym. In the following letter (*ca.* 1630), Europe is a mythological person, a statuette of her, and a continent.

> Je ne comprends pas comme cela m'ait pu arriver mais la lettre et le présent qui vinrent de votre part me firent oublier tous mes maux, et je reçus la petite Europe avec autant de contentement que si l'on m'eût donné celle qui fait une des trois parties du monde et que l'on divise en plusieurs royaumes. Aussi vaut-elle davantage, puisqu'elle vous ressemble. Et Mme la marquise, sous ce prétexte, me l'ôta par force, et jura Styx qu'elle ne sortirait point de son cabinet. Ainsi, Europe a été ravie pour la seconde fois, et beaucoup plus glorieusement, ce me semble, que lorsqu'elle fut enlevée par Jupiter.

Next we realize that while Europe was, of course, a *demoiselle*, so also are the spaniel lapdogs of the early seventeenth century, because of

---

7. This is from the revised, 1619 edition. Saint François de Sales, *Oeuvres*, Bibliothèque de la Pléiade (Paris: Gallimard, 1969), 23–24.

their round much-kissed faces and long silky ears hanging like hair on either side of their faces: "Il est vrai que pour m'apaiser l'on m'a donné deux chiens qui ont le museau si long qu'à mon avis ils valent bien une demoiselle, et je ne sais s'il y en a une dans Paris pour qui je les voulusse donner. Aussi bien, en l'humeur où je me trouve, je ne dois plus converser avec les créatures raisonnables; et dans le désespoir où je suis, je voudrais être en un désert entre les griffes du plus cruel des lions, moi qui disais qu'on ne devait aimer que les chiens."[8] Voiture preferred greyhounds to spaniels, as it emerges, but to them even, he prefers the recipient of his letter, Mlle Paulet, who was known familiarly as *la lionne*.

The next letter, to Mlle de Rambouillet in 1636, is grander; it evokes the Thirty Years' War and the voice heard crying over the sea, at the coming of Christ, that Great Pan was dead. The occasion for it was the quibble in literary circles over whether *car*, being replaceable by *parce que* (*pour ce que*), could be dispensed with in French. As in the preceding letter, a bipartite quality is often perceptible in the sentences, promoting wit here as well as the elegance it has elsewhere in ornamented prose.

> Mademoiselle, *car* étant d'une si grande considération dans notre langue, j'approuve extrêmement le ressentiment que vous avez du tort qu'on veut lui faire, et je ne puis bien espérer de l'Académie dont vous me parlez, voyant qu'elle se veut établir par une si grande violence. En un temps où la fortune joue des tragédies par tous les endroits de l'Europe, je ne vois rien de si digne de pitié que de faire le procès à un mot qui a si utilement servi cette monarchie et qui, dans toutes les brouilleries du royaume, s'est toujours montré bon Français. Pour moi, je ne puis comprendre quelles raisons ils pourront alléguer contre une diction qui marche toujours à la tête de la raison, et qui n'a point d'autre charge que de l'introduire. Je ne sais pour quel intérêt ils tâchent d'ôter à *car* ce qui lui appartient pour le donner à *pour ce que*, ni pourquoi ils veulent dire avec trois mots ce qu'ils peuvent dire avec trois lettres. . . . Qui m'eût dit, il y a quelques années, que j'eusse dû vivre plus longtemps que *car*, j'eusse cru qu'il m'eût promis une vie plus longue que celle des patriarches. . . . Je n'attends plus que l'heure d'entendre en l'air des voix lamentables, qui diront: *le grand car est mort*, et le trépas du grand *Cam* ni du grand *Pan* ne me semblerait pas si important ni si étrange.[9]

8. Vincent Voiture, *Lettres* (2 vols.; Paris: Librairie des Bibliophiles, 1880), I, 41–42.
9. *Ibid.*, I, 170–73.

The fundamental pun is that, in the French throne's shifting alliances with Protestant and Catholic German princes, it was not always possible to be patriotic in the sense of reconciling the Catholic tradition of one's country with one's allegiances to the king; *car*, however, was as much a *bon Français* as *bon français*. Furthermore, serving to introduce causative explanatory clauses, it always led the advancing army of Reason, almost as important an object of veneration as church or state. The death of the great Khan helps prolong the resonances of Voiture's extended metaphor, from the devastating Thirty Years' War, catastrophic to even secure-seeming princes, into fabulous history and then mythology. We see here a far more poetic letter than our preceding one: the mock-heroic mode is closer to Pope's elegant imagery than to Voiture's puns on Europa or the homely talent of Boileau's *héroïcomique*, and therein lies its exemplarity for the ornamented French *précieux* middle style, as distinguished from the merely witty or clever.

We have discovered strains of densely figured language from the early renaissance until well into the seventeenth century; they contrast to the fully realized Ciceronian high style of Guicciardini or Hooker by their self-consciously brilliant tone and detail—often there is a first person, a raconteur even, of whom we are intensely aware—but they do not stand in any chronologically contrastive position to high Ciceronianism. Lyly precedes Hooker, and Browne follows him; there is no easily derivable formula here, especially as Lyly looks forward to prose in a lesser version of his mode in Italian and Spanish, and Browne looks back to the aureation of the sixteenth century. Two authors, however, we have avoided mention of, despite their importance: Montaigne and Donne.

When we see Montaigne against the larger picture of sixteenth- and seventeenth-century prose, especially in the Romance languages, we are struck more acutely by the element of somewhat rough plain style in him and by the idiosyncracy of his style: he has plenty of figures and even ornaments, but these cannot be assimilated to those of others. With one exception perhaps. Much attention has been given precisely to the English Senecan styles, which, in contrast to Romance ornamented ones, even though many figures are shared by both, repeatedly strike the ear as having something of an abrupt spoken tone. The most splendid of these writers is Donne, who can mingle, in his pulpit oratory, the most elaborate conceits with a kind of brutally colloquial quality (the italics are Donne's).

> For the first *generall* sale by *Adam* wee complaine now that *Land* will not sell; that 20. is come to 15. yeares purchase; but doe wee not take too late a *Medium*, too low a time to reckon by? How cheape was *Land* at first, how cheape were *we*? what was *Paradise* sold for? . . . But what had *I* for *Heaven*? Adam sinnd and I suffer. . . . And *God* was displeased with *me* before *I* was I: I was built up scarse 50. years ago, in my Mothers womb, and I was cast down, almost 6000 years agoe, in *Adams* loynes; I was *borne* in the last *Age* of the world, and *dyed* in the first. How and how justly do we cry out against a Man, that hath sold a *Towne*, or sold an *Army*. And *Adam* sold the World.

There is no mistaking this for the ordinary worms-and-cadavers or dripping-blood imagery of the realist baroque sermon such as we have seen in French. Besides the metaphor, however, we see immediately in this sermon (preached February 24, 1625) the parataxis we recognize as Senecan; but how different it is from the "Verba, selecta, propria, significantia" of Justus Lipsius' elegant summary of the Senecan style. This English Seneca uses the cool asyndeton of Latin for violent outbursts: "But when this *Discipline* prevailed not upon them, *God sold* them away, *gave* them away, *cast* them away, in the tempest, in the whirlewinde, in the inundation of his indignation, and scattered them as so much dust in a windy day, as so many broken strawes upon a wrought Sea." We conclude readily that Seneca was perhaps greatest in the tremendous range of his influence, and that this aspect of it deserves some special qualification. The term *mannerist* has been imported from art criticism precisely in an attempt to suggest the strain and intensity of such language; the word refers originally to the muscular contortion and discomfort of Michelangelo's figures. A study of Williamson's book suggests that English seventeenth-century prose has some important characteristics we do not find elsewhere, save in Montaigne, and that we might well have a particular term for it.[10]

As we have seen, the progression baroque-neoclassicism would be

10. George Williamson, *The Senecan Amble: A Study in Prose Form from Bacon to Collier* (Chicago: University of Chicago Press, 1951).

impaired by the place of Hooker and Guicciardini, if we were to take their Ciceronianism as identical to neoclassicism. It is not the case, however; there are important kinds of neoclassicism independent of it, such as French middle styles of the later seventeenth century and, as we shall now see, related kinds of writing in Italian, or, to anticipate briefly, in English, the plain style of narration encountered in *Gulliver's Travels* or the elegant colloquial manner of Addison and Steele.

While in Italian literature we do not find the same cluster of eminent Senecans as elsewhere, some movement toward a more clipped colon shows up in the work of Bernardo Davanzati (1529–1606), a translator of Tacitus and thereby a contributor to the anti-Ciceronian current. The brief passage that follows, from the *Orazione in Morte del Granduca Cosimo I* is not, strictly speaking, anti-Ciceronian, but Davanzati's peroration uses the most condensed Ciceronian form of style; what he aims at imitating is not the orator's copiousness so much as the brief sententious manner, which is quite as proper to Cicero as the flowing period, with which it often alternates: "Col medesimo animo sopportò la sua malattia, lunga e compassionevole; che gli tolse il favellare, e lo scrivere, e'l muover delle membra; stando sempre la mente intera e viva, insino all' ultim'ora, che lo spirito ne volò al cielo; ond'era sceso poco meno di cinquant'anni innanzi. Età, se tu riguardi al corso di natura, non lunga; al desiderio de' mortali, brevissima; alle cose fatte, lunghissima." [11] Davanzati achieves a wonderful and ambiguous middle position between the segmented manner and a deeper continuity: there is only one main verb (*sopportò*), but the participle (*stando*) and the apposition (*età*) are punctuated so as to seem to some degree independent of it.

Brevity prevails in the characteristic eighteenth-century styles in Italian, if we overlook any surviving *boccacceschi*. Here are lines from a preface to *Favole Esopiane* on the *je ne sais quoi* of beauty, an esthetic

11. Quoted in Giacomo Leopardi, *Crestomazia Italiana: La Prosa* (Turin: Einaudi, 1968), 250–51. "With the same courage he bore his illness, long and worthy of compassion, which took away his speech and his ability to write and the movement of his limbs; his mind, however, remaining whole and lively until the last hour, when his spirit flew off to heaven, whence it had descended less that fifty years before. A life which is not long, if you consider the course of nature; most short, in comparison with the desire of mortals; very long, when you see what he had accomplished."

notion that had steadily gained favor as the limitations of rhetorical theory and definition came to be more acutely felt: "La favoletta debbe esser graziosa; cioè debbe ben parere entro i suoi poveri e schietti ornamenti, per un certo portamento, per una certa abitudine, per una certa aria, per una certa lusinga, in cui la grazia è riposta, che tocca l'animo, anzi per entro all'animo discende e s'insinua, e tutto lo ricerca soavissimamente."[12] There is, finally, *style coupé* in Italian, and the following elegantly written portrait should make us see just how different were the resources of French and Italian. Where La Bruyère adheres to natural word order, relying on the acute *coupes* of French to underscore his images, Gozzi employs, rather, an expressive collocation of terms.

> Cornelio poco saluta; salutato, a stento risponde: non fa interrogazioni che non importino; domandato, con poche sillabe si sbriga. Negl'inchini è sgarbato, o non ne fa; niuno abbraccia: per ischerzo mai non favella; burbero parla. Alle cirimonie volge con dispetto le spalle. Udendo parole che non significano, si addormenta o sbadiglia. Nell'udire le angosce di un amico, si attrista, imbianca, gli escono le lagrime. Prestagli, al bisogno, senza altro dire, opera e borsa. Cornelio è giudicato dall'universale uomo di duro cuore. Il mondo vuol maschere, ed estrinseche superstizioni.[13]

While the theory of natural word order had been put forth in Italian, we sense that it is "natural," on the contrary, in Italian, to make use of an initial object or adverb or subject modifier, in keeping with its roots in Latin, where the first place is one of emphasis not necessarily accorded to the subject. Gozzi's style is unquestionably inspired directly by La Bruyère, but we see how the French manner, which is at

---

12. Giovanni Batista Roberti, *Favole Esopiane*, quoted in Leopardi, *Crestomazia*, 107. "The fable should be graceful; that is, that quality should appear amidst its poor and plain ornaments by a certain movement, a certain habit, a certain air, a certain caressful way in which gracefulness is concealed, which touches the spirit, descends into the soul, and penetrates it completely and delicately."

13. Gasparo Gozzi, *Osservatore*, III, quoted in Leopardi, *Crestomazia*, 453. "Cornelius barely greets one; greeted, he scarcely responds: he does not ask idle questions; questioned, he hastily says a few syllables. Bowing, he is graceless, or he does not bow at all; he embraces no one; he never jokes; he speaks in a crabby fashion. On ceremonies he turns his back with annoyance. Hearing meaningless words, he falls asleep or yawns. Upon hearing of a friend's troubles, he grows sad, turns pale; tears come forth. He lends him, if necessary, without saying anything, his purse and aid. Cornelius is judged a hardhearted man by the generality. The world wants masks and superficial false beliefs."

least distantly Senecan in origin, recaptures automatically in Italian a certain spontaneous Latinity.

The most distinctive thing in English neoclassicism will be not so much the light, brief styles but rather Johnson's prose. However, we must not imagine English neoclassicism as entirely subsequent to the French in any chronological sense; Dryden's *Essay of Dramatic Poesy* (1666) is contemporary with the beginning literary phases of the period of Louis XIV: "It was that memorable day, in the first summer of the late war, when our navy engaged the Dutch; a day wherein the two most mighty and best appointed fleets which any age had ever seen, disputed the command of the greater half of the globe, the commerce of nations, and the riches of the universe . . ." We recognize the eloquent appositional construction we have seen going back through French neoclassicism to Guicciardini and beyond. The background of Dryden's style is not, of course, so much English as all the frequently forgotten or unobtrusive work of stylistic refinement that had been going on in France for half a century. When a large number of distinguished English styles emerge in the early eighteenth century, we see in them, however, a further adaptation, to the particular character of English, of the unceasing experimentation in language that continued in France throughout the later seventeenth century and beyond. While the lighter styles are entirely English in feeling, it is not surprising that grander styles should demonstrate some appreciable consonance with French ideas on elevated writing, and Edward Gibbon is the most prominent example. His years in Lausanne and his assimilation of French to the point of writing the *Essai sur l'étude de la littérature* (1761) help account for his style. As in French, his words are seldom exceptional, but rather his effort goes into epitheton and balance: "The licentious soldiers who had raised to the throne the dissolute son of Caracalla, blushed at their ignominious choice, and turned with disgust from that monster to contemplate with pleasure the opening virtues of his cousin Alexander, the son of Mamaea." This is, of course, exactly in keeping with our example of Perrault's distinguished common style, the step above ironic *style coupé*, and if Gibbon has won greater celebrity than his French antecedents, it must be attributed to the not inconsiderable part of style in the important new sense Buffon had just given the term: not *pensées fines*, *idées légères*, *déliées*, but sustained movement, transitions, graded repetition, and a larger design.

The most distinctive style of the English eighteenth century, one whose consequences can be felt on varied and subsequent kinds of writing, is Samuel Johnson's. His initial strong point is sentence structure, then the combination of varied structures in an often periodic paragraph, and, finally, notably in the preface to the *Dictionary*, a formidable sense of composition, in the *buffonesque* manner.

And is a very important word for Johnson; on it is based the expanded normal sentence that we might call Johnson's basic or major pattern, as in the first period here.

> In this part of the work [spelling], where caprice has long wantoned without control, and vanity sought praise by petty reformation, I have endeavored to proceed with a scholar's reverence for antiquity, and a grammarian's regard to the genius of our tongue. I have attempted a few alterations, and among those few perhaps the greatest part is from the modern to the ancient practice; and I hope I may be allowed to recommend to those whose thoughts have been perhaps employed too anxiously on verbal singularities, not to disturb, upon narrow views, or for minute propriety, the orthography of their fathers.[14]

The second structure is three independent clauses with polysyndeton, arranged according to the *Gesetz der wachsenden Glieder*; it is an expansion to the level of the clause of the sonorous nexus with *and*, which Johnson so favors. However, the third independent clause exemplifies within it the disjunctive principle, which is the contrary of *and*: syntactic suspension, indicated by the commas. Furthermore, suspensions and *incisae*, or parenthetical elements, are often joined with a second minor pattern, here observable, that of hyperbaton, as when *orthography*, the direct object, is placed very late in the word order. Here is another example of suspension and hyperbaton of the object: "In examining the orthography of any doubtful word, the mode of spelling by which it is inserted in the series of the dictionary is to be considered as that to which I give, perhaps not often rashly, the preference."

14. Examples are from the preface to the *Dictionary*. See Samuel Johnson, *Selected Poetry and Prose*, ed. Frank Brady and William K. Wimsatt (Berkeley: University of California Press, 1977), 280, 279, 285, 283.

The principle Johnson follows in his minor patterns is the Latin one that an element placed exceptionally in the initial or final position is emphasized; here are both kinds of emphasis: "Other words there are, of which the sense is too subtle and evanescent to be fixed in a paraphrase; such are all those which are by the grammarians termed expletives." The position of *termed expletives* in relation to the agent is unusual indeed, but the principle remains the simple one. Likewise, a lengthy initial direct object, though here most emphatic for opprobrious intent, is just the type *other words there are* expanded: "The words which our authors have introduced by their knowledge of foreign languages, or ignorance of their own, by vanity or wantonness, by compliance with fashion or lust of innovation, I have registered as they occurred, though commonly only to censure them, and warn others against the folly of naturalizing useless foreigners to the injury of the natives." Much exception has been taken to some of Johnson's prepositional phrases placed at the head of the sentence by hyperbaton ("Of composition there are different methods" [*Life of Pope*]), but these are essentially verb complements of the same semantic order as direct objects or predicate nominatives and follow the same English minor pattern as object-subject-verb.

I have mentioned Latin in connection with the initial and final positions in the sentence having the greatest emphasis, but, of course, what is normal in Latin (some 60 percent of the sentences end with a verb, for example) is the unusual or the prohibited in Johnson. Even Hooker's *is in the bosom of the earth concealed* is too daring for him, nor does he favor subject-verb inversions. Basically, Johnson uses normal word order with the minor variations of *incisae* or suspensions and a movable complement of the verb. Compared with, say, Hooker's grammar, this is a highly neoclassical system, and absolute limits are clearly worked out. There is nothing idly or casually peculiar in Johnson's syntax.

Within his formalized grammar, Johnson worked out a lexical esthetic that has no analogies in neoclassical styles outside English and considerable importance for the range of word choice in later English writers. Johnson's preference for the polysyllabic and Latinate is well known, but the historical situation of it demands some comment. There are no Latinate words in French after the aureate phase of sixteenth-century style; the ideal of a regular, circumscribed vocabulary prevailed. Italian has Latinate words, but since the language is phonetically consubstantial with Latin, they do not have the same effect as the alternative or, to some, alien system of Latinate terms in English. Finally, Latin uses no Latinisms, which may seem like a truism or paradox, as one defines Latinism; but, in any case, Cicero had at his disposal, with the minor exception of some Hellenisms, only words that were native and of a piece. Johnson's exotic vocabulary represents, on the other hand, a quite peculiar notion that one is classical (that is, follows an eternal, immutable system of elegance and concinnity) if one uses the words that happened to occur in a particular language at a particular time. The ideal is, of course, one of allusion to the existence of Latin rather than mere designation and is not surprisingly related to the polysyllabism of English poetry, one of its greatest stylistic resources. It is interesting that the earlier English prose writer from whom Johnson is said to derive the most is Browne, an aureate, almost *attardé* figure, who perpetuated the lexical profusion of the English renaissance.[15] The systematic emphasizing of the polysyllabic and Latinate is a peculiar heritage of English, unique in the Western European languages by and large, and contributory, in no small degree, to effects of tone characteristic of that language. It is one of the reasons why "classicism" has such confused connotations in English, whereas the word in French can evoke very precise notions of general esthetic values not tied necessarily to a moment of linguistic history. This confrontation with one of the greatest representatives of English neoclassicism suggests why the latter forms less of a comprehensive rhetorical system than the original movement in France.

In the early seventeenth century, French abandons the inner rimes, homeoteleutha, and prominent alliterations that persist in English, Spanish, and Italian writers; their baroque would seem to have a limited relation to even an embellished stylist like Balzac. However, if we reflect on the manner more closely, it becomes apparent that sound is

15. See William K. Wimsatt, *The Prose Style of Samuel Johnson* (Hamden, Conn.: Shoe String Press, 1972), 117–18.

a major concern in France. Pascal's word repetition and polyptoton are very obtrusive; Balzac's isocolon has analogies with baroque balanced phrasing and bipartition elsewhere, and, finally, the most distinctive new idea of style, multisegmented *style coupé*, derives its curiously mordant effect from the phrase or word accent on the ultima peculiar to French. There comes a later phase of neoclassicism, however, when no new rhythmic discoveries are to be made and writers fluently work on in *style coupé*, pure or modified, while a more original talent, Rousseau, revives rather than creates oratorical periods. With Chateaubriand, nevertheless, what must have seemed impossible happened: a new kind of prose was created, new in rhythm as well as diction.

II ✍ FROM ROMANTICISM TO THE TWENTIETH CENTURY

9 *Chateaubriand*

Chateaubriand is a significant writer not only for the high quality of his prose but also for his place at the beginning of the art-prose orientation of French literature in the course of the nineteenth and early twentieth centuries. His importance goes beyond the immediate domain of romanticism, and there is no equivalent figure in other literatures.

Chateaubriand inherited the notions of poetic prose that grew up in the early eighteenth century—especially the borrowing of vocabulary, figures, and descriptiveness from poetry—and these account for some of the effects we associate with him, although his success in handling them is such that he seems to belong altogether to another category than Bernardin de Saint-Pierre and other predecessors. While one of his works, *Les Martyrs* (1809), was a prose epic in the neoantique, eighteenth-century fashion, he early found a new vein; the prose poems in *Le Génie du Christianisme* (1802) demonstrate what connects Chateaubriand with eighteenth-century practice as well as what separates him from it.

> Une heure après le coucher du soleil, la lune se montra au-dessus des arbres, à l'horizon opposé. Une brise embaumée, que cette reine des nuits amenait de l'orient avec elle, semblait la précéder dans les forêts comme sa fraîche haleine. L'astre solitaire monta peu à peu dans le ciel: tantôt il suivait paisiblement sa course azurée; tantôt il reposait sur des groupes de nues qui ressemblaient à la cime de hautes montagnes couronnées de neige. Ces nues, ployant et déployant leurs voiles, se déroulaient en zones d'écume, ou formaient dans les cieux des bancs d'une ouate éblouissante, si doux à l'œil qu'on croyait ressentir leur mollesse et leur élasticité. (I, 5, xii)

A related description from the *Mémoires d'outre-tombe* shows a more advanced form of innovation in diction.

> A mesure que sur mon rivage natal elle [la lune] descend au bout du ciel, elle accroît son silence, qu'elle communique à la mer: bientôt elle tombe à l'horizon, l'intersecte, ne montre plus que la moitié de son front qui s'assoupit, s'incline et disparaît dans la molle intumescence des vagues. Les astres voisins de leur reine, avant de plonger à sa suite, semblent s'arrêter, suspendus à la cime des flots. (I, ii, 1)

In these scenes of night in the New World and in Brittany, we observe poetic vocabulary (*astre, course, voile*), a figure (*reine des nuits, astres voisins de leur reine*), and color indications. The dominant rhetorical mode is personification; Chateaubriand employs effects derived from mythology, while avoiding mythology itself on principle. At the same time, we are aware of another of Chateaubriand's characteristic innovations; the rare *intumescence* had belonged only to technical vocabulary; the verb *intersecter* is a neologism not to be found in ordinary dictionaries; *élasticité* is one of the numerous specialized terms that came into use in the eighteenth century and had no tradition of high literary usage, and *ouate*, finally, is, by neoclassical standards, a low word, fit only for practical use. Neologism, increasingly common in the eighteenth century, was not Chateaubriand's invention, but the assembling of a literary and even poetic vocabulary from the arsenal of technical terms was very much a new esthetic conception: Chateaubriand expanded the lexical figures to include rare words, not simply elevated ones as in neoclassical diction. By the standards of the latter, Chateaubriand's style is distinctly heteroclite. In this respect we see a kinship with the humanist poetic prose of the sixteenth century: the esthetic of the rare term has distinguished ancient antecedents to recommend it. The justification for such unusual words lies as much in sound as in their lack of complete synonymity with more ordinary ones; *intumescence* and *intersecter*, *mollesse* and *élasticité* make striking combinations of the dissimilar from the phonetic standpoint.

Chateaubriand's new words contribute powerfully to the imagistic value of his prose, and it is in general the effect of sensorial immediacy that gave his prose its hold over later generations. This is the quality the nineteenth century found poetic in his works, as distinguished from the *courses, voiles,* and *reines des nuits.* Sensory impressions were implied in the eighteenth-century notion of the role of description in poetic prose, but the language of the visual, to say nothing of the auditory or tactile, remained somewhat dim through lexical inadequacy, as it did in the poetry of the period. The most interesting thing is that it should have been in prose, not verse, that a new vocabulary of sensations was worked out; Chateaubriand was far in advance of the poets of his day. While one should hardly judge all styles, as Remy de Gourmont did, on their imagery, sensory values constituted one of the most important ideas in writing of the nineteenth century, increasing rather than diminishing as literature evolved from romantic to realist and symbolist modes. The reaction to neoclassicism's pallid imagery went far beyond the immediate concerns of the first romantic generation, and this reaction constitutes a major unifying element of the whole period from Chateaubriand to Zola, Huysmans, the prose poets, and Proust.

Chateaubriand did not always write such highly innovative prose. The *A and B* doublings we observe in the first example above suggest an affinity with much common neoclassical style (Flaubert's descriptions, by contrast, will rarely use *A and B*), and when we study the long speech which is *René,* we are further struck by Chateaubriand's mediating position between older prose and a new kind. The language is not infrequently periphrastic and metonymic: "J'ai coûté la vie à ma mère en venant au monde; j'ai été tiré de son sein avec le fer." As in Rousseau, *style coupé* is used for many narrative passages: "J'accompagnai mon père à son dernier asile; la terre se referma sur sa dépouille; l'éternité et l'oubli le pressèrent de tout leur poids: le soir même l'indifférent passait sur sa tombe; hors pour sa fille et pour son fils, c'était déjà comme s'il n'avait jamais été." The poetic figures are dense, as in *La Nouvelle Héloïse*: metaphor, poetic diction (*dépouille*), and hyperbole (*passait sur sa tombe*). The *style coupé* consists of clauses that tend to form pairs; a basically bipartite movement underlies the disjunction of the syntax. In the periodic developments the patterning in twos is again found: "Vaincu par la glorieuse douleur de la sainte, abattu par les grandeurs de la religion, tous mes projets de violence s'évanouirent; ma force m'abandonna; je me sentis lié par une main toute-puissante, et, au lieu de blasphèmes et de menaces, je ne trouvai dans mon cœur que de profondes adorations et les gémissements de l'humilité." The dangling or anacoluthonic participles *vaincu* and *abattu* show the asyndeton with twos that becomes more frequent in the nineteenth century; the four verbs are paired, and the fullness of the concluding phrase depends on a noun doubling. Rousseau's prose provides the rhetorical model for pairings, with parallelisms or antitheses, and of words and clauses, anaphora, and the impassioned use of these figures, which otherwise are not always above a more pedestrian level of amplification. This style, reinforcing the influence of Rousseau, is one source of an essentially conservative movement in nineteenth-century prose, that of Lamartine's *Confidences*, for example, contrasting with the sensorial, imagistic side of Chateaubriand.

Still in the earlier phase of Chateaubriand's literary development, that of *Le Génie du Christianisme*, we find in the famous opening passage of *Atala* an entirely different conception of sentence sequence and a brilliant, inventive new sense of syntax. Here the sentences are not bound together, as they are so often in *René*, by parallelisms, but stand in a contrasting relation to one another.

> Les deux rives du Meschacebé présentent le tableau le plus extraordinaire. Sur le bord occidental, des savanes se déroulent à perte de vue; leurs flots de verdure, en s'éloignant, semblent monter dans l'azur du ciel où ils s'évanouissent. On voit dans ces prairies sans bornes errer à l'aventure des troupeaux de trois ou quatre mille buffles sauvages. Quelquefois un bison chargé d'années, fendant les flots à la nage, se vient coucher, parmi les hautes herbes, dans une île du Meschacebé. A son front orné de deux croissants, à sa barbe antique et limoneuse, vous le prendriez pour le dieu du fleuve, qui jette un œil satisfait sur la grandeur de ses ondes et la sauvage abondance de ses rives.

Two variables govern the sentence forms: the opening syntactic unit and the position of the verb in regard to the total structure. As for the beginnings, we see a noun, a prepositional phrase, a pronoun and verb, an adverb, and a combination of two long prepositional phrases. Verbs vary in position as complements and present participles occur, and the longest postverbal unit is in the final sentence, forming a kind of grammatical cadence. Furthermore, the semantic content of the verbs is both connected and diversified; *présentent, se déroulent à perte de vue, on voit, vous le prendriez*, all deal with seeing.

Some doublings of nouns or adjectives occur above, but these yield to a more elaborate use of syntactic elements in series, a conspicuous feature of the second paragraph.

> Telle est la scène sur le bord occidental; mais elle change sur le bord opposé, et forme avec la première un admirable contraste. Suspendus sur le cours des eaux, groupés sur les rochers et sur les montagnes, dispersés dans les vallées, des arbres de toutes les formes, de toutes les couleurs, de tous les parfums, se mêlent, croissent ensemble, montent dans les airs à des hauteurs qui fatiguent les regards. Les vignes sauvages, les bignonias, les coloquintes s'entrelacent au pied de ces arbres, escaladent leurs rameaux, grimpent à l'extrémité des branches, s'élancent de l'érable au tulipier, du tulipier à l'alcée, en formant mille grottes, mille voûtes, mille portiques. Souvent égarées d'arbre en arbre, ces lianes traversent des bras de rivières, sur lesquels le magnolia élève son cône immobile; surmonté de ses larges roses blanches, il domine toute la forêt, et n'a d'autre rival que le palmier, qui balance légèrement auprès de lui ses éventails de verdure.

We have three past participles in asyndeton with a variation in number of complementary phrases, three *de* phrases in asyndeton modifying *arbres*, and three verbs (*se mêlent, croissent* . . .) in asyndeton with complements increasing in length. A triplet of nouns in asyndeton opens the second sentence, but the verbs are four in number, still asyndetic however, with complements of varied length, and the sentence ends in a strict asyndetic group of three (*mille grottes* . . .). The final sentence contains none of the previous figures.

The asyndetic triplet, the most formal series arrangement, is used in the second paragraph almost to the point of mannerism; suddenly, in the third section, it gives way to other figures.

> Si tout est silence et repos dans les savanes de l'autre côté du fleuve, tout ici, au contraire, est mouvement et murmure: des coups de bec contre le tronc des chênes, des froissements d'animaux qui marchent, broutent ou broient entre leurs dents les noyaux des fruits; des bruissements d'ondes, de faibles gémissements, de sourds meuglements, de doux roucoulements, remplissent ces déserts d'une tendre et sauvage harmonie. Mais quand une brise vient à animer ces solitudes, à balancer ces corps flottants, à confondre ces masses de blanc, d'azur, de vert, de rose, à mêler toutes les

couleurs, à réunir tous les murmures; alors il sort de tels bruits du fond des forêts, il se passe de telles choses aux yeux, que j'essayerais en vain de les décrire à ceux qui n'ont point parcouru ces champs primitifs de la nature.

After the opening doublets (*silence et repos* . . .) and the triplet of verbs with *ou*, six nouns represent the movement of the eastern bank of the Mississippi. Then five infinitives, one with a complement of four nouns of color, and the dynamic doublet in asyndeton (*il sort* . . . and *il se passe* . . .—inversion creates a last, new grammatical *tournure*) conclude the description in which no sentences are alike and in which Chateaubriand demonstrates a consciousness of syntactic variation that recalls but goes beyond Bossuet and La Bruyère's studied periods. This is a clear foretaste of the esthetic of syntax governing *Madame Bovary*, and one recalls Flaubert's concern that his novel might seem like *du Balzac chateaubrianisé*; it is in passages like the prologue to *Atala* more than in Chateaubriand's oratory in *René* or in his descriptive vocabulary that we see a major development to come.

Nine of the sixteen sentences in the prologue to *Atala* end in isocolonic phrases, a phenomenon that recalls Bossuet and brings us to the very important rhythmic patterns in Chateaubriand's prose. I shall illustrate the latter from the *Mémoires d'outre-tombe*, in which Chateaubriand's most striking effects are to be found. The general principle informing Chateaubriand's mature prose rhythms is clear definition of phrase and frequent isocolon. It is evident that Chateaubriand recited his prose at least to himself, for we never have any hesitancy over finding the natural articulation of the sentence. Within the general pattern, we find that many of the most arresting sentences are weighted in meaning toward the end, a structural device suggested in places in Bossuet but less systematically exploited.

Dans certains abris [5], le myrte et le laurier-rose [7] croissent en pleine terre [4] comme en Grèce [3]; la figue mûrit [4] comme en Provence [4]; chaque pommier [3], avec ses fleurs carminées [7],///ressemble à un gros bouquet [7]//de fiancée/de village [7].

La lune n'est pas plus tôt couchée [8], qu'un souffle venant du large [7] brise l'image des constellations [8],///comme on éteint les flambeaux [7]// après une solennité [7].

Je répète [3] encore aujourd'hui [5] ces méchantes rimes [4] avec autant de plaisir [7] que des vers d'Homère [5]; une madonne [3] coiffée d'une couronne gothique [7], vêtue d'une robe de soie bleue [7], garnie d'une frange d'argent [6],///m'inspire plus de dévotion [7]//qu'une vierge/de Raphaël [7].

We have used slashes to indicate rhythmic elements other than isocolon or near isocolon, for this prose has complex, interreacting factors. There is a closer relation between the last two isocolonic groups: they can be seen as one phrase in relation to what precedes and therefore are separated from it by a comma; at the same time, their grammatical structure suggests the subdivision. Thus, within an isocolonic system, there is also a long final phrase created by the difference between the full pause, marked by the comma and by my three slashes, and the small intonational shift indicated by the double slash.

A further rhythmic factor in the sentence is the intonational drop at the end, marked by my single slash. Classical rhetoric recognized special rhythmic effects for the end of the period called *clausulae*, and beginning with Chateaubriand, some French writers carefully planned the relation of words with the intonational fall, producing an irregular or asymmetric element as characteristic of the final phrase as its length. These *chutes de phrase* may be as long as seven syllables (*après une solennité*), although fewer is more typical. We have usually in Chateaubriand's long final phrases a contrast between the length of the ascending intonational section and the briefer, descending one, so that in contrast to a possible isocolonic subdivision, an overall asymmetrical division occurs. These effects belong in potential to French prose, but only a writer of particular subtlety of ear will make something of them and make us realize what French prose rhythms are capable of.

In keeping with the general principle that Chateaubriand strove most of all for clear rhythmic articulation, he has equally well defined variants on his characteristic type of sentence. The long final phrase may at times not be susceptible of any isocolonic subdivision: "Madame de Sévigné [6] vantait de son temps [5] ces vieux ombrages [4]; depuis cette époque [5]///cent quarante années [5]//avaient été ajoutées/à leur beauté [11]." Another variation is the inversion of the customary rhythmic pattern: a phrase shorter than the immediately preceding one forms the conclusion: "Mais je devais être agité [8], même dans mon enfance [5]; comme le dattier de l'Arabe [7],///à peine ma tige était sortie du rocher [11]//qu'elle fut battue/du vent [6]."

All these sentences have in common the exposition of Chateaubriand's *thèmes privilégiés* from which his distinctive sentences are not to be separated.[1] Proust maintained that what gave Chateaubriand's prose its characteristic effect was the contrast between the solid, enduring form of his sentences and the fugacity of beauty that they so often record.

> Lorsque le soir [4] élevait une vapeur bleuâtre [7] au carrefour des forêts [6], que les complaintes ou les lais du vent [9] gémissaient dans les mousses flétries [8],///j'entrais en pleine possession [7]//des sympathies/de ma nature [8]. Rencontrais-je quelque laboureur [8] au bout d'un guéret [5]? je m'arrêtais [4] pour regarder cet homme [6] germé à l'ombre [4] des épis [4] parmi lesquels [4] il devait être [4] moissonné [4], et qui [2] retournant la terre de sa tombe [8] avec le soc de la charrue [8],///mêlait ses sueurs brûlantes [7]//aux pluies glacées/de l'automne [7]: le sillon qu'il creusait [6]///était le monument [6]//destiné/à lui survivre [7].

In this last example we observe, beyond the interplay of isocolon and asymmetry, the strong structural element of antithesis. The combination of these factors suggests the extent to which Chateaubriand's prose, so new in many respects, builds on the rhetorical tradition. Isocolon was part of the early eighteenth-century conception of poetic prose, however different Chateaubriand's style seems from his predecessors of a century before, and, finally, the combination of isocolon and antithesis belongs to the oldest, Gorgian theory of artistic prose. Such high style would not in itself, however, be anything more than a forgotten monument, were it not for Chateaubriand's assumption of the sensuous lyric style, which was, in the nineteenth century, to come to seem the highest form of literary art.

---

1. For Chateaubriand's typical sentence, see Jean Mourot, *Le Génie d'un style: Chateaubriand: Rhythme et Sonorité dans les Mémoires d'outre-tombe* (Paris: Armand Colin, 1969), 273–313. For Chateaubriand's style, see Jean-Maurice Gautier, *Le Style des Mémoires d'outre-tombe de Chateaubriand* (Geneva: Droz, 1959).

10 *Romantic Prose*

Despite Chateaubriand's great reputation, the most distinctive romantic prose does not especially reflect his influence: the sentence structure with sense emphasis at the end, the taste for a long, sonorous concluding clause, and the character of tranquil grandeur that has always linked Chateaubriand with Bossuet and Rousseau as one of the great creators of high style in French. Instead, romantic prose of the 1830s and beyond leans toward more excited rhythms and a frequently agitated tone. The idiosyncratic voice becomes of the greatest importance, even in third-person narratives. While there persists a great deal of traditional rhetoric, ranging from the figures of Vigny's *Stello* and the Rousseauesque prose of Lamartine's *Confidences* to a famous set piece like Renan's "Prière sur l'Acropole," some entirely new directions in style are to be found, and I designate these, rather than simply anything dating from the early and middle decades of the nineteenth century, as romantic prose.

French romantic prose was in part the creation of poets engaged in a continuous search for new stylistic domains in verse, and, as Hugo stands at the beginning of romantic poetry, he is also identified with the first manifestations of a new prose. In *Notre-Dame de Paris* (1831), Hugo attempted both to write an objective essay on medieval culture and, through the story, to give an image of that culture. To hold together what might seem the disparate expository and narrative modes, he employs a distinctive tone, an authorial presence that is brilliant, serious, and amused in turn. There is a kind of variety in sentence structure which had scarcely existed in neoclassical prose: "Cette figure, qu'on eût crue scellée dans la dalle, paraissait n'avoir ni mouvement, ni pensée, ni haleine. Sous ce mince sac de toile, en janvier, gisante à nu sur un pavé de granit, sans feu, dans l'ombre d'un cachot dont le soupirail oblique ne laissait arriver du dehors que la bise et jamais le soleil, elle ne semblait pas souffrir, pas même sentir. On eût dit qu'elle s'était faite pierre avec le cachot, glace avec la saison" (VI, 3). The longer middle sentence and the brief final one are both characteristic; what distinguishes Hugo's prose is not length but the asymmetrical, heterocolonic tendency, the numerous pauses, and the enumeration of detail. One looks in vain for any sign of balancing, equilibrated effects. The second sentence, in particular, with its long accumulation of modifiers before the subject, has a kind of suspension, different from that of earlier centuries and anticipating Flaubert and Proust; Hugo belongs to a new phase of style following upon the dominance of natural word order. Asyndeton of twos, a device becoming more common in the nineteenth century, suggests the spontaneity of a mind in movement, of narrational improvisation (the figure often conveys the feeling that the second member develops from the first, as one thinks further). Unexpected details come forth as the sentence unwinds; the final picture in the following one is like Proust's unforeseen images coming forth at the end of subordinate constructions: "Il y avait à peine deux jours que la dernière cavalcade de ce genre, celle des ambassadeurs flamands chargés de conclure le mariage entre le dauphin et Marguerite de Flandre, avait fait son entrée à Paris, au grand ennui de M. le cardinal de Bourbon, qui, pour plaire au roi, avait dû faire bonne mine à toute cette rustique cohue de bourgmestres flamands et les régaler, en son hôtel de Bourbon, d'une *moult belle moralité, sotie et farce*, tandis qu'une pluie battante inondait à sa porte ses magnifiques tapisseries" (I, 1). This is the descending or loose period in the sense that in the context, where Hugo is speaking of the day and of public entertainments, the logically relevant part of the sentence ends with *Paris*; what follows has no direct bearing on the question at hand. But the principle behind the period is that of creating poetic and imagistic wholes. We even find the *tandis que*, almost emptied of meaning, so often used by Flaubert and others in the nineteenth century to attach a striking visual detail to what precedes. Mention of Flaubert and Proust in regard to *Notre-Dame* is far from idle: many sentences in the novel suggest that it must have been a work of genuine influence on them.

Triads are quite frequent at times, often in asyndetic form and combined with doublets or with a longer series: "Puis il se fit un grand remue-ménage, un grand mouvement de pieds et de têtes, une grande détonation générale de toux et de mouchoirs; chacun s'arrangea, se posta, se haussa, se groupa; puis un grand silence; tous les cous restèrent tendus, toutes les bouches ouvertes, tous les regards tournés vers la table de marbre" (I, 1). It is the triad and enumeration, not the antithesis, the figure always associated with Hugo, that dominates in *Notre-Dame de Paris*. The combination of it, however, with twos and fours makes for the somewhat complicated patterns that give density to Hugo's prose. Density also comes from his fondness for verbless or elliptical expressions such as *puis un grand silence*. These have an important role in *Notre-Dame* and anticipate the great freedom later prose will show in their use.

The triads cannot be said to constitute truly idiosyncratic movement, as they tend, because of their Latin origin, to have a rather formal, calculated air. Where we find the unexpected, *primesautier* effect again, the unforeseeable accumulation, is in the handling of adjectives. There are series of adjectives, remarkable for their unusual juxtaposition, that appear in irregularly shaped sentences; and sometimes we even find adjectives in syntactic fragments as well, combined in the following example with apposition, another characteristic device for amassing nouns and adjectives.

Elle n'est pas, comme la cathédrale de Bourges, le produit magnifique, léger, multiforme, touffu, hérissé, efflorescent de l'ogive. Impossible de la ranger dans cette antique famille d'églises sombres, mystérieuses, basses et comme écrasées par le plein cintre; presque égyptiennes au plafond près; toutes hiéroglyphiques, toutes sacerdotales, toutes symboliques; plus chargées dans leurs ornements de losanges et de zigzags que de fleurs, de fleurs que d'animaux, d'animaux que d'hommes; œuvres de l'architecte moins que de l'évêque; première transformation de l'art, tout empreinte de discipline théocratique et militaire, qui prend racine dans le bas-empire et s'arrête à Guillaume le Conquérant. (III, 1)

The rhetorical figure anadiplosis (*que de fleurs, de fleurs*) epitomizes the fanciful, "efflorescent," and surprising movement of the prose. What is interesting is Hugo's way of handling imposing oratorical structures in such a way as to blend with the lighter, more nimble

manner: the colloquial *impossible de* phrase joins with formal apposition. Of course, we must remember that all oratorical effects are in
origin intended to be suggestive of a distinctive persona, called the
ethos of the speaker, and that the idea of rhetoric as being standardized to the point of impersonality only applies to its debased form.

The elastic, free sentence is casually constructed at times with such
superabundance of detail that repetition of the subject is used:
"Gringoire, de plus en plus effaré, pris par les trois mendiants
comme par trois tenailles, assourdi d'une foule d'autres visages qui
moutonnaient et aboyaient autour de lui, le malencontreux Gringoire
tachait de rallier sa présence d'esprit pour se rappeler si l'on était à un
samedi" (II, 6). The suspensional effect is combined with the oral, improvisational manner. The voice informing the novel ranges from the
grandiose to the informal, the unity of style coming from the feeling
that it is indeed that of an individual speaker. Technically, there is an
important resemblance to Rabelais' prose: great variety in sentence
structure and subject matter is dominated by a distinctive, often jocular narrative figure.

Hugo's prose assumed another form at times in his later career,
which is a stripped down, also often colloquial sentence, used in moments of the greatest intensity. Here is the octopus in *Les Travailleurs
de la mer*: "Une forme grisâtre oscille dans l'eau, c'est gros comme le
bras, et long d'une demi-aune environ; c'est un chiffon; cette forme
ressemble à un parapluie fermé qui n'aurait pas de manche. Cette
loque avance vers vous peu à peu. Soudain, elle s'ouvre, huit rayons
s'écartent brusquement autour d'une face qui a deux yeux; ces rayons
vivent; il y a du flamboiement dans leur ondoiement; c'est une sorte
de roue; déployée, elle a quatre ou cinq pieds de diamètre. Epanouis-
sement effroyable. Cela se jette sur vous" (II, iv, 2). This vision of evil
is the center of the novel, breaking the humorous or realistic texture.
The language becomes rudimentary; the *c'est* construction replaces
elle est or *il est* in conversational fashion; the images are strange and
abrupt. While this is the extreme form taken by Hugo's later prose
style, we notice the same tendency toward parataxis in many narrative passages. Similar in grammatical form is a rhetoric of aphorisms,
metaphors, antitheses, and personifications: "Wellington, c'est la

guerre classique qui prend sa revanche. Bonaparte, à son aurore, l'avait rencontré en Italie, et superbement battu. La vieille chouette avait fui devant le jeune vautour. L'ancienne tactique avait été non seulement foudroyée, mais scandalisée" (*Les Misérables*, II, i, 16). This style, of which my example is intended to be a characteristic piece rather than the finest expression, is closely related to that of Hugo's metaphysical poems of the 1850s and is justified by a view of language as divine and visionary, one found more often among poets than prose writers: this is poetic prose, in a special sense.

Because of its large essayistic content, much of Hugo's fiction could be said to belong to a mixed genre, and the mixed genre is frequent in French romantic literature. Michelet's history of France, likewise, seems to have a certain heterogeneous quality: it is at once a documentary work and an often visionary narrative. As early as the *Introduction à l'histoire universelle* (1831), Michelet conceived of a dialectic narrative in which the characters were entities—The Revolution, The People, or Christianity. Increasingly, the stage of history became not the real France but a visionary mental space.

> Les yeux s'ouvrirent sous Louis XV, se refermèrent sous Louis XVI, la question s'obscurcit encore. L'espoir du peuple se plaça encore une fois dans la royauté. Turgot espéra, Voltaire espéra... Ce pauvre jeune roi, si mal né, si mal élevé, aurait voulu pouvoir le bien. Il lutta, et fut entraîné. Ses préjugés de naissance et d'éducation, ses vertus mêmes de famille, le menèrent à la ruine... Triste problème historique!... Des justes l'ont excusé, des justes l'ont condamné... Duplicité, restrictions mentales (peu surprenantes sans doute dans l'élève du parti jésuite), voilà ses fautes, enfin son crime, qui le mena à la mort, son appel à l'étranger... Avec tout cela n'oublions pas qu'il avait été longtemps anti-autrichien, anti-anglais, qu'il avait mis une passion réelle à relever notre marine, qu'il avait fondé Cherbourg à dix-huit lieues de Portsmouth, qu'il aida à couper l'Angleterre en deux, à créer une Angleterre contre l'Angleterre. Cette larme que Carnot verse en signant son arrêt, elle lui reste dans l'histoire; l'histoire et la justice même, en le jugeant, pleureront. (*Histoire de la Révolution française*, Introduction, II, 7)

Here the form is frankly that of an inner monologue, with violent breaks, tangential association of ideas, asyndeton in abundance marking developing thought, *points de suspension* indicating the trailing off of an idea, personifications mingling with real people, ellipti-cal sentences, little hypotaxis, and other peculiarities. More so than *Notre-Dame* even, this history of the Revolution is given to authorial interventions, with only intermittent indications of objective, imper-sonal facts. Again, an effect of spontaneity and improvisation carries the reader along. Although not every page of Michelet's history in its later parts shows such strong monologuelike characteristics and such dolorous involvement, the effect of these passages is to color the en-tire historical undertaking. In Proust's pastiche of Michelet, the most salient trait is Michelet's interjection of himself into the stream of French history, between the reader and documentary realities.

The visionary style of Hugo and Michelet in their later works reveals new possibilities for prose in the domain of abruptness, discon-tinuity, implied rather than explicit connection between sentences, and uses of disruptive punctuation like the dash and suspension points. In Gautier's work, the creation of a spontaneous, improvisa-tional air, which we encounter in Hugo and Michelet, is not entirely a matter of calculation, given the hasty conditions under which he wrote prose. He made of journalistic necessity a virtue, however; in *Made-moiselle de Maupin* the resulting unvaried sentences, the parataxis, and abrupt punctuation of dashes contribute to an appropriate, excited, somewhat blurting, epistolary style. Although Gautier frankly did not concern himself with rhythm, he had a natural tendency toward isocolon, and phrases of similar length often occur in passages that, by their diction, represent Gautier at his best. Here is one of the many impressive developments in *Mademoiselle de Maupin*: "Je suis un homme/des temps homériques;/—le monde où je vis/n'est pas le mien,/ et je ne comprends rien/à la société qui m'entoure./ Le Christ n'est pas venu pour moi;/je suis aussi païen/qu'Alcibiade et Phi-dias./—Je n'ai jamais été cueillir/sur le Golgotha/les fleurs de la pas-sion,/et le fleuve profond/qui coule du flanc du crucifié/et fait une ceinture rouge au monde/ne m'a pas baigné de ses flots." The iso-colon often takes on an aphoristic coloring, and the novel is full of sharply phrased statements. At the same time, there is a whole ironic side to this: the above passage, for example, is not a disinterested moral and esthetic affirmation but part of an apology for homosexual inclinations. The main character, D'Albert, is at once an esthete expounding Gautier's doctrine of art for art's sake and something of a fool, a parodic version of Adolphe, René, and fictional men of enthusiasm and sensibility who are totally absorbed in themselves. It is part of the romantic irony governing the work that the author's ideas are given to such a character, that the sententiousness of the novel is at once serious in the abstract and comic in situations. The lack of articulations in presenting ideas, stated bluntly in sentences tending toward brevity and parataxis, makes for a texture that inspires a mixture of assent and distrust on the part of the reader; this rhetoric of ambiguity is joined to a curious narrational technique, self-consciously casual, disordered, but yet quite extraordinary in stylistic detail. The genre is a mixed one in that the expository preface is an integral part of the work, and the colloquial and the poetic are often side by side. Gautier achieves a perfect example of the ambivalent effect called romantic irony, taking familiar stylistic elements and giving them unexpected nuances of meaning through the total context of the work.

Gautier was a maker of elegant metaphors, as may be judged from the passage above, but in the long run, for his place in the history of French prose, his cult of the interesting and unusual word is more important: throughout his life he read specialized books just for their vocabulary, and the result is a tendency to write in such a way as best to display such terms, to the point that his vocabulary has even been studied for the new words he introduced or helped to disseminate.[1] Here is a pertinent passage.

On lit dans les contes de Nathaniel Hawthorne la description d'un jardin singulier, où un botaniste toxicologue a réuni la flore des plantes vénéneuses. Ces plantes aux feuillages bizarrement découpés, d'un vert noir ou minéralement glauque, comme si le sulfate de cuivre les teignait, ont une beauté sinistre et formidable. On les sent dangereuses malgré leur charme; elles ont dans leur attitude hautaine, provocante ou perfide, la conscience d'un pouvoir immense ou d'une séduction irrésistible. De leurs fleurs féro-

---

1. See Georges Matoré, *Le Vocabulaire et la Société sous Louis-Philippe* (Geneva: Droz, 1951), 113–213.

cement bariolées et tigrées, d'un pourpre semblable à du sang figé ou d'un
blanc chlorotique, s'exhalent des parfums âcres, pénétrants, vertigineux;
dans leurs calices empoisonnés la rosée se change en aqua-tofana, et il ne
voltige autour d'elles que des cantharides cuirassées d'or vert, ou des
mouches d'un bleu d'acier dont la piqûre donne le charbon. L'euphorbe,
l'aconit, la jusquiame, la ciguë, la belladone y mêlent leurs froids virus aux
ardents poisons des tropiques et de l'Inde; le mancenillier y montre ses petites pommes mortelles comme celles qui pendaient à l'arbre de science,
l'upa y distille son suc laiteux plus corrosif que l'eau-forte. (*Fusains et Eaux-
fortes*, "Charles Baudelaire")

We notice here, if not so much isocolon, an avoidance of striking heterocolon, and the syntax as well offers characteristic traits: the sentences tend to have little or no subordination, and the verbs are generally colorless, varied ways of expressing the copula or *il y a*, for
Gautier's major effort is toward interesting nouns and adjectives. The
prose is nominal in spirit and descriptive in method; it shows the
dominant tendency in Gautier's style which contemporary writers
like Baudelaire, Flaubert, and Mallarmé so admired. Judged unsym-
pathetically, this is a pure rhetorical development from a much
plainer, more summary kind of statement in Hawthorne's "Rappac-
cini's Daughter"; one could call it a spectacular example of the figure
called *enargeia*, or vivid representation. The word color, applied to
style as early as Quintilian and the highest criterion of writers from
Gautier to Proust's Bergotte, suggests the parallel with the visual arts
that lies behind the traditional rhetorical theory of description.

Gautier's style is an especially good example of the decadent-
descriptive side of romanticism, with its sometimes morbid tableaux
and its tendency toward neologism, which, in the early nineteenth
century, meant innovation in figurative language as much as the use
of new words. Interestingly enough, at least one widely read contemporary, Sainte-Beuve, found much the same sort of effect in Balzac's
"style si souvent chatouilleux et dissolvant, énervé, rosé et veiné de
toutes les teintes, ce style d'une corruption délicieuse, toute asiatique
comme disaient nos maîtres."[2] Balzac is fond of unusual expressions:
old families are *familles primordiales*, and tanneries and laundries are

2. Charles-Augustin Sainte-Beuve, quoted in André Allemand, *Unité et Structure de
l'univers balzacien* (Paris: Plon, 1965), 25.

commerces aquatiques; Lucien Chardon fancies that he will *s'impatro-niser chez Mme de Bargeton*. Quotations and allusions often occur: "Quand elle [une femme aimante] est sur le point d'être quittée, elle devine plus rapidement le sens d'un geste que le coursier de Virgile ne flaire les lointaines corpuscules qui lui annoncent l'amour." One of the extreme examples of elaborate and strange style in Balzac is the peculiar reversal by which Mme de Beauséant, about to be abandoned by her lover, resembles the stallion in the *Georgics* who smells a mare. He is not always successful in imitating the metaphoric style of Gautier, which he much admired: "Aussitôt l'amour des poètes déplia ses ailes blanches: mille souvenirs environnèrent de leurs horizons bleuâtres le grand homme d'Angoulême qui retomba dans la rêverie." At the same time Balzac is capable of very fine uses of figurative language: "La rue Neuve-Sainte-Geneviève surtout est comme un cadre de bronze, le seul qui convienne à ce récit." The end of the second part of *Illusions perdues* is likewise impressive: "Bérénice se sauva sans que Lucien pût savoir par où elle avait passé; car, il faut le dire à sa louange, cet argent lui brûlait la main et il voulait le rendre; mais il fut forcé de le garder comme un dernier stigmate de la vie parisienne."

One must not underestimate the elements of irony and humor in Balzac's language. When he lists among Mme de Bargeton's bizarre words *poétiser* and *synthétiser*, he is including words he uses himself, and he is perfectly aware, as Rastignac is, that fancy *phrases de coiffeur* are absurd, if useful, in many circumstances. Balzac, while making fun of his characters who do the same thing, assumed the noble *particule*, thereby epitomizing the extremely ambiguous character of many of his linguistic effects. Balzac's intense awareness of language shows up in the brilliant and corrupt lessons in rhetoric the journalists give Lucien in *Illusions perdues*; he seems to have been quite conscious of the effect of stylistic devices on the reader, whether the latter cares for them or not, and the fact that Sainte-Beuve so enjoyed Balzac's style establishes clearly that the decadent-neologistic taste was by then largely formed. Essentially, Balzac's ornaments are those of other romantics but pushed to an extreme degree and made especially striking by their juxtaposition with various levels of spoken language in the dialogue of his novels.

The styles we have been examining are the advanced romantic ones, those which self-consciously negate the values of neoclassical language, as Hugo does with his fanciful, unpredictable sentence structure, Michelet with his borrowing of colloquial abruptness and alogical sequence of thoughts, and Gautier and Balzac with novelties of vocabulary and image. These innovations represent the most obvious aspect of romantic historical consciousness in style. There is, however, another side to being aware of the historicity of language: one may prize stylistic qualities of the past, without being a *pasticheur* or epigonus; one may create something new whose advanced character depends in part on salvaging effects of earlier literary language that everyone else has abandoned. Stendhal's limited vocabulary, suggestive of eighteenth-century middle style, is the first manifestation of such a stylistic mode, and its very existence can be said to constitute an ironic commentary on the romantic idea of color in style.

Nabokov said that Stendhal was for those who took their French neat, and the idea that his language constitutes some kind of neutral medium is widespread. It is necessary, however, to remember the historical moment when *Le Rouge et le Noir* (1830) was written to see how wrong a notion this is. The novel was conceived in relation to the most admired prose of its day, which was that of Chateaubriand, and *René* in particular; its style is a negative reference to *René*. This peculiar timeliness makes Stendhal a very difficult author to pastiche or parody: we cannot easily recapture the exact balance of elements determined by the time when the book was written.

Stendhal's background, like Chateaubriand's, lay in neoclassicism, and we find in *Armance* (1827) an elegant language derived from earlier high style: "Mme de Malivert fit amener dans l'écurie un superbe cheval anglais dont la jeunesse et la grâce firent un étrange contraste avec les deux anciens chevaux normands, qui, depuis douze ans, s'acquittaient du service de la maison." This kind of diction and tone recur in Stendhal, but only for local effect. For example, in the farewell scene between Julien and Mme de Rênal in part I of *Le Rouge et le Noir*, we find the expressions "Ah! voilà un cœur dans lequel il est doux de régner!" "L'amour qui est sans doute dans ces yeux charmants sera donc perdu pour moi?" and "Tu ne m'aurais pas parlé ainsi avant ce cruel départ pour le séminaire." The Racinian metaphor of reigning in a heart and the objectifying, deictic construction in place of *ses yeux* and *mon départ* are customary devices of the grand manner. *Le Rouge et le Noir*, largely constituting an evolution away from this elevated style, is best understood if we keep works like *Armance* and *René* in mind. The famous abrupt, jerky quality of the sentences in *Le Rouge* directly, consciously counters the aims of *distingué* writing; it is, furthermore, not an illusion but consists, as shown with a little statistical sampling, of cola averaging about seven syllables in length, whereas in *La Chartreuse de Parme*, closer to the ideal of smooth style, the cola tend, on the average, toward nine syllables. The asyndeton and triplets of formal style are uncommon, and the binary arrangements of words, phrases, and clauses so prominent in the oratorical manner of *René* are generally absent. Sentence forms are not especially varied, but they do not repeat each other in such a way as to make one aware of parallelism.

Stendhal, on the other hand, keeps the small vocabulary of neo-classicism, and we sense that he was aiming deliberately at an effect of understatement with respect to newer trends in French literature. His dryness is not the natural one of the eighteenth century but constitutes a self-conscious device in 1830. Just as the small vocabulary is a quite positive element of style, so is the paucity of description. Stendhal commented on his contemporaries' genuine taste for detailed accounts of the look of things,[3] and in this respect he wrote against the prevailing fashion: nothing makes us more aware of this than trying to read the slower moving works of his coevals. At the same time, he made effective use of small, concrete details; he is not an abstract writer.

Stendhal uses a rhetorical expression, "coloris modéré," to describe *Le Rouge* and explain the absence of lurid material. We can summarize the characteristics of his middle style as consisting of short phrases, with less hypotaxis than in *La Chartreuse*, for example; as avoiding the phonetic and syntactic devices of emotive prose; and as using less imagery than the work of his contemporaries. Insofar

3. See Matoré, *Le Vocabulaire*, 123*n*.

abruptness in rhythm characterizes romantic prose, he is very much in the same movement with Gautier and Michelet. Some of the interior monologues in *Le Rouge* show the same devices we find in them: "Mais un vrai prêtre, un Massillon, un Fénelon... Massillon a sacré Dubois. Les Mémoires de Saint-Simon m'ont gâté Fénelon; mais enfin un vrai prêtre... Alors les âmes tendres auraient un point de réunion dans le monde... Nous ne serions pas isolés... Ce bon prêtre nous parlerait de Dieu. Mais quel Dieu? Non celui de la Bible, petit despote cruel, et plein de la soif de se venger . . . mais le Dieu de Voltaire, juste, bon, infini . . ." (II, 44). Incomplete sentences and a special punctuation convey the drifting of thought. There is, furthermore, a very positive kind of movement in Stendhal's prose which is the reverse of descriptive prolongation; we observe rapid alternations of thought and speech: "Cette demande frappa le maire. Puisque Sorel n'est pas ravi et comblé de ma proposition, comme naturellement il devrait l'être, il est clair, se dit-il, qu'on lui a fait des offres d'un autre côté; et de qui peuvent-elles venir, si ce n'est du Valenod? Ce fut en vain que M. de Rênal pressa Sorel de conclure sur-le-champ: l'astuce du vieux paysan s'y refusa opiniâtrement; il voulait, disait-il consulter son fils, comme si, en province, un père riche consultait un fils qui n'a rien, autrement que pour la forme" (I, 4). Five devices occur in close succession: a third-person statement about M. de Rênal's reaction, a first-person thought, a third-person summary of speech, an indirect quote, and a comment coming from the narratorial voice. This is a particularly dense example of what we find generally true in *Le Rouge*: all details count, and the reader's attention is constantly solicited; there are no repetitive passages or leisurely descriptions to skim lightly. This kind of effect gives one the impression of short, rapid sentences quite as much as any real shortness of phrase and absence of hypotaxis. The style of *Le Rouge* is sometimes said to be more rudimentary in grammar than it actually is because we especially remember effects of brevity; the impression made on us is as much a part of Stendhal's art as the devices by which the impressions are created.

Stendhal is sometimes compared with the *moralistes*, and his tendency to repeat certain words and concepts over and over in *Le Rouge et le Noir* is certainly reminiscent of their work. His repeated terms and ideas fall into antitheses: *âme de feu/prudence, hypocrisie/sincérité, mépris/orgueil, courage/lâcheté (timidité), ambition/bonheur, vanité/sincérité, devoir/bonheur.* They can form various pairs among themselves, as is obvious, and some ideas have no single term: impulsiveness and calculation, knowledgeableness and ingenuousness, acting and sincerity, impassivity and sensibility. The more general notions of illusion and reality subsume many of these antithetical situations, and frequently the contrast is between an inner feeling and an exterior display. Quite naturally, two devices are associated with the antitheses.

> Julien ne faisait paraître devant lui que des sentiments pieux. Qui eût pu deviner que cette figure de jeune fille, si pâle et si douce, cachait la résolution inébranlable de s'exposer à mille morts plutôt que de ne pas faire fortune. (I, 5)

> En un mot, ce qui faisait de Julien un être supérieur fut précisément ce qui l'empêcha de goûter le bonheur qui se plaçait sous ses pas. (I, 15)

> Le bonheur de Julien fut, ce jour-là, sur le point de devenir durable. Il manqua à notre héros d'oser être sincère. Il fallait avoir le courage de livrer bataille, mais *sur-le-champ.* (I, 16)

> Dans ce cas, se dit-il, je dois être sensible à sa beauté; je me dois à moi-même d'être son amant. Une telle idée ne lui fût pas venue avant les confidences naïves faites par son ami. (I, 13)

The contrary-to-fact condition or hypothesis and the authorial intervention, often occurring together, produce the effect of a double plane: that of the action and that of possible alternatives having a validity of their own. This twofold psychological level is, rhetorically, a constant source of wit and functions like the *moralistes'* antitheses to reveal the nature of truth as being complex rather than simple. Before his final realization of his nature in the novel, Julien is often arbitrary and blind in his self-affirmations. Furthermore, many pages of the novel contain abundant antitheses, though not formulated in an obvious fashion. These tend to create that feeling of constant rhetorical activity so basic to Stendhal's art. The sense of game, of improvisation, is always with us. The term *analyse psychologique,* so often used of Stendhal, could not be more misleading; whereas a novelist like Constant presents a more or less stable situation and then comments on it, the situations are constantly being created in *Le Rouge et le Noir*, and the mode is one of progressive synthesis. There is everpresent change: "Après leur depart, Julien n'était plus le même homme. Toute sa colère contre lui-même avait disparu. La douleur atroce, envenimée par la pusillanimité, à laquelle il était en proie depuis le départ de Mme de Rênal, s'était tournée en mélancolie" (II, 44). The traditional criticism that Julien Sorel is an inconsistent character derives from such mutability. There is no prior state open subsequently to analysis but a steady improvisation. The *imprévu*, a favorite word, is the guiding esthetic idea. The brief paragraphs, the short chapters, Stendhal's way of putting down "etc., etc." when he does not wish to prolong a speech, all suggest the continual search for new effect. Romantic irony is the general term under which we may subsume the contrasting play of moods and ideas, and its most striking specific figure is literary allusion.

Of all the antitheses which inform the novel, that between books and life is perhaps the most prominent. We are told that Julien's nearfirst words ("Je ne veux pas être domestique") come from Rousseau's remarks in the *Confessions*. The *Mémorial de Sainte-Hélène* is his source of wisdom. Mathilde tries to compare her feelings for Julien with those in novels: "Elle repassa dans sa tête toutes les descriptions de passion qu'elle avait lues dans *Manon Lescaut, La Nouvelle Héloïse*, les *Lettres d'une Religieuse portugaise*, etc., etc. Il n'était question, bien entendu, que de la grande passion; l'amour léger était indigne d'une fille de son âge et de sa naissance" (II, 11). The text of *Le Rouge* is filled with references to literature, and epigraphs, notably those from Byron, constitute a sort of commentary.[4] One of the aspects of literary allusion and preconceived ideas is what we might call Julien's projective mode of thought; when, for example, he conceives the idea of holding Mme de Rênal's hand in the garden, he sees it not as a pleasure but as one of the duties, part of the code of honor, he has read about: "Julien pensa qu'il était de son *devoir* d'obtenir que l'on ne retirât pas cette main quand il la touchait. L'idée d'un devoir à accom-

4. For literary allusions see the notes to Stendhal, *Le Rouge et le Noir*, ed. P.-G. Castex (Paris: Garnier, 1973).

plir, et d'un ridicule ou plutôt d'un sentiment d'infériorité à encourir si l'on n'y parvenait pas, éloigna sur-le-champ tout plaisir de son cœur" (I, 8). Julien's mind is full of maxims for conduct he has not entirely evolved by himself. It is not altogether surprising therefore that the commonplaces of deliberative rhetoric, such as we find them in plays, inform his thoughts when he is about to seize Mme de Rênal's hand: "Dans sa mortelle angoisse, tous les dangers lui eussent semblé préférables. Que de fois ne désira-t-il pas voir survenir à Mme de Rênal quelque affaire qui l'obligeât de rentrer à la maison et de quitter le jardin! . . . L'affreux combat que le devoir livrait à la timidité était trop pénible pour qu'il fût en état de rien observer hors lui-même . . . Julien, indigné de sa lâcheté, se dit: Au moment précis où dix heures sonneront, j'exécuterai ce que, pendant toute la journée, je me suis promis de faire ce soir, ou je monterai chez moi me brûler la cervelle" (I, 9). Here, as in the previous example, we see the antitheses in action. Sometimes the deliberative rhetoric is frankly in monologue form, stressing the theatrical and mock-heroic effect. All this formal planning of one's actions is quite remote from the *analyse psychologique* texture as epitomized in a work like *Adolphe*.

"La vie de Julien se composait . . . d'une suite de petites négociations." The structure of *Le Rouge et le Noir*, with its brief chapters, reflects Julien's habit of making existence into a series of deliberations, projects, or self-affirmations, often with some model in mind. He improvises himself much as Stendhal improvises the novel. There is little feeling of orderly progression in long stretches of *Le Rouge*, and its composition, in the traditional sense, has been criticized. Stendhal does not hesitate to bring in some accessory effect like the *chapelle ardente* episode, with its parody of Chateaubriand's religiosity, or the secret note chapter, with its contemporary allusion. This improvisational mode Stendhal shares with other romantic prose writers, and we must not think of it as the result of some habit of writing less organized than that of other authors, but as a willed effect. The improvisational structure permits many distinctive, striking units in succession; it sacrifices massive effects for frequent ones. *La Chartreuse de Parme*, however, will not be based entirely on the same principle.

In *Le Rouge et le Noir*, the allusions to Napoleon and to Mathilde's

ancestor and the sixteenth century function as comparisons, part of
the system of antitheses and double levels, or aspects of psychological and moral life. In *La Chartreuse de Parme*, allusion is the dominant
figure, and it works somewhat differently. There is, to be sure, a series of comparisons between Napoleonic times and Europe after the
Congress of Vienna, and, as in *Le Rouge*, allusion is not so much to
some sort of historical reality as to an archetype, like allusions to the
golden age in renaissance literature. The pseudohistorical reference is
reinforced in *La Chartreuse* by geographical allusion, which again involves an ideal: the Italian lake country and the view from the tower
represent perfect types like the place names in classical poetry. Bel-
girate, Grianta, La Cadenabia, Villa Melzi, the sacred wood of Le
Sfondrata, the wood of San Giovanni, Laveno, Vico, Durini, Belagio,
Managio, and the Resegon di Lek are words that Stendhal uses as if
he were alluding to reality, when he is really creating a world. It has
been observed that the great detail concerning the geography of Lake
Como and its environs derives as much from books as from personal
memories,[5] and this savant, scarcely casual use of toponymy has as
much imagistic value as the protracted descriptions of contemporary
writers. While Stendhal limits himself to conventional phrasing ("Les
eaux et le ciel étaient d'une tranquillité profonde; l'âme de Fabrice ne
put résister à cette beauté sublime"), the many place names have an
exceptionally rich evocative power, as Hugo, Gautier, and other romantics were also discovering.

     Although literary reference is less frequent in *La Chartreuse* than in
Le Rouge, there is one striking example of it that illuminates a whole
side of the novel. In Chapter 22, a sonnet that Fabrice sends to Clelia
is paraphrased; the subject and conceit are baroque and in the erotico-
religious vein. We realize that the religious themes of the book are
distinctly Counter Reformation in character and that many differences mentioned between France and Italy can best be summarized
by the Voltairean versus the baroque. The sonnet polarizes the cultural contrasts.

     The less antithetical style of *La Chartreuse* has only *bonheur* and *sub-*

     5. See the notes to Stendhal, *La Chartreuse de Parme*, ed. Antoine Adam (Paris: Gar-
nier, 1973).

lime as key words; it is also more markedly *style négligé*, in the sense that conversational repetitions are common, and colloquial habits like the use of *affreux* and other terms in a hyperbolic fashion are frequent. The reason behind the stylistic differences between *La Chartreuse* and *Le Rouge* is that the recounting effect, the impression of someone telling a story, is more sustained. There are fewer authorial intrusions, less brilliant alternation between inner and outer, and more of a relaxed but not wordy air of oral narration, which is reflected in the longer, less puppetlike interior monologues. We note how Stendhal chooses to use secondary narrators at times in the novel to stress the recounting quality: Lieutenant Robert in Chapter 1, an anonymous Milanese in Chapter 6, Fabrice describing his escape from the Citadel, and the duchess telling how she wishes the illumination of Sacca and the flooding of Parma to be brought off. Stendhal does use representational narrative at times with great vividness, as in Fabrice's crossing the Po or the torchlit parade in the Fausta episode, but he obviously feels the recounting tone to have a value in itself. Similarly, he uses summary narration with frequency and brilliance: this perhaps is the kind of texture in which the authorial voice is clearest. The key to the narrative method lies in the introductory *Avertissement*, where Stendhal associates the civilized pleasure of telling stories with Italian society, so that the style of the book reflects its subject matter. Indeed, one has only to imagine the novel written in a more sustained representational fashion to see how much would be lost.

In *La Chartreuse de Parme*, as in *Notre-Dame de Paris* and some other romantic books, we find brilliant writing used to characterize a historical epoch, one of the very new kinds of subject matter in nineteenth-century fiction. Nerval's *Sylvie* opens with a similar, almost epigrammatic presentation of the mood of the 1830s.

> Nous vivions alors/dans une époque étrange,/comme celles qui d'ordinaire/succèdent aux révolutions/ou aux abaissements des grands règnes/ . . . quelque chose/comme l'époque/de Pérégrinus/et d'Apulée./ L'homme matériel/aspirait au bouquet de roses/qui devait le régénérer/par les mains de la belle Isis/ . . . Vue de près,/la femme réelle/révoltait notre ingénuité;/il fallait/qu'elle apparût reine ou déesse,/et surtout n'en pas approcher./ Quelques-uns d'entre nous néanmoins/prisaient peu ces paradoxes pla-

toniques,/et à travers nos rêves/renouvelés d'Alexandrie/agitaient parfois
la torche/des dieux souterrains/qui éclairent l'ombre/un instant/de ses
traînées d'étincelles.

As we saw in Stendhal, allusion is a powerful trope, functioning
much like a metaphor or simile; here Nerval uses it to evoke a belief
in mysteriously supernatural phenomena, something that the reference to the *Golden Ass* accomplishes succinctly. The tendency to isocolon and the striking sound repetitions of certain phrases (*prisaient
peu ces paradoxes platoniques, de ses traînées d'étincelles*) contribute to the
epigrammatic sharpness of the passage.

The sacred and profane are the dominant categories of imagery in
Sylvie, but these are not straightforward or unambiguous. In the
opening reflections on women or Woman, we see the contrasting
views of the actress as goddess or mere flesh: Nerval, however, does
not make of this an antithesis neatly epitomizing the story; there are
three women in it, and the narrator is not faced with a simple choice.
As soon as Nerval establishes his initial references to mystery re-
ligions, we move from them into a pastoral world, with hints of a
golden age, allusions to old chateaux, folk songs, and the narrator's
crowning a queen—an act of infidelity to Sylvie, compensated for by
their dressing themselves in wedding costumes from the eighteenth
century and singing ancient amoebean-idyllic songs: "Elle retrouva
même/dans sa mémoire/les chants alternés,/d'usage alors,/qui se ré-
pondaient/d'un bout à l'autre/de la table nuptiale,/et le naïf épi-
thalame/qui accompagnait les mariés/rentrant après la danse./Nous
répétions ces strophes/si simplement rhythmées,/avec les hiatus/et
les assonances du temps;/amoureuses et fleuries/comme le cantique/
de l'Ecclésiaste;/—nous étions l'époux et l'épouse/pour tout un beau
matin d'été." The past is brought back to life in this magic moment,
and Sylvie and the narrator are archetypal man and woman, king and
queen. The references to antiquity (*chants alternés, épithalame*) and the
Song of Songs continue the metaphorical method of the opening of
Sylvie, and again isocolon contributes vividness. A new world is created, as in the best romantic fiction, and the element of color in style
has a richness in its indirect, discreet handling, which the more advanced and neological romantic styles often lack.

We are led to the climax of the pastoral section by a series of references to the eighteenth century, including ones to Watteau and to a temple built to Urania; later, there are allusions to Virgil, Rousseau, a Temple to Philosophy, and other things suggestive of an age that is not so much the Enlightenment as a pastoral era filled with ancient piety for nature. We see the mythic sense of history being established, by which the nineteenth century and contemporary life represent a fall, the desperate age of an Apuleius and esoteric cults searching to recapture primordial unity. The prose Nerval uses is an attempt to recreate the pastoral style purged of cliché. The imagery is precise, charming, but carefully chosen so as not to be gaudy.

> Parfois nous rencontrions sous nos pas les pervenches si chères à Rousseau, ouvrant leurs corolles bleues parmi ces longs rameaux de feuilles accouplées, lianes modestes qui arrêtaient les pieds furtifs de ma compagne. (V)
>
> La Thève bruissait à notre gauche, laissant à ses coudes des remous d'eau stagnante où s'épanouissaient les nénuphars jaunes et blancs, où éclatait comme des pâquerettes la frêle broderie des étoiles d'eau.
>
> . . . .
>
> Je suis entré au bal de Loisy à cette heure mélancolique et douce encore où les lumières pâlissent et tremblent aux approches du jour. Les tilleuls, assombris par en bas, prenaient à leurs cimes une teinte bleuâtre. La flûte champêtre ne luttait plus si vivement avec les trilles du rossignol. (VIII)

We have seen the pastoral style going back through *La Nouvelle Héloïse* and *Télémaque* to Sannazaro. Nerval very deftly suggests older prose by epitheton (*lianes modestes, pieds furtifs, frêle broderie, flûte champêtre*), while the nineteenth-century touches, like color adjectives or indications of light, are discreet. Although this is a very nineteenth-century style through its allusiveness, it consciously eschews the intense color one associates with the romantics. What Nerval is doing is to create a prose appropriate to his theme, which is all in half-shades and hints: we know that there has been a fall in the narrator's life from his earlier condition, but we can only surmise the roles of Adrienne and Sylvie in this; we do not know whether Adrienne is the actress or whether she really died. We realize that the profane world of the theater, Sylvie's domestic life, and the revolution in cottage industry have transformed existence by the end of the story, but we do not know exactly if there has been some corresponding fault on the narrator's part. Understatement, to the point of mystery, is Nerval's method, and it is a device we shall find again, although with a very different effect, in Baudelaire.

Baudelaire's prose poems are more self-consciously differentiated from highly colored romantic prose than are Nerval's. This may be shown especially well by a comparison of Aloysius Bertrand's prose poem style, which Baudelaire professed to admire, with a characteristic passage from *Le Spleen de Paris*. Bertrand writes largely descriptive pieces.

> Aussitôt la lune courut se cacher derrière les nuées, et une pluie mêlée d'éclairs et de tourbillons fouetta ma fenêtre, tandis que les girouettes criaient comme des grues en sentinelle sur qui crève l'averse dans les bois.
> . . . .
> Cette effrayante lueur peignait des rouges flammes du purgatoire et de l'enfer les murailles de la gothique église, et prolongeait sur les maisons voisines l'ombre de la statue gigantesque de saint Jean.
> Les girouettes se rouillèrent; la lune fondit les nuées gris de perle; la pluie ne tomba plus que goutte à goutte des bords du toit, et la brise, ouvrant ma fenêtre mal close, jeta sur mon oreiller les fleurs de mon jasmin secoué par l'orage. ("La Ronde sous la cloche")

Here we have a kind of elegant common romantic style derived from Hugo's poetry in its imagery and rather self-consciously trying to reach the condition of poetry through stanza divisions, poeticisms such as "la gothique église," and the use of a striking final image. Baudelaire's stylistic resources, on the other hand, are ironically used and scarcely contemporary.

> Je voyageais. Le paysage au milieu duquel j'étais placé était d'une grandeur et d'une noblesse irrésistibles. Il en passa sans doute en ce moment quelque chose dans mon âme. Mes pensées voltigeaient avec une légèreté égale à celle de l'atmosphère; les passions vulgaires, telles que la haine et l'amour profane, m'apparaissaient maintenant aussi éloignées que les nuées qui défilaient au fond des abîmes sous mes pieds; mon âme me semblait aussi vaste et aussi pure que la coupole du ciel dont j'étais enveloppé; le souvenir des choses terrestres n'arrivait à mon cœur qu'affaibli et diminué, comme le son de la clochette des bestiaux imperceptibles qui paissaient loin, bien loin, sur le versant d'une autre montagne. ("Le Gâteau")

The comparisons are intentionally bland; the use of doublets such as *grandeur* and *noblesse, vaste* and *pure, affaibli* and *diminué*, are deliberate recreations of the redundant balanced style; Baudelaire seeks an effect of insipidity with his suggestions of the *style noble* (*la coupole du ciel*) according to Buffon. The mountain setting is the very archetype of the eighteenth-century sublime. All this gives the effect of a conventional exaltation, which will form the most bizarre contrast with the following scene of violence. Uniting the unexpected is Baudelaire's essential method, as in the following, where the apposition has its frequent lyric feeling, before the grotesque final comparison: "La petite vieille ratatinée se sentit toute réjouie en voyant ce joli enfant à qui chacun faisait fête, à qui tout le monde voulait plaire; ce joli être, si fragile comme elle, la petite vieille, et, comme elle aussi, sans dents et sans cheveux" ("Le Désespoir de la vieille"). The sudden mention of precise details, teeth and hair, at the end of the apposition creates a superb example of the mordant period in which the final words are essential.

The creation of a dramatic character for the *I* of the poem—most of *Le Spleen de Paris* uses the first person—is customary in Baudelaire's conception of the prose poem. Often an introductory section will begin quite reasonably and deceptively: "Il y a des natures purement contemplatives et tout à fait impropres à l'action, qui cependant, sous une impulsion mystérieuse et inconnue, agissent quelquefois avec une rapidité dont elles se seraient crues elles-mêmes incapables" ("Le Mauvais Vitrier"). The *cependant* and the doublets suggest a very settled mind; the prose is in the mold of the anonymous rational style we have seen in Perrault. But the glazier's cry in the street leads, on the narrator's part, to the very mysterious impulse he has spoken of, and he orders the former to come up, "non sans quelque gaîté," for "la chambre étant au sixième étage et l'escalier fort étroit, l'homme devait éprouver quelque peine à opérer son ascension et accrocher en maints endroits les angles de sa fragile marchandise." A certain contained madness expresses itself in understatement, as we find litotes: *non sans . . . quelque peine*. Increasingly there is a distance between the narrator's manic pleasure and the distant character of his language: *opérer son ascension* is like the neoclassical joining of a verbal noun to a verb (*il en fit la remarque*), except that here the verb is almost technical in feeling and the expression exact and formal. *Fragile marchandise* follows the neoclassical pattern of ennobling with an epithet, although the noun could hardly occur in a neoclassical context. The peculiar mixture represented by *opérer son ascension* and *fragile marchandise* continues as, with growing excitement, the narrator continues in his detached fashion; the following occurs after the glazier has descended again: "Je m'approchai du balcon et je me saisis d'un petit pot de fleurs, et quand l'homme reparut au débouché de la porte, je laissai tomber perpendiculairement mon engin de guerre sur le rebord postérieur de ses crochets; et le choc le renversant, il acheva de briser sous son dos toute sa pauvre fortune ambulatoire, qui rendit le bruit éclatant d'un palais de cristal crevé par la foudre." The words are maniacally precise, almost scientific, on the one hand—*perpendiculairement, rebord postérieur*—and, on the other, elevated after the neoclassical fashion—*engin de guerre, palais de cristal*. This peculiar combination of two kinds of vocabulary gives the characteristic savor of Baudelaire's prose: they have in common the avoidance of color and emotional intensity. But we must remember that Baudelaire's poem would not have its full force were it not for the context of romanticism: his style is historicized in the sense that the narrator, with his romantic violence, is a kind of classicist in language and surely abominates the *frénétique* side of nineteenth-century literature.

Although he avoids it in most of *Le Spleen de Paris*, Baudelaire was not an enemy of the elaborate romantic metaphor or simile, as we know from his verse. Indeed, in the preface to *Le Spleen de Paris*, Baudelaire compares his book at length to a snake, which, cut up, will rejoin or form a new head and tail virtually anywhere. We notice something in this comparison which is characteristic of romantic figurative language and goes against the classical tradition. Aristotle pointed out that one usually compares whatever is the immediate, first term to something larger, more general, more intense, or more elevated, the opposite being true in vituperative language. One moves a step up, so to speak. Thus eyes blaze like the sun, not the sun like an eye, unless one is personifying the cosmos. A woman's teeth can be like pearls, but not her pearl necklace like teeth. Baudelaire's comparison of his book to a snake, however, strikes one as more miscellaneous than anything else. It does not ennoble or diminish the book; it merely surprises.

The elaborate comparison is a characteristic device of romantic prose; it does not always clarify or elevate like the similes we have seen in Chartier, Rabelais, Du Vair, Boccaccio, Saint François de Sales or the less frequent ones of neoclassical prose such as *Adolphe.* Our first example is from Chateaubriand, who, in the *Avant-propos* to the *Mémoires d'outre-tombe,* shows himself a creator of effects like those of his younger contemporaries: "Ces Mémoires ont été l'objet de ma prédilection: saint Bonaventure obtint du ciel la permission de continuer les siens après sa mort; je n'espère pas une telle faveur, mais je désirerais ressusciter à l'heure des fantômes, pour corriger au moins les épreuves. Au surplus, quand l'Eternité m'aura de ses deux mains bouché les oreilles, dans la poudreuse famille des sourds, je n'entendrai plus personne." The allusion to Saint Bonaventura follows the traditional principle of elevation, but a dissonant anachronism comes from comparing the drudgery of the printing process with the saint's special favor. Moreover, the subsequent metaphor is an odd mixture of the grand style (*la poudreuse famille*) and the concrete, familiar *de ses deux mains* added to *boucher les oreilles à quelqu'un.* Chateaubriand is evolving away from his distant and noble manner toward grotesque romantic taste.

The form of romantic metaphors often makes them as unexpected as the terms of them: "Quatre-vingt-quatorze sonnait à l'horloge du dix-huitième siècle, quatre-vingt-quatorze, dont chaque minute fut sanglante et enflammée. L'an de terreur frappait horriblement et lentement au gré de la terre et du ciel, qui l'écoutaient en silence. . . . Alors les hommes s'écartaient les uns des autres, ou s'abordaient brusquement comme des combattants. Leur salut ressemblait à une attaque, leur bonjour à une injure, leur sourire à une convulsion, leur habillement aux haillons d'un mendiant, leur coiffure . . ." (Vigny, *Stello,* Chapter 20). Vigny's comparison of a century to a day might seem to be a diminishing one: a century is only a day in the larger view of human history, and therefore insignificant. But the violence of the accompanying imagery belies this, and, in any case, the day-

century metaphor is so elliptic as to be negligible, and one is supposed to think of the equivalence of a specific hour with fatal happen-
ings. The clock evokes the idea of inevitability. What we find here is
something like the *pensée neuve* of baroque conceits rather than the
elevating figurative language of classical tradition.

The elaborate metaphor appears in a comic form as well, again like
the fancies of the seventeenth century, when *métaphores filées* were acceptable provided they were witty.

> Chacun comprendra mieux l'espèce particulière à laquelle appartenait
> Poiret dans la grande famille des niais, après une remarque déjà faite par
> certains observateurs, mais qui jusqu'à présent n'a pas été publiée. Il est
> une nation plumigère, serrée au budget entre le premier degré de latitude
> qui comporte les traitements de douze cents francs, espèce de Groenland
> administratif, et le troisième degré, où commencent les traitements un peu
> plus chauds de trois à six mille, région tempérée, où s'acclimate la gratifica-
> tion, où elle fleurit malgré les difficultés de la culture.

This passage from *Le Père Goriot*, in which Balzac is trying to explain
the behavior of clerks and *petits fonctionnaires* with a geographical
simile, is very much in the neological style of the romantic era, combining a neologism of figurative language with the peculiar coinage
plumigère, to describe the birds of the cool zone with their *plumes* and
the government employees who spend their days copying things
with *plumes*. Comic metaphor is found quite widely in romantic prose,
and it is sometimes difficult for the modern reader to perceive immediately what tone is being aimed at, for the serious and the humorous
share a certain tendency toward elaboration and length. There is a
kind of irony which partakes of both, as in this sarcastic yet lyrical
speech from *Les Caprices de Marianne* (II, 1).

> Je croyais qu'il en était du vin comme des femmes. Une femme, n'est-elle
> pas aussi un vase précieux, scellé comme ce flacon de cristal? Ne renferme-
> t-elle pas une ivresse grossière ou divine, selon sa force et sa valeur? Et n'y
> a-t-il pas parmi elles le vin du peuple et les larmes du Christ? Quel miséra-
> ble cœur est-ce donc que le vôtre, pour que vos lèvres lui fassent la leçon?
> Vous ne boiriez pas le vin que boit le peuple; vous aimez les femmes qu'il
> aime; l'esprit généreux et poétique de ce flacon doré, ces sucs merveilleux
> que la lave du Vésuve a cuvés sous son ardent soleil, vous conduiront chan-
> celant et sans force dans les bras d'une fille de joie; vous rougiriez de boire

un vin grossier; votre gorge se soulèverait. Ah! vos lèvres sont délicates, mais votre cœur s'enivre à bon marché.

Musset's comparison is in the baroque taste for surprising, insistent logic. The conceit lies in the lengthy equivalence of a bottle of wine and a woman, which is a reversal of usual values in that wine turns out to be more precious than a human being, the one being lachrymae Christi, the other a trollop. Considerable stylistic care is brought to enhancing the image of the bottle, so that the passage has a lyric quality as well as diminishing the values of Octave, to whom it is addressed.

Flaubert, we know from his correspondence, was very proud of the following comparison in *Madame Bovary*.

> Dès lors, ce souvenir de Léon fut comme le centre de son ennui; il y pétillait plus fort que, dans un steppe de Russie, un feu de voyageurs abandonné sur la neige. Elle se précipitait vers lui, elle se blottissait contre, elle remuait délicatement ce foyer près de s'éteindre, elle allait cherchant tout autour d'elle ce qui pouvait l'aviver davantage; et les réminiscences les plus lointaines comme les plus immédiates occasions, ce qu'elle éprouvait avec ce qu'elle imaginait, ses envies de volupté qui se dispersaient, ses projets de bonheur qui craquaient au vent comme des branchages morts, sa vertu stérile, ses espérances tombées, la litière domestique, elle ramassait tout, prenait tout, et faisait servir tout à réchauffer sa tristesse.
>
> Cependant les flammes s'apaisèrent, soit que la provision d'elle-même s'épuisât ou que l'entassement fût trop considérable . . . (II, 7)

There is even more to the comparison than is quoted here. The point of departure is an elevating simile, in which Emma's ennui is like the Russian steppe; the requisite vastness and tone are present, and the fire, to which the memory of Leon is compared, is usually a dignified and even vivid term of comparison for its archetypal-elemental value. The activity of feeding a fire, however, is not necessarily a grand or intense occupation, and as the material considerations of finding fuel are elaborated, the general elevation of the comparison turns into an effect more of ingeniousness. Taking it as a *pensée neuve*, one might criticize the passage, in contrast to the Vigny metaphor we have looked at, for not being sufficiently concise and brilliant. A *pensée neuve* should be surprising enough that we are not bothered by grotesque visual elements, since it is supposed to be an intellectual rather than a sensorial figure.

The peculiarities of romantic imagery and the double strain of advanced neological styles and those searching to recapture some virtue of neoclassical diction combine to form a literary era whose styles are often surprising when juxtaposed; the general reason for this is the mutiplication of curious, frequently mixed genres, to which the manner of writing has been closely adapted. Novels include the essayistic *Notre-Dame de Paris*; the mixture of expository preface, letters, and dialogue of *Mademoiselle de Maupin*; Vigny's fiction with a philosophical framework in *Stello*; the interventional *Le Rouge et le Noir*; and the oral-recounting technique of *La Chartreuse de Parme*. Romantic irony, the tendency toward a self-consciously arbitrary form or parody of other novels, is often present. The monologue acquires a new life, assuming a paradoxically autobiographical and mythic form in *Une Saison en enfer* and Nerval's *Aurélia*; the dream element of the latter is related to the oneiric *Smarra* by Nodier; and here and there in other works—*Sylvie*, *Le Rouge et le Noir*, Michelet's history of France— the monologue is employed. *Le Spleen de Paris* is a whole anthology of genres. Works in Biblical versets like Ballanche's *Vision d'Hébal* or Lamennais' *Paroles d'un croyant* are another prose form put to unexpected ends, and the play for reading, like Musset's *Comédies et Proverbes* and Flaubert's *Tentation de Saint Antoine*, is a characteristically mixed genre. A texture suggestive of on-the-spot invention provides another shade of romantic irony in many works—calculated improvisation. Such a plethora of esthetically significant prose forms cannot be matched in the eighteenth century or in the literary period just after the romantics.

The multiple forms and styles of romantic imaginative literature reveal one tendency that differentiates them from previous prose genres: they tend to create a world that is not merely an imitation of the real one, like what we find in the novel of manners. Often, this world is presented in historical terms, as in Hugo, Stendhal, Gautier, and Nerval, but the historical element is pseudo objective and could better be called mythic; the action of *Mademoiselle de Maupin*, for example, takes place in a synthesis of baroque, eighteenth-century, and romantic cultures. The element of historicism, however, provides an important point of departure for stylistic invention, as in Nerval's fantasy of an eighteenth-century pastoral world. Diverse as the concrete details of French romantic writing are, there are underlying, unifying tendencies.

11 *Flaubert*

While working on *Madame Bovary*, Flaubert read a volume by Michelet and made the following comment: "J'ai lu, avant-hier, tout un volume du père Michelet, le sixième de sa *Révolution*, qui vient de paraître. Il y a des jets exquis, de grands mots, des choses justes; presque toutes sont neuves. Mais point de plan, point d'art. Ce n'est pas clair, c'est encore moins calme, et le calme est le caractère de la beauté, comme la sérénité l'est de l'innocence, de la vertu. Le repos est attitude de Dieu" (letter to Louise Colet, September 12, 1853). Flaubert's remarks are applicable to a number of romantic prose writers, such as Gautier, Stendhal, Hugo, Musset, and Balzac. We observe Flaubert's customary conception of style as not embodied in the striking phrase or passage but as a large, sustained movement inseparable from the notion of general form or *plan*. In his overall characterization of the greatest writing as serene, we see how Flaubert conceives of high style, and his is, indeed, the first important such notion of style in the nineteenth century after Chateaubriand's.

When Flaubert indicated what he did not like in prose, it was not, however, the agitated romantic styles that offended him; rather, it was the *style coulant*, the term and the thing epitomizing bourgeois notions of fine writing. Well before he reached his first mature style in *Madame Bovary*, Flaubert had identified the flowing style as a false ideal, and it is significant that his first thinking about prose concerned rhythm, not imagery or level of style.[1] In reading aloud, Flaubert ignored stagey effects of expression and concentrated his efforts on the definition of intonational phrases.[2] In *Bovary* the gov-

1. See Flaubert's letter of June 7, 1844, to Louis de Cormenin.
2. See Emile Zola, *Les Romanciers naturalistes*, in *Oeuvres complètes* (Paris: Bernouard, 1927), XXXVI, 216.

erning principle of style he worked out was the syntactico-rhythmic one of segmentation, with an attendant concern for variety in movement. Any page of *Bovary* contains sentences with numerous rhythmic pauses marked by commas, and a little analysis will show that Flaubert also likes the contrastful element of heterocolon, when it can be conveniently obtained; in this respect his prose differs basically from Chateaubriand's. To break up a French sentence into small phrases and to avoid a flowing effect, it is useful to introduce modifiers, of which adverbial ones are especially helpful, provided that they be placed exactly where one would never put them in speech or traditional prose: "Les carreaux, chaque matin, étaient chargés de givre, et la lumière, blanchâtre à travers eux, comme par des verres dépolis, quelquefois ne variait pas de la journée" (I, 9). The sentence receives its characteristic Flaubertian sound from the positioning of adverbs between subject and verb, and, to a lesser extent, from the rhythmically detached adjective modifying *lumière*. In addition, the second clause contains an almost hyperbatic effect; the abundance of material between subject and verb places the latter near the end of the sentence, after a kind of suspension, such as we saw in examples of much earlier French prose. The whole might best be characterized as belonging to a new era of postnatural word order, in which hyperbatic adverbial expressions between subject and verb and multiple indications of time and place are frequent: "La nouvelle bonne obéissait sans murmure pour n'être point renvoyée; et, comme Madame, d'habitude, laissait la clef au buffet, Félicité, chaque soir, prenait une petite provision de sucre qu'elle mangeait toute seule, dans son lit, après avoir fait sa prière" (I, 9). Sometimes Flaubert chooses a sequence of complements for the verb which one would be hard put to arrange in a normal-sounding order, keeping them all: "Elle décachetait ses lettres, épiait ses démarches et l'écoutait, à travers la cloison, donner ses consultations, dans son cabinet, quand il y avait des femmes" (I, 1). The essential adverbial clause is allowed to dangle like some element optional for the sense, and the multiplication of prepositional phrases is typical, because they lend themselves to segmentation. "Il la voyait par derrière, dans la glace, entre deux flambeaux" (I, 8).

Asyndeton is an excellent method of bringing about segmentation:

"Emma devenait difficile, capricieuse" (I, 9). Aside from the fact that the asyndetic construction has special shades of sense, as one can see by substituting *difficile et capricieuse* for it, the juxtaposition eliminates one of the commonest forms of balance and symmetry, the *A and B* construction, increasing the asymmetrical quality we can feel in our previous examples of sentence structure. With Flaubert begins a great era of asyndetic constructions, which had been growing in frequency in preceding decades. Of course, asyndeton would not have its values if it did not contrast with the regular serial form, and Flaubert, as we have already seen in the sentence beginning *Elle décachetait*, employs *A, B, and C*, though frequently in combinations with asyndeton: "Elle dévorait, sans en rien passer, tous les comptes rendus de premières représentations, de courses et de soirées, s'intéressait au début d'une chanteuse, à l'ouverture d'un magasin" (I, 9); "Enjouée jadis, expansive et tout aimante, elle était, en vieillissant, devenue (à la façon du vin éventé qui se tourne en vinaigre) d'humeur difficile, piaillarde, nerveuse" (I, 1). Here we see a typical effect of asyndeton: *dévorait* and *s'intéressait* have an air of random activities, not of an exhaustive indication like *dévorait et s'intéressait*. The three adjectives (*difficile* . . .) overlap somewhat, another nuance of asyndeton.[3] The various assertions that have been made about the triadic pattern in romantic prose tend to overlook the fact that what distinguishes prose in the nineteenth century, especially in and after Flaubert, is the very free combination of twos and threes in regular and asyndetic form. The following examples are distinctly exceptional.

> Les garnitures de dentelles, les broches de diamants, les bracelets à médaillon frissonnaient aux corsages, scintilaient aux poitrines, bruissaient sur les bras nus.
>
> . . . .
>
> Un homme, au contraire, ne devait-il pas tout connaître, exceller en des activités multiples, vous initier aux énergies de la passion, aux raffinements de la vie, à tous les mystères? Mais il n'enseignait rien, celui-là, ne savait rien, ne souhaitait rien. Il la croyait heureuse; et elle lui en voulait de ce calme si bien assis, de cette pesanteur sereine, du bonheur même qu'elle lui donnait. (I, 8)

3. See Marcelle-Denise Hubert, *Effets stylistiques de la construction asyndétique dans quelques œuvres du 18e, 19e, et 20e siècle* (Zurich: Juris Verlag, 1967). According to this study, elements in asyndeton are not exhaustive, not present at the same time, or not on the same plane.

The first sentence employs a rhetorical device of distribution of subjects and verbs, confined for the most part to sixteenth- and seventeenth-century poetry. The first sentence of the second example would represent a usage suggested by Chateaubriand and La Bruyère, were it not for the peculiar persistence of the triad in the next two sentences, which gives the whole passage an exceptional, mannered quality. In *L'Education sentimentale* we find nothing so odd in serial usage; *Madame Bovary*, in certain respects, shows experimentation with effects Flaubert was later to give up.

Sometimes with so few as three elements of a kind, Flaubert creates distinctive one-time constructions: "Elle lui interdit les bonnets de coton, lui apprit qu'il fallait vous parler à la troisième personne, apporter un verre d'eau dans une assiette, frapper aux portes avant d'entrer, et à repasser, à empeser, à l'habiller, voulut en faire sa femme de chambre" (I, 9). It would take a diagram to describe neatly such syntax. When more than three in a series occurs, still more possibilities are open, and Flaubert further develops the device of the irregularly constructed series, which La Bruyère was the first to devise and which Chateaubriand used in the prologue to *Atala*. In the following example, Flaubert complicates the enumeration with a semicolon in the middle and varied treatment of the verbs as they are transitive or intransitive: "Elle allait chez les avoués, chez le président, se rappelait l'échéance des billets, obtenait des retards; et, à la maison, repassait, cousait, blanchissait, surveillait les ouvriers, soldait les mémoires, tandis que, sans s'inquiéter de rien, Monsieur, continuellement engourdi dans une somnolence boudeuse dont il ne se réveillait que pour dire des choses désobligeantes, restait à fumer au coin du feu, en crachant dans les cendres" (I, 1). The complexly varied series is more interesting than a normal one; the semicolon prevents the sequence from progressing mechanically; and, finally, the massive main clause is the climax of a paragraph of verbs having Madame Bovary *mère* for subject and contrasting with the single *restait* characterizing her husband.

This last example contains much that is noteworthy besides the series: the *tandis que* is a common alternative to *mais*, *et*, or a semicolon in joining clauses; the final image exemplifies Flaubert's concern for the concluding words of a sentence, and, finally, there is a distinct effect of suspension created by the abundance of material between *tandis que* and *restait*. Sometimes the suspension occurs in an independent clause merely from the accumulation of adjectival and adverbial modifiers before the verb or, as here, before the subject and verb: "Et alors, sur la grande route qui étendait sans en finir son long ruban de poussière, par les chemins creux où les arbres se courbaient en berceaux, dans les sentiers dont les blés lui montaient jusqu'aux genoux, avec le soleil sur ses épaules et l'air du matin à ses narines, le cœur plein des félicités de la nuit, l'esprit tranquille, la chair contente, il s'en allait ruminant son bonheur, comme ceux qui mâchent encore, après dîner, le goût des truffes qu'ils digèrent" (I, 5). What distinguishes this sentence is not only the extraordinary number of modifiers preceding the grammatical nucleus but the *et* Flaubert felt suitable at the beginning of it. The sentence concludes a paragraph and represents Flaubert's great fondness for tying together clauses with what has been called an *et de mouvement*, which does not necessarily join things on the same plane at all. Furthermore, the *et* is commonly preceded by a semicolon—stronger than a mere comma—and followed by a comma introducing a modifier: "Elle renversa son cou blanc, qui se gonflait d'un soupir; et, défaillante, tout en pleurs, avec un long frémissement et se cachant la figure, elle s'abandonna" (II, 9). The *et* is thrown into relief by the punctuation, heterocolon is emphasized, and the element of suspension in the final clause is distinctly increased by the presence of a linked preceding clause.

It is often said that Flaubert favored ternary groups of clauses, such as the following: "Il faisait chaud, l'enfant s'endormait; et le bonhomme, s'assoupissant les mains sur son ventre, ne tardait pas à ronfler, la bouche ouverte" (I, 1). Certainly such sentences are not characteristic of Chateaubriand, Hugo, or any earlier user of triple constructions. Flaubert's grammar here has, however, an element of ambiguity: according to ordinary grammar the compound sentence is triadic; but a present participle can count as much as a finite verb in another method of syntactic analysis—a situation underscored by the phrasing here—and so from that point of view, the sentence is quadripartite. Actually, there is no absolute statistical dominance of the ternary in Flaubert; what is more characteristic is the formula *; plus et*

<u>plus</u> , or part of it, followed by a modifier before the last main verb. (A peculiarity of the formula is the use of the semicolon before *et*, creating a stronger pause than the normal comma.) The modifier may be a clause: "Charles, par galanterie, se précipita et, comme il allongeait aussi son bras dans le même mouvement, il sentit sa poitrine effleurer le dos de la jeune fille, courbée sous lui" (I, 2). This bipartite sentence constitutes a verbal triad. Sometimes there are variations with ellipsis: "Une fois, il manqua la visite, le lendemain son cours, et, savourant la paresse, peu à peu, n'y retourna plus" (I, 1). *Mais* may be substituted for *et*: "Ils venaient se délaisser dans les beaux-arts des inquiétudes de la vente; mais, n'oubliant point les *affaires*, ils causaient encore cotons, trois-six, ou indigo" (II, 15). As many as four or five verbs are sometimes used: "Le *boc* de Charles s'arrêta devant le perron du milieu, des domestiques parurent, le Marquis s'avança, et, offrant son bras à la femme du médecin, l'introduisit dans le vestibule" (I, 8). From the rhythmic viewpoint these series are commonly arranged in clauses of increasing length: "On était au commencement d'avril, quand les primevères sont écloses; un vent tiède se roule sur les plates-bandes labourées, et les jardins, comme des femmes, semblent faire leur toilette pour les fêtes de l'été" (II, 6). Here we recognize the Chateaubrianesque use, sporadic in Flaubert, of a long final phrase divided syntactically in the center (*semblent faire . . .* is one of those alexandrines with cesura belying the notion that verse lines are avoided in French prose). This example has a modifier, but not a verbal one before the *semblent faire* phrase; all manner of variations are possible, such as the introduction of subordinate clauses before the conjunction (*cf. elle renversa . . .* above), but the essential unity of the sentence type is assured by the *et* or *mais* as a sign of compounding. This is Flaubert's major sentence form, one by which we recognize his prose; and, however frequent the division into three, the number of elements is less regular than the fact of the coordinating conjunction or *et de mouvement* settling us into the concluding section, with its air of saying something definitive, of reaching the end of a certain order of actions, impressions, or ideas. This solid use of the conjunction in a clause sequence of *A and B* or *A, B, and C* contrasts interestingly with Flaubert's fondness for asyndeton

with words in twos or a series; while asyndetic clause sequences exist in Flaubert, the hesitant or dramatic character of asyndeton is reserved usually for another type of sentence. Both handlings of series, however, as well as the placing of modifiers, give one that strong feeling of craft and control we associate with Flaubert's prose.

Just as Flaubert varied his favorite sentence form, he also was greatly concerned with variety in the sequence of sentences, so that a paragraph often has a distinctive pattern. We have already seen the conclusion to the paragraph about Charles' mother's activities in contrast to his father's idleness. A paragraph devoted to the father illustrates a typical kind of variety.

> Son père, M. Charles-Denis-Bartholomé Bovary, ancien aide-chirurgien-major, compromis, vers 1812, dans des affaires de conscription, et forcé, vers cette époque, de quitter le service, avait alors profité de ses avantages personnels pour saisir au passage une dot de soixante mille francs, qui s'offrait en la fille d'un marchand bonnetier, devenue amoureuse de sa tournure. Bel homme, hâbleur, faisant sonner haut ses éperons, portant des favoris rejoints aux moustaches, les doigts toujours garnis de bagues et habillé de couleurs voyantes, il avait l'aspect d'un brave avec l'entrain facile d'un commis voyageur. Une fois marié, il vécut deux ou trois ans sur la fortune de sa femme, dînant bien, se levant tard, fumant dans de grandes pipes en porcelaine, ne rentrant le soir qu'après le spectacle et fréquentant les cafés. (I, 1)

The first two sentences contain a string of modifiers, much segmented, before the verb; however, the position of the subject with regard to the modifiers changes from one to the other sentence. In the third sentence, the accumulated modifiers come after the verb: nothing is more characteristic of Flaubert than the concern we have already seen in the prologue to *Atala* for varying the position of the various elements of the sentence.

As also in *Atala*, we find that Flaubert gives especial attention to the beginning of his sentences. Descriptions, for example, typically contain the diversified elements *on* plus *verb*, *il y avait*, *c'était*, and an inversion of subject and verb: "*C'était* une ferme de bonne apparence. *On voyait* dans les écuries, par le dessus des portes ouvertes, de gros chevaux de labour qui mangeaient tranquillement dans des râteliers neufs. Le long des bâtiments *s'étendait un large fumier*, de la buée s'en élevait, et, parmi les poules et les dindons, *picoraient* dessus *cinq ou six paons*, luxe des basses-cours cauchoises. La bergerie était longue, la grange était haute, à murs lisses comme la main. *Il y avait* sous le hangar deux grandes charrettes . . ." (I, 2). These are Flaubert's basic tools for description, and, it must be said, their recurrence in *Madame Bovary* verges on the mannered. Another characteristic device is to vary nouns and pronouns and the kind of pronoun at the beginning of clauses in series; this example is from *L'Education sentimentale*: "*Beaucoup* de bourgeois avaient des imaginations pareilles; *on* croyait que des hommes, dans les catacombes, allaient faire sauter le faubourg Saint-Germain; des rumeurs s'échappaient des caves; *il* se passait aux fenêtres des choses suspectes" (III, 2).

We have incidentally seen some of the striking examples of the *chute de phrase* in Flaubert: the image of Charles' father spitting into the fire, his unexpected resemblance to a *commis voyageur*, and the moment when Emma *s'abandonna*. Just as the *et de mouvement* and suspensions at the beginning of a clause heighten the later elements of the sentence, Flaubert chooses frequently to use striking words at the end as well: "Pour lui épargner de la dépense, sa mère lui envoyait chaque semaine, par le messager, un morceau de veau cuit au four, avec quoi il déjeunait le matin, quand il était rentré de l'hôpital, tout en battant la semelle contre le mur. Ensuite il fallait courir aux leçons, à l'amphithéâtre, à l'hospice, et revenir chez lui, à travers toutes les rues. Le soir, après le maigre dîner de son propriétaire, il remontait à sa chambre et se remettait au travail, dans ses habits mouillés qui fumaient sur son corps, devant le poêle rougi" (I, 1). The unity of this paragraph lies in the use of images at the end of the sentences, which are, furthermore, synecdoches, standing for a whole complex of mood and feeling.

Recurrent sentence structures, the principle of variation, devices like the image at the *chute de phrase*—what one might call Flaubert's rhetoric, in short—serve as elements of unity, of course; but the need of elements of unity is a special matter in *Bovary*, compared with most previous fiction. Much of the dialogue is frankly in clichés; whole episodes are conceived of as an exchange of banalities, like Emma's approaching the priest in II, 6. Between these ironic passages and the most poetic descriptions in the novel lie the realistic descriptive passages and Emma's daydreams, both often somewhat ironic and related at once to the poetic and to the banal. The sentence structure serves as a common element effectuating transitions among all the nondialogue sections. For example, Emma's fantasy about her coming life with Rodolphe is cast, in part, in elegant ternary sentences: "Ils se promèneraient en gondole, ils se balanceraient en hamac; et leur existence serait facile et large comme leurs vêtements de soie, toute chaude et étoilée comme les nuits douces qu'ils contempleraient. Cependant, sur l'immensité de cet avenir qu'elle se faisait apparaître, rien de particulier ne surgissait; les jours, tous magnifiques, se ressemblaient comme des flots; et cela se balançait à l'horizon, infini, harmonieux, bleuâtre et couvert de soleil" (II, 12). There is something ambiguous here: a blend of genuine sumptuousness and facile lyricism that risks confusing the reader. In fact, Flaubert was so aware of this double aspect of much of the novel that he, intrusively, devotes a paragraph to the notion of language; it concludes thus.

> Parce que des lèvres libertines ou vénales lui [à Rodolphe] avaient murmuré des phrases pareilles, il ne croyait que faiblement à la candeur de celles-là; on en devait rabattre, pensait-il, les discours exagérés cachant les affections médiocres; comme si la plénitude de l'âme ne débordait pas quelquefois par les métaphores les plus vides, puisque personne, jamais, ne peut donner l'exacte mesure de ses besoins, ni de ses conceptions, ni de ses douleurs, et que la parole humaine est comme un chaudron fêlé où nous battons des mélodies à faire danser les ours, quand on voudrait attendrir les étoiles. (II, 12)

The unexpected cluster of hypotactic constructions along with the simile give great prominence to these lines, and they are among the most important of Flaubert's theoretical statements about *Madame Bovary*. To a certain degree, the images of romanticism became banalized so that what started out as unusual and fresh language turned into a particularly undesirable form of cliché. The more that romantic language had aspired to renovate literature, the more offensive its kinds of expressions, fallen a prey to inept imitation, turned out to be. Most problematic for the writer are thoughts and images that retain something of their original lyricism while the process of devaluation is already underway. Here Flaubert, recognizing the difficulty inherent in language like Emma and Rodolphe's, seems to lead one away from words proper into a consideration of motive or psychological authenticity. This curious passage also suggests, by its form, the peculiar function figurative language plays in the novel.

There are elements of rhetoric that by their absence contribute to the consistency of the texture of *Madame Bovary*: antithesis is rare, as are anaphora and parallel clauses; isocolon is incidental, not systematic; asymmetry dominates. However, one traditional figure very much present is metaphor, or the simile, in such an insistent form as is not common in prose immediately before the romantic period. Flaubert's images often derive from traditional categories—animals and storms are the most frequent—but they tend to exhibit a certain detail not common in prose.

> Si Charles l'avait voulu cependant, s'il s'en fût douté, si son regard, une seule fois, fût venu à la rencontre de sa pensée, il lui semblait qu'une abondance subite se serait détachée de son coeur, comme tombe la récolte d'un espalier quand on y porte la main.
> . . . .
> Mais elle, sa vie était froide comme un grenier dont la lucarne est au nord, et l'ennui, araignée silencieuse, filait sa toile dans l'ombre à tous les coins de son coeur. (I, 7)

> Son voyage à la Vaubyessard avait fait un trou dans sa vie, à la manière de ces grandes crevasses qu'un orage, en une seule nuit, creuse quelquefois dans les montagnes. (I, 8)

> Au fond de son âme, cependant, elle attendait un événement. Comme les matelots en détresse, elle promenait sur la solitude de sa vie des yeux désespérés, cherchant au loin quelque voile blanche dans les brumes de l'horizon. Elle ne savait pas quel serait ce hasard, le vent qui le pousserait jusqu'à elle, vers quel rivage il la mènerait, s'il était chaloupe ou vaisseau à trois ponts, chargé d'angoisses ou plein de félicités. (I, 9)

Flaubert's images are variously rare, commonplace, grotesque, elegant, and so forth, much in the fashion of Victor Hugo's imagery between *Les Orientales* (1829) and *Les Rayons et les Ombres* (1840). These volumes, which had a decisive effect on Flaubert's notions of simile and metaphor, exhibit a tendency toward multiplication of detail beyond the strictly necessary. The following extracts are from Hugo's *Les Feuilles d'automne*.

[There pours on his head:]
Comme les feuilles d'arbre au vent de la tempête
Cette neige des jours qui blanchit notre tête. ("A M. Louis B.")

Il [le peuple] sait tirer de tout d'austères jugements,
Tant le marteau de fer des grands événements
A, dans ces durs cerveaux qu'il façonnait sans cesse,
Comme un coin dans le chêne enfoncé la sagesse! ("Rêveries")

Le ciel, bleu pavillon par Dieu même construit,
Qui, le jour, emplissant de plis d'azur l'espace
Semble un dais suspendu sur le soleil qui passe,
Et dont on ne peut voir les clous d'or que la nuit. ("Bièvre")

Hugo particularizes his images as much as possible, not merely being content with hair being snowy white, wisdom beaten into thick brains, and the stars resembling gold studs. Images that may have their source in some traditional comparison are elaborated in a way unknown for a century and a half before.

The presence of metaphor and simile in *Madame Bovary* is linked to a special problem in style. In many places Flaubert uses the representational technique by which the reader must divine the character's feeling from description. This is often considered his major innovation in fictional technique and is exemplified by the section wherein Charles repeatedly visits the farm before actually becoming engaged to Emma. Representation, however, or "showing," is not a concise technique, and Flaubert frequently resorts to the comments on feelings and summaries that are termed "psychological analysis" in French. Yet Flaubert clearly felt the pure analytic style to be lacking in poetry and color, so in most cases it is analysis that entails the use of metaphor and simile in the novel.

The savor of romantic poetry that Flaubert is credited with having introduced into the novel goes beyond the presence of metaphor and simile, however; it is found in descriptions such as that of the sky after Léon's departure from Yonville or the last evening Rodolphe and Emma spend together.

Ils [les nuages] s'amoncelaient au couchant, du côté de Rouen, et roulaient vite leurs volutes noires, d'où dépassaient par derrière les grandes lignes du soleil, comme les flèches d'or d'un trophée suspendu, tandis que le reste du ciel vide avait la blancheur d'une porcelaine. Mais une rafale de vent fit se courber les peupliers, et tout à coup la pluie tomba; elle crépitait sur les feuilles vertes. Puis le soleil reparut, les poules chantèrent, des moineaux battaient des ailes dans les buissons humides, et les flaques d'eau sur le sable emportaient en s'écoulant les fleurs roses d'un acacia. (II, 6)

La lune, toute ronde et couleur de pourpre, se levait à ras de terre, au fond de la prairie. Elle montait vite entre les branches des peupliers, qui la cachaient de place en place, comme un rideau noir, troué. Puis elle parut éclatante de blancheur, dans le ciel vide qu'elle éclairait; et alors, se ralentissant, elle laissa tomber sur la rivière une grande tache, qui faisait une infinité d'étoiles; et cette lueur d'argent semblait s'y tordre jusqu'au fond, à la manière d'un serpent sans tête couvert d'écailles lumineuses. Cela ressemblait aussi à quelque monstrueux candélabre d'où ruisselaient, tout du long, des gouttes de diamant en fusion. (II, 12)

These magnificent passages constitute a problem in interpretation which is not always correctly envisaged: Flaubert has with great care explained that Emma is "de tempérament plus sentimentale qu'artiste, cherchant des émotions et non des paysages" (I, 6). Indeed, clichés are more to Emma's taste than grand language in Flaubert's manner; her preference in poetry is not for Hugo's verse but for Lamartine's, which is often pallid. The descriptions belong to high romantic poetry, but Emma has no high romantic poetic experiences. In other words, these passages represent not the landscape Emma sees or at least sees in all its beauty; they are there for the reader, as a means of communicating between Flaubert and his audience that circumvents the characters. The seduction scene with Rodolphe is a peculiarly arresting example: in its four pages the landscape moves from having a sky like a pale lake with black rocks through a setting of brown light and russet, gold, tawny, and tobacco-colored leaves alternating with patches of violets, and ends with the red evening. But Emma, we know, is not contemplating the melancholy landscape; she is overwhelmed by the great change in her life that has her inwardly repeating, "J'ai un amant! un amant!" The fact is that Emma is not only not of an esthetic temperament, she is not given to the rich melancholy Flaubert's descriptive prose often conveys; spleen, boredom, and catatonic depression are more her lot when she is discouraged.

Even Emma's hallucinatory experiences seem more calculated to interest the reader nurtured on romantic poetry than to render her in-many-ways-dull mind: "Dans l'avenue, un jour vert rabattu par le feuillage éclairait la mousse rase qui craquait doucement sous ses pieds. Le soleil se couchait; le ciel était rouge entre les branches, et les troncs pareils des arbres plantés en ligne droite semblaient une colonnade brune se détachant sur un fond d'or; une peur la prenait, elle appelait Djali, s'en retournait vite à Tostes par la grande route, s'affaissait dans un fauteuil, et de toute la soirée ne parlait pas" (I, 7). This extraordinary passage hardly represents color as we actually see it; Flaubert's technique is almost expressionistic. In Emma's hallucinatory visions toward the end of the novel, especially that of globules of fire just before her suicide (III, 8), we encounter a grandeur not present in the depiction of her daydreams and find Emma's life raised to a higher plane that Flaubert obviously meant us to take as tragic. This ambiguity about the seriousness and significance of Emma's fate stems from the two extremes of language: the ironic one of the daydreams and the visionary one of hallucinations. While her daydreams, with their frequent clichés, tend to be presented as inauthentic experience, the hallucinations are perfectly serious; they are not a debased mental activity.

At the same time, there is no ultimate disparity of style in *Madame Bovary*. The fact is that in all examples of representational technique the language does not render a character's sensibility so much as it reveals the author's, even if in an ironic form. As a work like *Madame Bovary* recedes in time, its style has ceased to seem like a neutral psychological medium through which Emma's world is conveyed and shows itself as a Flaubert-language, in which every word is part of the continuity of his sense of life. No better demonstration exists of Flaubert's dominating the novel than the scenes which Emma does not see: the white bits of paper on red clover at the end of III, 1, the day of her burial, or Charles' melancholy gazing through the window when he is a student: "Dans les beaux soirs d'été, à l'heure où les rues tièdes sont vides, quand les servantes jouent au volant sur le seuil des portes, il ouvrait sa fenêtre et s'accoudait. La rivière, qui fait de ce quartier de Rouen comme une ignoble petite Venise, coulait en bas, sous lui, jaune, violette ou bleue, entre ses ponts et ses grilles. . . . En face, au-delà des toits, le grand ciel pur s'étendait, avec le soleil rouge se couchant. Qu'il devait faire bon là-bas!" (I, 1). Venice has nothing to do with Charles' thoughts and preoccupations as we see them elsewhere, and the stance at the window is pure Emma. In other words, the passage fits the tonality of the novel perfectly but hardly represents Charles as an individual.

Continuity of style, then, is a principle taking precedence over the depiction of Charles and Emma, and we see in our last examples some of its characteristics: the verb brilliantly placed at the end of a paragraph (*ne parlait pas*), an inimitable sequence of complements after the verb (*coulait* . . .), the systematic use of unusual present participles to avoid multiplication of relative clauses (*le soleil rouge se couchant*), and the use of as many as three adverbial elements at the beginning of the sentence (*Dans les beaux soirs* . . .). When Flaubert started working on *Madame Bovary*, and as he kept working out what were to be his characteristic stylistic touches, he lamented frequently in his letters that he was not writing in his "natural" style, the one he had used in the early version of *La Tentation de Saint Antoine*.[4] This, like his complaints about the subject matter—which, as he said elsewhere, should not matter to an artist—constituted a self-defense in case *Madame Bovary* should not turn out as he hoped; but, as he worked, periods of cheerfulness interrupted the *affres du style*, and he even came to see that *La Tentation* was a poor piece of writing. The natural style he so frequently told himself and his correspondent about quietly vanished from consideration when it became evident that *Madame Bovary* was an utterly superior piece of work. It disappeared so completely that in *Salammbô*, where one would expect Flaubert's earlier, "oriental" style, he continued to use the stylistic devices of *Madame Bovary*. The reader may feel a certain malaise at finding the sentence structures of *Bovary* fitted out with garnerings from Carthaginian archeology; for *L'Education sentimentale*, however, Flaubert did some rethinking about style.

Of course, certain basic principles do not change in Flaubert's books after *Madame Bovary*. He remained sensitive to the clatter of *qui* and

4. See, for example, the letter of June 1, 1853, to Louise Colet. For Flaubert's later view, see the letter of late July or early August, 1856, to Louis Bouilhet.

que, choosing often to substitute present participles for relative clauses in a way unknown in the previous two centuries of French prose; *le soleil se couchant* and analogous expressions sometimes seem like merely idiosyncratic variations and sometimes have a hard-to-define grammatical beauty. The period frequently contains no hypotactic elements, the avoidance of explanations in representational narrative technique diminishing the need for subordinate clauses. Sometimes there are new prepositional substitutes for clauses, as in "Mais les hommes de Caussidière, avec leur sabre et leur écharpe, l'effrayaient un peu."[5] In general, however, Flaubert does not lean to an excessively nominal syntax in which finite verbs are avoided. Despite seemingly anticipatory expressions in *Bovary* like *Il y eut une agitation sur l'estrade* or *les lendemains de mariage ont de plus suaves paresses,* the verbal noun and the plural of nouns not normally taking a plural do not increase in Flaubert's later work, as they increased in French prose generally after 1860. Flaubert, like Hugo, was an early user of such constructions, but their occurrence is quite exceptional. Only once in a while, as in a phrase like *le reflet des ors décorant la nervure des penditifs* (*Education sentimentale,* III, 4), does the combination of the odd plural with the peculiar participle and the rare substantives suggest the eccentric art-prose of the later nineteenth century.

In general there is less minute segmentation of the sentence in *L'Education sentimentale* than before, and adverbial expressions are placed less often directly after the subject. Metaphors and similes become uncommon, and there is a certain increase in phrase length. These features cohere in a new continuity of style, which, like that of *Bovary,* takes precedence over all technical questions of point of view in fiction and even, interestingly, of representational narrative method itself.

The larger number of characters, the important ideological subject matter forming a counterbalance to Frédéric's sentimental education, make the gradual revelation of character we see in *Madame Bovary* impracticable in the later novel. Psychological commentary is frequent and found from the beginning; we know that Frédéric is enthusiastic

5. See Marcel Cressot, *La Phrase et le Vocabulaire de J.-K. Huysmans* (Paris: Droz, 1938), 58–59. One alternative form of the sentence could be *Mais le sabre et l'écharpe que portaient les hommes de Caussidière l'effrayaient un peu.*

and melancholy. Since his background and verbal culture are superior to Emma's, there is little need of the tentative, exploratory method used in the earlier novel. Nor are Frédéric's fits of boredom and despondency at such a vague, generalized level of consciousness as Emma's; it is usually quite clear what, in the realm of possibility, might relieve them. Finally, the irony is of a different, less mordant kind than that of *Madame Bovary*: whereas there is an extreme discrepancy between Emma's social condition and her dreams, Frédéric is a privileged person whose aspirations are by no means out of keeping with his station in life. Even his exotic daydreams, for example, are not impossibilities: in later life he travels, like Flaubert, to what appears to be Italy, Greece, and the Near East. Irony in *L'Education sentimentale* comes from the ambiguous relative value of Frédéric's experiences and, in the case of his friends, from the contrast between ideology and human nature.

If representational narrative is not consistently the means of rendering Frédéric's consciousness, another kind of representation assumes enormous importance in *L'Education sentimentale*: the conveying of movement through rhythmic means. While it has been claimed that there are imitative effects of sound in *Madame Bovary*, these are far more elusive than the rendering of a ship's movement, carriages stopping and starting, a crowd's various actions, fencing motions, a train arriving at a station, and so forth. The first page of *L'Education sentimentale* contains an especially brilliant example of imitative sound: "Des gens arrivaient hors d'haleine; des barriques, des câbles, des corbeilles de linge gênaient la circulation; les matelots ne répondaient à personne; on se heurtait; les colis montaient entre les deux tambours, et le tapage s'absorbait dans le bruissement de la vapeur, qui, s'échappant par des plaques de tôle, enveloppait tout d'une nuée blanchâtre, tandis que la cloche, en avant, tintait sans discontinuer." Flaubert makes careful distinctions between the cumulative period, in which sentences are separated by semicolons, and disjunct actions marked by periods. Here we are building up to the ship's departure. The short phrases through *les colis . . .* render breathlessness, the chaos on the deck, and bluntly bumping into someone. With the *et* comes the hiss and release of steam: a long clause of fifteen syllables is followed by two medium length ones (*s'échappant* . . .; *enveloppait* . . .) for additional whistles of steam. The bell sound is contained in the nasal vowels and nasal consonants of *tinter* and *discontinuer*.

Flaubert's entertainment is not over yet, however. First a one-sentence paragraph depicts, with a long phrase after shorter ones, the ship's gliding out into and up the river: "Enfin le navire partit; et les deux berges, peuplées de magasins, de chantiers et d'usines, filèrent comme deux larges rubans que l'on déroule."

Next some quiet comes in short phrases followed by a long phrase depicting smoke: "Le tumulte s'apaisait; tous avaient pris leur place; quelques-uns, debout, se chauffaient autour de la machine, et la cheminée crachait avec un râle lent et rhythmique son panache de fumée noire; des gouttelettes de rosée coulaient sur les cuivres; le pont tremblait sous une petite vibration intérieure, et les deux roues, tournant rapidement, battaient l'eau." The splash of water is conveyed by the concluding short phrases.

We must elaborate briefly on the principles of Flaubert's phrasing. While relativity is important in one's perception of phrase lengths, and sense and tone certainly contribute to one's impression, I would say that here short and long phrases lie on either side of a mean of ten syllables. With the long ones we have a further distinction to make. When intonational phrases break without a pause, Flaubert uses no punctuation; this is, of course, true most of all with the break between a substantial noun subject and its verb, where the shift of phrasing (marked often by a comma in the seventeenth century) entails no pause. In general, in *L'Education sentimentale* the really long sequences of words without commas consist of phrases continuous in time, much like the phrases meeting at the unpunctuated cesura of many classically constructed alexandrines. I shall refer, however, for convenience, to anything enclosed in punctuation marks as one phrase. For Flaubert the comma, and even more so the semicolon, is not a casual, conventional unemphatic sign but an important articulation of rhythm and sense. When we encounter a commaless clause like *et la cheminée crachait avec un râle lent et rhythmique son panache de fumée noire*, its three sections, which depict the long plume of smoke, must be connected.

The relation of syntax and rhythm is nicely illustrated by the paragraph immediately following the above one: "La rivière était bordée par des grèves de sables. On rencontrait des trains de bois qui se mettaient à onduler sous le remous des vagues, ou bien, dans un bateau sans voiles, un homme assis pêchait; puis les brumes errantes se fondirent, le soleil parut, la colline qui suivait à droite le cours de la Seine peu à peu s'abaissa, et il en surgit une autre, plus proche, sur la rive opposée." The first unemphatic sentences with imperfect tenses conclude with short equal phrases, in an alexandrine cadence. But a great sense of movement follows; in phrases of widely varying lengths, *passé simple* verbs are grouped in close pairs. The phrasing, in conjunction with the verbs, is designed to suggest first speed (*fondirent, parut*), then a suspenseful tension broken by the shifting of hills from one bank to another; quiet returns at the end. Although the boat perhaps moves no faster, the changing banks give the sense of heightened motion. The stylistic method is one of contrasting phrase lengths sharpened by punctual tenses.

Elsewhere tense and phrase length are used for similar effect: "Un coupé bleu, attelé d'un cheval noir, stationnait devant le perron. La portière s'ouvrit, une dame y monta et la voiture, avec un bruit sourd, se mit à rouler sur le sable." The carriage stops at the concierge's loge and Frédéric looks inside it: "Les vêtements de la dame l'emplissaient; il s'échappait de cette petite boîte capitonnée un parfum d'iris et comme une vague senteur d'élégances féminines. Le cocher lâcha les rênes, le cheval frôla la borne brusquement, et tout disparut." As Frédéric inhales the scent of Mme Dambreuse's boudoir-vehicle, the phrase lengthens, only to end with her departure in short phrases and *passé simple* verbs. In two substantial passages in *L'Education sentimentale*, Flaubert describes, with rhythmic devices, carriages filling the Champs-Elysées, coming to a halt in the jam, and starting to move once more (I, 3, and II, 4).

The indications furnished by punctuation can be significant, as in this series of mostly short phrases (the populace has entered the Tuileries Palace in the 1848 revolution): "On n'entendait plus que les piétinements de tous les souliers, avec le clapotement des voix. La foule inoffensive se contentait de regarder. Mais, de temps à autre, un

coude trop à l'étroit enfonçait une vitre; ou bien un vase, une statuette déroulait d'une console, par terre. Les boiseries pressées cra-
quaient. Tous les visages étaient rouges; la sueur en coulait à larges
gouttes; Hussonnet fit cette remarque: 'Les héros ne sentent pas
bon!'" The full stops are disjunctions, holes in the fabric of events.
With the words *tous les visages*, a focus suddenly occurs, a rudimentary period forms. The use of punctuation is of especial interest in all
the passages depicting crowds in the opening months of the Second
Republic.

As much ingenuity as Flaubert uses in mimicking action in sentence rhythms, this aspect of his style is less remarkable than the imitation of psychological states or events in *L'Education sentimentale*.
There is, of course, no necessary simple correspondence preestab-
lished between states of mind and prose rhythm; the art lies, once a
context is established, in manipulating long, medium, and short
phrases so that they seem, momentarily at least, to have a necessary
correlation. We do not have difficulty in seeing languor depicted in
the following sentences: "Il y avait dans le ciel de petits nuages blancs
arrêtés, et l'ennui, vaguement répandu, semblait alanguir la marche
du bateau et rendre l'aspect des voyageurs plus insignifiant encore"
and "Ainsi les jours s'écoulaient, dans la répétition des mêmes ennuis
et des habitudes contractées." On the other hand, the long phrase
suggests in this case that Frédéric is impressed by the importance of
Arnoux's review, *L'Art Industriel*: "Frédéric avait vu ce titre-là, plusieurs fois, à l'étalage du libraire de son pays natal, sur d'immenses
prospectus, où le nom de Jacques Arnoux se développait magistrale-
ment." Long adverbs, disdained as awkward and heavy by writers
before Flaubert, play an important role in the prose of *L'Education sentimentale*. Sometimes the adverb is like a decisive clause in itself: "Il
avait ordre de ramener Frédéric, définitivement."

More interesting though than isolated sentences are places where
Flaubert chooses different rhythmic means to convey similar effects.
In I, 2, in successive paragraphs, Flaubert wants to express the after-
effects of excitement: ". . . ils travailleraient ensemble, ne se quit-
teraient pas; et, comme délassement à leurs travaux, ils auraient des
amours de princesses dans des boudoirs de satin, ou de fulgurantes

orgies avec des courtisanes illustres. Des doutes succédaient à leurs emportements d'espoir. Après des crises de gaieté verbeuse, ils tombaient dans des silences profonds." After the ample *ils auraient . . . illustres*, the shorter clauses render doubts, the weariness that overcomes Frédéric and Deslauriers after imaginary debauches. The mechanism is clear: a short phrase after a long one means failing power. But in the next paragraph we find a description of the boys returning to the *collège* after lying in the fields dreaming of their future life: ". . . les rues désertes sonnaient sous leurs pas; la grille s'ouvrait, on remontait l'escalier; et ils étaient tristes comme après de grandes débauches." Here a long phrase clearly indicates the worn-out, supine body and imagination. As it works out, long phrases have contradictory associations. On the positive side they are a full release of energy after constraint, confidence, a desired result, and grandeur; the negative connotations, on the other hand, include a drop of intensity, melancholy, resignation, and lack of vitality. Short phrases are also paradoxical in effect, and for both long and short phrases there exists a possible dimension of ironic meaning.

Frédéric's life as a student in Paris is at first far from agreeable, thanks to its contrast with his cozy, comfortable, adequately staffed home in Nogent: "Mille choses nouvelles ajoutaient à sa tristesse. Il lui fallait compter son linge et subir le concierge, rustre à tournure d'infirmier, qui venait le matin retaper son lit, en sentant l'alcool et en grommelant. Son appartement, orné d'une pendule d'albâtre, lui déplaisait. Les cloisons étaient minces; il entendait les étudiants faire du punch, rire, chanter." Only the first phrase of the second sentence is of real length; the subdued movement of parataxis and general brevity represents Frédéric's disgruntlement. When he goes to look up Martinon, an acquaintance from school, he finds him placidly installed, with mistress, in a *pension bourgeoise* and not very comprehending: "Comme les ennuis de Frédéric n'avaient point de cause raisonnable et qu'il ne pouvait arguer d'aucun malheur, Martinon ne comprit rien à ses lamentations sur l'existence. Lui, il allait tous les matins à l'Ecole, se promenait ensuite dans le Luxembourg, prenait le soir sa demi-tasse au café, et, avec quinze cents francs par ans et l'amour de cette ouvrière, il se trouvait parfaitement heureux." Here, a few lines from the preceding paragraph, the expansive voice of reason, with its language of cause and effect, explains away Frédéric's moodiness; two long phrases setting forth the premises of any sound conclusion (*Comme les ennuis . . .; avec quinze cents francs . . .*) are followed by relatively shorter phrases, which here seem decisive and logical in virtue of their comparative brevity. The last one, above all, is almost aphoristic in its confident demonstration of how happiness is possible. "'Quel bonheur!' exclama intérieurement Frédéric."

Short phrases nicely render awkwardness and irritation when Frédéric calls on Arnoux in the absence of the latter's wife and while a woman is concealed somewhere in the apartment: "Ils ne trouvèrent, ensuite, absolument rien à se dire. Arnoux, qui s'était fait une cigarette, tournait autour de la table, en soufflant. . . . Un morceau de journal, roulé en boule, traînait par terre, dans l'antichambre; Arnoux le prit; et, se haussant sur la pointe des pieds, il l'enfonça dans la sonnette, pour continuer, dit-il, sa sieste interrompue. Puis, en lui donnant une poignée de main: 'Avertissez le concierge, s'il vous plaît, que je n'y suis pas!'" In one memorable passage in short phrases Frédéric meets soldiers as he enters Paris during the June, 1848, insurrection: "Quatre barricades formaient, au bout des quatre voies, d'énormes talus de pavés; des torches çà et là grésillaient; malgré la poussière qui s'élevait, il distingua des fantassins de la ligne et des gardes nationaux, tous le visage noir, débraillés, hagards. Ils venaient de prendre la place, avaient fusillé plusieurs hommes; leur colère durait encore." In this depiction of physical threat, asyndeton combines strikingly with short phrases to produce a tense, terse effect.

Long phrases and short can make interesting combinations when their value shifts. Here is Frédéric poverty stricken, resigned to living in Nogent and working as a law clerk: "Ces lamentations se répétèrent vingt fois par jour, durant trois mois; et, en même temps, les délicatesses du foyer le corrompaient; il jouissait d'avoir un lit plus mou, des serviettes sans déchirures; si bien que, lassé, énervé, vaincu enfin par la terrible force de la douceur, Frédéric se laissa conduire chez maître Prouharam." The long concluding phrases express Frédéric's surrender of his dreams of living in Paris, but in the next paragraph the long phrase depicts the exaggerated expectations of his fellow *nogentais*: "Il n'y montra ni science ni aptitude. On l'avait considéré jusqu'alors comme un jeune homme de grands moyens qui devait être la gloire du département. Ce fut une déception publique." Here the final short phrase has no energy, but merely a dropping effect—an example of the influence of meaning on the value of rhythm.

For short phrases conveying determination, there is Frédéric's frame of mind before his duel with Cisy: "Il fut pris d'un paroxysme de bravoure, d'une soif carnassière. Un bataillon ne l'eût pas fait reculer. Cette fièvre calmée, il se sentit, avec joie, inébranlable." Whereas Frédéric is depicted in *style coupé*, in Cisy's juxtaposed lament the phrases are not so much long as connected syntactically, as his mind races on in fear and anguish: "Il souhaita que Frédéric, pendant la nuit, mourût d'une attaque d'apoplexie, ou qu'une émeute survenant, il y eût le lendemain assez de barricades pour fermer tous les abords du bois de Boulogne, ou qu'un événement empêchât un des témoins de s'y rendre; car le duel faute de témoins manquerait." This device of shifting styles with a change of paragraph to produce some ironic effect is highly characteristic of Flaubert's method, which relies a good deal on suggestion by context and contrast.

We have been observing a kind of local rhythmic effect, but there is a larger, more general aspect of prose rhythm in *L'Education sentimentale*. We are aware, right from the first line, of a very special voice speaking, well before Frédéric's consciousness is focused upon; the opening sentence is cast in the grand Chateaubrianesque mold with four delaying, shorter phrases followed by a longer final one divided symmetrically: "Le 15 septembre 1840, vers six heures du matin, la *Ville-de-Montereau*, près de partir, fumait à gros tourbillons devant le quai Saint-Bernard." We perceive a disparity between the magnificence of the rhythm—usually saved in Chateaubriand for special, poetic moments—and the commonplaceness of the subject matter. We hear the same voice in many descriptions in the novel, such as this one of Frédéric's table, when he is about to receive his friends after his inheritance: "Un domestique en longues guêtres ouvrit la porte, et l'on aperçut la salle à manger avec sa haute plinthe en chêne relevée d'or et ses deux dressoirs chargés de vaisselle. Les bouteilles chauffaient sur le poêle; les lames des couteaux neufs miroitaient près des huîtres; il y avait dans le ton laiteux des verres-mousseline comme une douceur engageante, et la table disparaissait sous du gibier, des fruits, des choses extraordinaires." In the description of Frédéric's table, one is struck by the heterogeneity of the exact remark on the high molding in oak and gold and the more general terms that follow, until the last words, *choses extraordinaires*, could hardly be less descriptive in a concrete sense. There is an interesting question here of the esthetic of the description in *L'Education sentimentale*. Besides the rather iconographic image of Madame Arnoux, some beautiful depictions of weather with great insistence on effects of light, and the pictures of the Seine, Flaubert tends in *L'Education sentimentale* to describe unevenly, a few striking details mingling with the most approximate terms. The office of *L'Art Industriel*, the Dambreuses' reception rooms, and Rosanette's apartment are all presented in this way. In general, sensory notations count less than rhythmic effects, and we observe that the memorable image in the *chute de phrase*, so characteristic of *Madame Bovary*, is absent from the later novel. There are reasons for this: Frédéric is sensitive to visual details, having a certain esthetic culture, but he is not quite an artist in his perceptions; things play an enormous role in the novel, not so much as beautiful objects in themselves, but as reminders that bourgeois society is founded on the notion of property and that one's identity is one's things; and, finally, the controlling, authorial voice in *L'Education sentimentale* conveys its meaning often through a disparity between vocabulary and rhythm.

The imagery of the ugly is quite striking, especially in the descriptions of the passengers on the boat and the outskirts of Paris as Frédéric returns to the city by stagecoach, at the beginning of Part II. The solemn grandeur of the latter is memorable: "Puis, la double ligne de maisons ne discontinua plus; et, sur la nudité de leurs façades, se détachait, de loin en loin, un gigantesque cigare de fer-blanc, pour indiquer un débit de tabac. . . . Des affiches couvraient l'angle des murs, et, aux trois quarts déchirées tremblaient au vent comme des guenilles. Des ouvriers en blouse passaient, et des haquets de brasseurs, des fourgons de blanchisseuses, des carrioles de bouchers; une pluie fine tombait, il faisait froid, le ciel était pâle, mais deux yeux qui valaient pour lui le soleil resplendissaient derrière la brume." Elaborate devices are present: the balancing phrase *un gigantesque . . . tabac*, the inversion of subject and verb, and the hinge expression ; plus *et* plus , ; three short noun phrases (*des haquets . . .*) elegantly precede three short clauses (*une pluie fine . . .*), and the final clause stretches out in a magnificent conclusion. Flaubert is specifically trying to render the contrast between concrete reality and Frédéric's inner excitement; but, more generally, he is conveying the contrast that results from a great sensibility, represented by the rhythmic aspect of the prose, acting on the inferior material which is life. Over and over again in the novel we find this effect, which is established right in the opening pages, of the grand spreading out or dying away rhythms depicting undistinguished sights and events. "La misère des propos se trouvait comme renforcée par le luxe des choses ambiantes"; the remark, made of one of Mme Dambreuse's receptions, has a certain general validity for the subject matter and rhythms of the novel.

While rhythmic luxury is often used ironically in the depiction of the second-rate, as in the many portraits in the novel, it also at times paints the truly beautiful or stately; but here we encounter Flaubert's important stylistic decision not to allow too brilliant a sensory vocabulary to distract from the controlling rhythms of the book or to form purple patches contrasting with their context. The presentation of the chateau and forest at Fontainebleau is an excellent example. The look of the rooms in the chateau is cursorily described rather than evoked in detail, Flaubert tending to summarize and comment: "Les résidences royales ont en elles une mélancolie particulière, qui tient sans doute à leurs dimensions trop considérables pour le petit nombre de leurs hôtes, au silence qu'on est surpris d'y trouver après tant de fanfares, à leur luxe immobile prouvant par sa vieillesse la fugacité des dynasties, l'éternelle misère de tout; et cette exhalaison des siècles, engourdissante et funèbre comme un parfum de momie, se fait sentir même aux têtes naïves." Both parts of the period conclude with relatively short clauses, and the second sentence as a whole is less long than the first. Diminishing, dying away rhythmic effects become almost regular and continue on into the description of the forest. The description, while it first may seem somewhat lengthy and unrelieved, shows Flaubert working to produce his most subtle effects. Long ago, Thibaudet pointed out that in the description of the trees the various elements in the sentence, both pictorial and grammatical, shift places from clause to clause:[6] "La diversité des arbres faisait un spectacle changeant. Les hêtres, à l'écorce blanche et lisse, entremêlaient leurs couronnes; des frênes courbaient mollement leurs glauques ramures; dans les cépées de charmes, des houx pareils à du bronze se hérissaient; puis venait une file de minces bouleaux, inclinés dans des attitudes élégiaques; et les pins, symétriques comme des tuyaux d'orgue, en se balançant continuellement, semblaient chanter." As we continue to read the paragraph, a new facet of the passage emerges. Whereas dying rhythms are half again as frequent as lengthening ones in the description of the forest, here we encounter mostly the latter.

> Il y avait des chênes rugueux, énormes, qui se convulsaient, s'étiraient du sol, s'étreignaient les uns les autres, et, fermes sur leurs troncs, pareils à des torses, se lançaient avec leurs bras nus des appels de désespoir, des menaces furibondes, comme un groupe de Titans immobilisés dans leur colère. Quelque chose de plus lourd, une langueur fiévreuse planait au-dessus des mares, découpant la nappe de leurs eaux entre des buissons d'épines; les lichens de leurs berges, où les loups viennent boire, sont couleur de soufre, brûlés comme par le pas des sorcières, et le coassement ininterrompu des grenouilles répond au cri des corneilles qui tournoient.

In the whole of the paragraph, which I have not quoted, seven periods as against three are of the augmenting sort: Flaubert is making this section of the forest description stand out as the high point before resuming the former, diminishing rhythmic structure.

The most famous passage of *L'Education sentimentale* makes use of the broadest contrast between the short clause and the long. It begins with a pronoun reference back to the preceding chapter, a device Proust pointed out as an extraordinary example of stylistic continuity between units and which links many paragraphs in the novel.[7]

6. See Albert Thibaudet, *Gustave Flaubert* (Paris: Gallimard, 1935), 234–36.

7. Marcel Proust, "A propos du style de Flaubert," in *Contre Sainte-Beuve précédé de Pastiches et Mélanges et suivi d'Essais et Articles*, Bibliothèque de la Pléiade (Paris: Gallimard, 1971), 588.

Il voyagea.

Il connut la mélancolie des paquebots, les froids réveils sous la tente, l'étourdissement des paysages et des ruines, l'amertume des sympathies interrompues.

Il revint.

Il fréquenta le monde, et il eut d'autres amours encore. Mais le souvenir continuel du premier les lui rendait insipides; et puis la véhémence du désir, la fleur même de la sensation était perdue. Ses ambitions d'esprit avaient également diminué. Des années passèrent; et il supportait le désœuvrement de son intelligence et l'inertie de son cœur.

It is characteristic of Flaubert to have avoided anything too simply or too obviously Flaubertian in this passage; there are no ternary groups for example: the second sentence has four complements, and binary periods occur later. In the sentence beginning *Il connut*, the complements are not only four in number, they are partly isocolonic, so that neither spreading nor diminishing effects occur; it is too soon for Flaubert to use a conclusive cadence, this paragraph being left open as the fourth one is closed. Typically the prepositional phrases modifying *mélancolie*, *réveils*, *étourdissement*, and *sympathies* are varied in form. Heterocolon takes over with the paragraph beginning *Il fréquenta*, and increases till the last sentence. Verb position varies, but the most interesting device is the placing of the complex *rendait insipides* and the forms *était perdue*, *diminué*, and *passèrent* in the *chute de phrase*, which, containing the verb, produces a more striking effect of dying away than anything we have considered up to now. Likewise the languorous, spreading clause of the end of the fourth paragraph is extreme in its effect, being all of twenty-three syllables long, as opposed to the immediately preceding six.

Proust called Flaubert's style a *trottoir roulant*, alluding to a means of conveyance invented for the visitors to one of the Paris Expositions Universelles. In a sense, the slow but steady-seeming pace at which events occur as Frédéric and his friends drift down the river of life justifies the comparison, but actually, as we have seen, the sentences seem to reflect another water movement, ebb and flow. Rhythmic oscillation between long and short, within or between sentences and paragraphs, is much more its motion, and, in fact, this is the real movement of Frédéric's life: he oscillates between love of Mme Arnoux and pique or indifference. Connected, but somewhat independent, is the alternation between psychic energy and languor, and, of course, there are lesser oscillations involving Deslauriers, Rosanette, and the Dambreuses. All of his shifts of direction are presented as virtually involuntary, like the many coincidences of which the plot is made. Frédéric can scarcely have a broad enough point of view to encompass the whole picture, and thus we have the authorial presence in specific passages of commentary and everywhere in the controlling rhythms. Even in the free indirect discourse, there is a tendency to modulate into something more eloquent than what could have been actually said, as we saw in the passage dealing with Martinon's reactions to Frédéric's self-pity. Free indirect discourse moves between the extremes of the character's words and the author's, and frequently Flaubert inclines toward the latter.

Many other passages in *L'Education sentimentale* have remarkable features, such as the portrait of Sénécal all in bipartite constructions to render his heavy, rigid, emphatic mind, or that of Rosanette principally in verbs to render her flighty temperament; but we have seen sufficiently the range of Flaubert's style to draw one important conclusion: Flaubert worked out a whole rhetoric for the novel—not just a stylistic manner suitable to one or two subjects, but an elaborate mimesis of action. The extent of Flaubert's influence, deep and pervasive, shows the broad usefulness of his devices, the completeness of his ensemble of techniques. These include the possibility of a high style, the first real one after Chateaubriand, and in this respect also, Flaubert's work stands out from that of other romantics. In *Bovary*, to be sure, we are still close to the grotesque and ironic principles first set forth by Hugo; Emma's death scene with the depiction of extreme unction, drawing on allusions to the appropriate prayers and constituting the grandest passage in the novel, concludes with the appearance of the leprous beggar, in an effect that probably seemed to Flaubert quite Shakespearean but which appears to us more in the romantic macabre vein. The heightened passages in *L'Education sentimentale*, however, such as that beginning *Il voyagea*, are strictly dependent for their effect on reference to the whole of the novel; there are no anthology pieces. Flaubert's task of unifying style continued in

Bouvard et Pécuchet, except that there the short phrase has taken over and the style is drier; with such sobriety of tone, high style is no longer possible. As Mallarmé said, "Style extraordinairement beau, mais on pourrait dire nul, quelquefois, à force de nudité imposante."[8]

8. Aside from the relevant chapter of the work of Thibaudet's cited above, there is a section on Flaubert's style in Ferdinand Brunot, *Histoire de la langue française des origines à nos jours* (13 vols.; Paris: Armand Colin, 1966), Vol. XIII, Pt. 2, pp. 7–46.

12 Decadent Style and Beyond

Decadent style received a rhetorical definition as early as the 1830s: writing about Latin authors of the Empire and French poets of his own day, the critic Désiré Nisard characterized decadent writing as abundant in description and detail, uneven in texture, and given to excessively brilliant local effects.[1] We have seen the romantic taste for the striking figurative passage, and it is obvious that Flaubert, with his overriding concern for continuity of style, represents, in one respect, a reclassicizing of literary language, although the multiplication of detail in his representational technique obviously prolongs the decadent-descriptive side of romanticism. The latter increases, in fact, to constitute the most important unifying element of late nineteenth-century French styles—realist, Parnassian, or symbolist—in prose or verse. All divisions into schools are secondary to this fact, which did not escape the student of French decadent art Max Nordau, who, in his once-famous *Entartung* (1892)—*Degeneration*—puts Flaubert, Leconte de Lisle, Zola, and Mallarmé much on the same plane.

After Nisard, the definition of decadence in art acquires biological and sociological analogies. Paul Bourget, in a famous essay, compared the excessive importance of the individual, isolated effect of a word or a sentence in recent literature to a society disintegrated into a collection of highly individualized members. This does not concern us here, but a word has to be said about the more complicated biological analogy. According to this, organisms in a degenerate state have

---

1. Désiré Nisard, *Etudes de mœurs et de critique sur les poètes latins* (2 vols.; Paris: Hachette, 1888), II, 210, 249, 389. A recent general survey of the idea of decadence in literature is found in Matei Calinescu, *Faces of Modernity: Avant-Garde, Decadence, Kitsch* (Bloomington: Indiana University Press, 1977), 149–221.

232

heightened sensory perceptions; hence we have the descriptiveness of late nineteenth-century writing. Of course, one might argue just as well that a decayed nervous system will make fewer fine discriminations and will not be capable of refined analysis at all: the biology of discussions of decadence is pseudoscience, a kind of literary biology.

In regard to sense impressions and their use in art, Nietzsche, who did not dwell on biology in cultural decadence, had some relevant observations. In his various comments on nineteenth-century art, especially that of Wagner, he stressed the extreme technical competence of the artist, who permits his competence to assume a certain autonomy. The temptation of confusing or synthesizing the arts becomes prominent, and "painting with words" is a particularly widespread form of it. Nietzsche was quite familiar with the whole tradition of French literature up through the mid-century at least, and after finding, for example, comparisons of Wagner with Hugo, one senses that he was thinking primarily of French writers, especially since he was generally indifferent to German literature. We must keep these notions about decadence in mind as we explore French prose styles after Flaubert, to which such ideas will be variously applicable.

Of the nineteenth-century novelists after Flaubert, Zola had the best developed, most consistent theories of narrative technique and coherence of style. There is variation in the way he used his principles, and some development from novel to novel occurs, but within each work the prose has a remarkable evenness. Zola early called himself a decadent for his excessive love of sensory perceptions,[2] and we can sense something of what he meant by it in a passage from *Le Ventre de Paris*, the one of his early novels whose style is most often referred to; it is a description of the fish stalls at the Halles.

> Puis, venaient les beaux poissons, isolés, un sur chaque plateau d'osier; les saumons, d'argent guilloché, dont chaque écaille semble un coup de burin dans le poli du métal; les mulets, d'écailles plus fortes, de ciselures plus grossières; les grands turbots, les grandes barbues, d'un grain serré et blanc comme du lait caillé; les thons, lisses et vernis, pareils à des sacs de cuir noirâtre; les bars arrondis ouvrant une bouche énorme, faisant songer à quelque âme trop grosse, rendue à pleine gorge, dans la stupéfaction de

2. Emile Zola, *Oeuvres complètes* (36 vols.; Paris: Bernouard, 1927), XXX, 55.

l'agonie. Et, de toutes parts, les soles, par paires, grises ou blondes, pullulaient; les équilles minces, raidies, ressemblaient à des rognures d'étain; les harengs, légèrement tordus, montraient tous, sur leurs robes lamées, la meurtrissure de leurs ouïes saignantes; les dorades grasses se teintaient d'une pointe de carmin . . .

This prose is indebted most of all to Gautier's descriptive technique, with its use of unusual words and especially the vocabulary of the artist's atelier. Gautier, however, almost never integrated his descriptions successfully into fiction of real power. Zola uses such passages as part of a total pattern of imagery in his novels, in this case a mythology of eating, of the fat and the thin as descendants of Abel and Cain. The sight of food, even the suggestion of gluttony, is part of the special color of *Le Ventre de Paris*, for Zola, like Flaubert, conceived of each work as having its own stylistic tonality. At the same time, such passages in Zola's early work have always struck critics as *hors-d'œuvre* and certainly belong to decadent style in that sense as well.

The finite verb, which in Flaubert had remained a strong element of the sentence, often yields in importance to nouns, adjectives, and participles in Zola's early descriptions.

Il répétait ce chiffre sur tous les tons, montant une gamme étrange, pleine de soubresauts. Il était bossu, la face de travers, les cheveux ébouriffés, avec un grand tablier bleu à bavette. Et le bras tendu, violemment, les yeux jetant des flammes:
—Trente-un! trente-deux! trente-trois! trente-trois cinquante!... trente-trois cinquante!...
Il reprit haleine, tournant la manne, l'avançant sur la table de pierre, tandis que des poissonnières se penchaient, touchaient le turbot, légèrement, du bout du doigt. Puis, il repartit, avec une furie nouvelle, jetant un chiffre de la main à chaque enchérisseur, surprenant les moindres signes, les doigts levés, les haussements de sourcils, les avancements de lèvres, les clignements d'yeux . . .

Zola is not writing true nominal style here, but there is an obvious imbalance in the parts of speech, with participles present and past used with a density that had been completely foreign to French syntax since the sixteenth century. The participle seems here to belong in many ways with the adjectives and nouns as a descriptive element, keeping some of its verbal dynamism, but in a blurred form without the punctual character of the *passé simple* tense. Of course, in French the imperfect tense can serve a similar function, and here is a passage, from *La Faute de l'abbé Mouret* (1875), in a more thoroughgoing nominal style, using nonpunctual tenses when a verb does occur.

> La vie rieuse du rose s'épanouissait ensuite: le blanc rose, à peine teinté d'une pointe de laque, neige d'un pied de vierge qui tâte l'eau d'une source; le rose pâle, plus discret que la blancheur chaude d'un genou entrevu, que la lueur dont un jeune bras éclaire une large manche; le rose franc, du sang sous du satin, des épaules nues, des hanches nues, tout le nu de la femme, caressé de lumière; le rose vif, fleurs en boutons de la gorge, fleurs à demi ouvertes des lèvres, soufflant le parfum d'une haleine tiède. Et les rosiers grimpants, les grands rosiers à pluie de fleurs blanches, habillaient tous ces roses, toutes ces chairs, de la dentelle de leurs grappes, de l'innocence de leur mousseline légère; tandis que, çà et là, des roses lie de vin, presque noires, saignantes, trouaient cette pureté d'épousée d'une blessure de passion.

This is the beginning of the section where Serge and Albine, forgetful of their former lives, enter the enchanted garden as virgin flower-creatures before the fall; the whole episode resembles in style and technique one of the symbolist dramas of the 1890s, and it is not surprising that Des Esseintes and Mallarmé particularly liked this novel (along with *La Curée*, in the exotic hothouse of which Renée and Maxime exchange sexes). Many analogies of syntax and imagery are to be found in contemporary poetry, including, for example, Mallarmé's "Les Fleurs."

The importance of *L'Assommoir* (1877) in Zola's development as an artist is well-known: familiar, even argotic words and turns of phrase enter the narrative part of the novel, so that there is only a thin line between narrative and the thoughts of the characters cast in free indirect discourse. The opening page of the novel is written in a literary style of its day: "Il y avait là un piétinement de troupeau, une foule que de brusques arrêts étalaient en mares sur la chaussée, un défilé sans fin d'ouvriers allant au travail, leurs outils sur le dos, leur pain sous le bras; et la cohue s'engouffrait dans Paris où elle se noyait, continuellement." We see here Flaubert's present participle, his semicolon followed by *et* and a concluding clause, his long adverb placed prominently at the end of the sentence. *Il y avait un piétinement* for *la foule piétinait* belongs to the common new style of the period. As the narrative progresses, however, such self-consciously literary devices recede, and the familiar color enters: "Copeau branla furieusement la tête. Lorilleux lui revaudrait cette soirée-là. Avait-on jamais vu un pareil grigou!" At times there is a surprising modulation back to the literary; here the wedding party is visiting the Louvre: "Fichtre! il ne faisait pas chaud; la salle aurait fait une fameuse cave. Et, lentement, les couples avançaient, le menton levé, les paupières battantes, en-tre les colosses de pierre, les dieux de marbre noir muets dans leur raideur hiératique." Flaubert did not like the "preciosity" of using slang in narrative, and, despite his general success, Zola does not en-tirely avoid an occasional clash of styles, as between *fichtre!* and *hiératique*. We must not, however, consider *L'Assommoir* as the end point of Zola's development away from the style of a novel like *Le Ventre de Paris*.

In *La Terre*, Zola reached a high point in the invention of stylized narrative idiom. Peasants during the Second Empire still spoke patois exclusively among themselves, so even the dialogue in *La Terre* had necessarily to be an artifice. But beyond this, there is an essential thematic cleavage in the novel between the beautiful and indifferent earth and the creatures who live on it and cultivate it. Especially in the passages describing the land, Zola uses distinctive language, slow and segmented. My first three quotations come from the open-ing pages; the fourth shows how the same stylistic tendencies recur regularly in the novel where the land is envisaged as a whole.

> Sous le ciel vaste, un ciel couvert de la fin d'octobre, dix lieues de cultures étalaient en cette saison les terres nues, jaunes et fortes, des grands carrés de labour, qui alternaient avec les nappes vertes des luzernes et des trèfles; et cela sans un coteau, sans un arbre, à perte de vue, se confondant, s'abaissant, derrière la ligne d'horizon, nette et ronde comme sur une mer.
> . . . .
> Au milieu, une route, la route de Châteaudun à Orléans, d'une blancheur de craie, s'en allait toute droite pendant quatre lieues, déroulant le défilé géométrique des poteaux du télégraphe.
> . . . .
> Le temps s'était mis brusquement au froid, un temps couleur de suie, sans

un souffle de vent, d'une lumière égale et morne sur cet océan de terre immobile.

. . . .

Un reflet jaunâtre semblait en être resté au ras du sol, une lumière louche, un éclairage livide d'orage: tout paraissait jaune, d'un jaune affreusement triste, la terre rôtie, les moignons des tiges coupées, les chemins de campagne, bossués, écorchés par les roues.

The essential devices are easily identified: appositions, often involving a repeated noun, neutral verbs, present participles, modifiers—including both adjectives and prepositional phrases—detached by commas, asyndeton, and a general accumulation of short elements after the verb. This is Zola's pensive, almost lethargic style, the appositions and repetitions imitating a kind of colloquial hesitation, the accumulations of the later part of the sentence observing no climax but, if anything, a descending order. This narrative language has little to do with Flaubert's segmented style, where, for example, apposition is found very seldom. Zola commented that Flaubert's sculptured ideal of prose aimed at the impossible and that, for his part, he found necessarily in prose "une mollesse de contours, une fluidité, qui la rend très pénible à couler dans un moule solide."[3] Of course, his failure to understand Flaubert's ambition was related to his own taste for a sentence avoiding suspensions and dying away with short, asyndetic modifying elements. We find in the passages from *La Terre* the same disequilibrium in parts of speech that we observed in our passage from *Le Ventre de Paris*: the verb is rather colorless and undynamic, while nouns and their modifiers bear the major weight of meaning. But here the nominalizing style is beautifully suited to its function, whereas in the depiction of the fish auction one might maintain that a greater degree of characterization with punctual verbs could have been, if not more appropriate, at least just as valid a technique. The descriptive manner of *La Terre* was not completely new in Zola's work by any means—we see the same tendency toward apposition and enumeration in our first quotation from *L'Assommoir*—but it stands out for its contrast with the portrayal of "la vermine sanguinaire et puante des villages déshonorant et rongeant la terre."

3. *Ibid.*, XXXVI, 114.

Almost all the mannerisms of other writers of Zola's day, notably of
Huysmans and the Goncourts, are to be found, with diligent searching, somewhere in his work, but the general impression is one of regularity, with the only persistent and quite new feature of grammar
being the abundance of prepositional phrases slowing and segment-
ing the sentence: "Et toujours, et du même pas, avec le même geste, il
allait au nord, il revenait au midi, enveloppé dans la poussière vi-
vante du grain; pendant que, derrière, la herse, sous les claquements
du fouet, enterrait les grains, du même train doux et comme ré-
fléchi."[4] Zola's later style, as distinguished from that of *Le Ventre de
Paris*, where we are so conscious of Gautier and the poetic movements of the mid-century, is a remarkable achievement but one little
discussed. Zola focused his publicizing efforts on the "experimental"
novel and not on language, whereas his contemporaries drew a good
deal of attention to what they had accomplished in fine writing, so
that, rightly or wrongly, they are still associated, more than Zola,
with stylistic imagination. At the same time, we do not often find in
other novelists of the period such beautiful descriptions as this one:
"Dans le ciel, une nuée laiteuse, uniforme, s'était épandue, et la
pleine lune, qu'on ne voyait pas, noyée derrière, éclairait toute la
voûte d'un reflet rougeâtre. Aussi distinguait-il nettement la campagne, dont les terres autour de lui, les coteaux, les arbres se dé-
tachaient en noir, sous cette lumière égale et morte, d'une paix de
veilleuse." This is from a late novel, *La Bête humaine*, the finest feature
of which is its writing.

The different character of Huysmans' prose in *A rebours* from Zola's
can be felt, in part, by comparing with the description of night in *La
Bête humaine* these lines on the rain perceived by Des Esseintes in a
cab: "La pluie entrait en diagonale par les portières; des Esseintes dut
relever les glaces que l'eau raya de ses cannelures, tandis que des
gouttes de fange rayonnaient comme un feu d'artifice de tous les
côtés du fiacre. Au bruit monotone des sacs de pois secoués sur sa
tête par l'ondée dégoulinant sur les malles et sur le couvercle de la
voiture, des Esseintes rêvait à son voyage" (Chapter 11). We notice a

---

4. Emile Zola, *La Terre*, I, 1. See Ferdinand Brunot, *Histoire de la langue française des
origines à nos jours* (13 vols.; Paris: Armand Colin, 1966), Vol. XIII, Pt. 2, pp. 150–52, 159.

good deal of unusual passing metaphor here: the grooves of the rain, the splashing like fireworks, and sacks of dried peas hitting the lid of the cab. This technique of constant, shifting metaphorical embellishment comes from Baudelaire, who of all the writers Des Esseintes admires is the most central to his imagination. The prose is not idly imagistic but conveys Des Esseintes' way of feeling through a kind of allusion to *Les Fleurs du mal,* and the reading of Huysmans' other novels shows that the prose of *A rebours* is quite special in his work.

Although the myth of decadent sensorial perception is used on the narrative level in the novel—perfumes, for example, give Des Esseintes the impression of various landscapes as he experiments with them—the principal stylistic idea of decadence in it is that the lexical structure of the French language is disintegrating. The analogy is drawn with Petronius, who wrote "dans un style d'une verdeur étrange, d'une couleur précise, dans un style puisant à tous les dialectes, empruntant des expressions à toutes les langues charriées dans Rome," and with Apuleius, in whose work "la langue latine battait le plein . . . elle roulait des limons, des eaux variées, accourrues de toutes les provinces, et toutes se mêlaient, se confondaient en une teinte bizarre, exotique, presque neuve." Huysmans, in keeping with this vision of Empire Latin, layered with the alluvia of different vocabularies, employs elaborate synonymity. Here is part of a discussion of Louis Veuillot's style.

> Tenu en défiance par l'Eglise qui n'admettait ni ce style de contrebande ni ces poses de barrière, ce religieux arsouille s'était quand même imposé par son grand talent, ameutant après lui toute la presse qu'il étrillait jusqu'au sang dans ses *Odeurs de Paris,* tenant tête à tous les assauts, se débarrassant à coups de soulier de tous les bas plumitifs qui s'essayaient à lui sauter aux jambes.
>
> Malheureusement, ce talent incontesté n'existait que dans le pugilat; au calme, Veuillot n'était plus qu'un écrivain médiocre; ses poésies et ses romans inspiraient la pitié; sa langue à la poivrade s'éventait à ne pas cogner; l'arpin catholique se changeait, au repos, en un cacochyme qui toussait de banales litanies et balbutiait d'enfantins cantiques.

Poses de barrière, that is, the stance of a thug, brings in the argotic *arsouille* or *voyou. Ameuter* is curiously followed by *étriller,* or "currycomb," in the sense of *malmener;* the image changes back with *coups de soulier* to the *voyou*; and *plumitifs* is a jocular formation common in the nineteenth century in the sense of *journaliste*. *Pugilat* is a specific sort of combat; *poivrade*, *s'éventait*, and *cogner* form a remarkable trio of substitutes, each a different kind of metaphor, for *forte*, *s'affaiblissait*, *se battre*. *Arpin* is a rare equivalent of *hercule de foire*, and *cacochyme* replaces the more common *valétudinaire*. Some might tax Huysmans with *cacozelon*, or tasteless affectation in language; it appears that such effects were obtained less through brilliant inspirations than by use of a *dictionnaire analogique* or thesaurus of synonyms, whence their somewhat mechanical quality.[5]

The *sermo cotidianus* of Petronius and Apuleius does not, as a matter of fact, have much resemblance to Huysmans' stylistic inventions; Huysmans' description of their Late Latin is more a dream of style than an actual representation of the language of the *Satyricon* or the *Golden Ass*. From the strictly historical point of view, Greek and Roman experimenters with words had, well before Apuleius at least, mixed vocabularies. Quintilian alludes to orators mingling old words, regional ones, and those peculiar to a métier (*Institutio* VIII, 2); he also compares the blending of dialects in Greek to a Latin combination of high and low, old and new, poetic and common (VIII, 3). One gathers that among the Roman writings that did not survive, there were some very curious attempts at a novel style and that these occurred before the full decadence. Like theirs, Huysmans' attempt at a new style was the result of a very artful *recherche* and quite unrelated to any objective feature of the history of French.

In sentence structure, we should note that Huysmans' language in *A rebours* does not follow the kind of decreasing, nominalizing segmented sentence we have observed in Zola. Rather, his segmented style is suspenseful after the manner of Flaubert: "Afin de jouir d'une œuvre qui joignît, suivant ses vœux, à un style incisif, une analyse pénétrante et féline, il lui fallait arriver au maître de l'Induction, à ce profond et étrange Edgar Poë, pour lequel, depuis le temps qu'il le relisait, sa dilection n'avait pu déchoir" (Chapter 14). We see that if Zola's syntax could be called decadent in the sense of being soft and fluid, this is not the case with Huysmans', whose phrasing is tense

5. See Marcel Cressot, *La Phrase et le Vocabulaire de J.-K. Huysmans* (Paris: Droz, 1938), 72.

and stiffened. Finally, we should note that *A rebours* is closer to traditional notions of elegance in language than are Huysmans' other books; in Cressot's study, few examples of bizarre grammar come from it.

We have seen that decadent style in the sense of employing unusual terms is connected in Zola with the idea of painting in words and in Huysmans with an historical analogy with Late Latin. The decadence of society is assumed but does not in itself motivate lexical innovations. The idea of decadence informing the Goncourt brothers' stylistic choices is, as in Zola, that of a decayed, exacerbated sensibility receiving intense sensorial stimuli; Edmond and Jules considered themselves "les Saint Jean-Baptiste de la nervosité."[6] I have already pointed out that this notion of a degenerate nervous system being a refined one is of dubious validity, and the case of the Goncourts will confirm this. When we read their descriptions, we are struck not by any hyperacute impression but merely by oddities of language, which are of purely grammatical origin and have nothing to do with any perception behind them; here is a passage from *La Faustin* (1882) written by Edmond after Jules' death.

> Cela commençait ainsi: d'abord l'allée et la venue d'une bottine colère, remuée dans le vide, puis deux ou trois mouvements de resserrement des coudes contre le corps, et du gris montant sous le rose de la peau du visage, et le tortillage nerveux d'une bouche qui se ferme pour s'empêcher de parler, et malgré ce cadenassement de tout son être, au bout de quelques secondes, de la femme jaillissait pour son amant une parole aigre, méprisante, empoisonnée, dite avec l'ironie sifflante d'une imprécation à la Camille, parole sur laquelle ses lèvres se refermaient, et sa bottine se mettait à rebattre le vide. (Chapter 38)

We are reminded of the passage quoted earlier from Saint-Simon (p. 109 herein) about the imperceptible movement in the crowd of courtiers waiting for the news of Monseigneur's death: the division of the individual into anatomical elements is similar, and the nominal style likewise prevails; but Saint-Simon is describing a more subtle phenomenon, one almost escaping attention. Here there is a discrepancy between the essentially ordinary picture of a tense, nervous

---

6. For a general treatment of the Goncourts' style, see Brunot, *Histoire de la langue,* Vol. XIII, Pt. 2, pp. 65–105.

woman and the syntactically odd enumeration of verbal nouns (*allée et venue, mouvements de resserrement, tortillage, cadenassement*). Furthermore, the use of the article in *l'allée et la venue* (instead of *les allées et venues*), the use of the adjective *colère* outside an expression like *voix colère*, and the peculiarity of the form *tortillage* (instead of *tortillement*), where the suffix seems like the wrong one for a frequentative, suggest that the language is being made complicated and rare purely for the sake of grammar and not for anything unusual in the thing designated or the way of apprehending it. There is no perceptual sensitivity here but merely a penchant for neologism; we find much less real color than in Gautier, Zola, and Huysmans. If the Goncourts were unusually open to sense impressions, their fiction does not succeed in conveying it, but their style certainly does reveal a studied approach to language. The suspicion that we are dealing with some sort of disparity between fancy words and ordinary things is confirmed by the extreme banality of conception behind the novel, with its caricature English lord and its clichés about how actresses love the theater because it is so theatrical.

The Goncourt brothers had no general theory of fictional technique or prose rhythm, unlike Flaubert or Zola, so that their makeshift narratives are not written with any clear total effect in mind. They are filled with interventions and allusions like the "imprécation à la Camille" in the above example or the grotesque notion that they were the "Saint Jean-Baptiste" of nervousness. In this, they are the heirs of Balzac, as well as of his neological tendencies. But their language pushed to the extreme certain tendencies perceptible here and there in Flaubert and especially Hugo, so that they serve as the pure type of what they called *écriture artiste*; if we did not have their influential work, we would have to posit its existence to explain tendencies widespread in the prose of the 1880s. Of these, the use of participles and verbal nouns, especially in conjunction, is perhaps the most striking: "C'était, cette maison, l'ancien grenier à sel de la ville. Les murailles, infiltrées et encore transsudantes de la gabelle emmagasinée pendant des siècles, disparaissant, à tout moment, sous le tourbillonnement de centaines d'oisillons donnant un coup de bec au crépi salé, puis montant dans le ciel à perte de vue, puis planant une seconde, puis redescendant entourer le noir bâtiment des circuits rapides de leur joie ailée. Et toujours, depuis l'aurore jusqu'au cré-puscule, le tournoiement de ces vols qui gazouillaient" (*La Fille Elisa*, Chapter 9). More than one device is at work here: the adjective be-comes a noun (*oisillons tourbillonnants* → *tourbillonnement d'oisillons*);[7] then a further replacement of noun by adjective can occur (*mouvement d'ailes joyeux* → *joie ailée*). The verbal noun can simply be substituted for the performer when some adjectival element is included to clarify the expression (*oiseaux volants et gazouillants* → *vols qui gazouillaient*). The conversion of adjectives and verbs into nouns has the peculiar feature that these nouns, while they normally would be classified as abstract ones, have some imagistic suggestion without definite out-lines. The peculiar effect of this style is to avoid visual sharpness, just as the syntax of nouns and participles diminishes movement and ten-sion on the grammatical plane. Coupled with an uncertain fictional technique, these effects make the Goncourt novels curiously static.

Although the Goncourts were not interested in poetry, feeling the novel was to replace it, poets read them, and some of the linguistic oddities of minor symbolist verse are doubtless owing to them. A cer-tain amount of fiction was written in poetic circles, and we may take the following as characteristic; it is from a volume by Paul Adam and Jean Moréas called *Le Thé chez Miranda* and consisting of stories told during "l'hiémale nuit et ses buées et leurs doux comas": "Cela se de-vine tout de suite qu'il ne l'aura point. Elle est honnête fatalement par sa blondeur tendre d'anémique, la matité du teint pur, la tendance à rester clapie très longtemps dans la même attitude. Elle le regarde venir. Sur l'orbe de son œil levé une nacrure luit, humide, puis se voile des cils baissés vite. Et cette luisance le pénètre, se darde par ses entrailles qui frémissent. Il la veut." The scene deals with a seduction in the Tuileries, with Maupassant-like material, but the accumulation

7. For the type *de froides pérennités de sources* and *des immensités de champs*, there is a Latin model: "Adde hunc frontium gelidas perennitates, liquores perlucidos amnium, riparum vestitus viridissimos, speluncarum concavas altitudines, immensitates campo-rum." "Add to these, cool fountains always flowing, transparent streams and rivers, their banks always green, deep, vaulted caverns, craggy rocks, sheer mountain heights, and plains of immeasurable extent." Cicero, *De Natura Deorum*, II, 39. To what degree the study of Latin contributed to the French expressions is difficult to ascertain.

of *matité*, *nacrure*, and *luisance*, ambiguously archaic or neologistic, sets off another range of connotations, that of the most rarefied and poetic, to say nothing of *clapie* (crouched), which is used, when at all, of rabbits. The taste for the realist-banal and the symbolist-exquisite is often presented in terms of successive literary movements in the late nineteenth century, but both show the same fondness for *recherché* writing and description, as one can see when they are side by side in Huysmans' *œuvre* or in this short passage. These supposedly antithetic styles are actually to be found in varying degrees of combination in the poetry and prose of the period.

A prose poem of Mallarmé's will illustrate a particularly charming combination of the rarefied and the argotic. In "Réminiscence," an orphan speaks to the child of acrobats passing through town, who is eating a sandwich of farmer cheese so white and snowlike it would make one soar inwardly with delight.

> Orphelin, j'errais en noir et l'œil vacant de famille: au quinconce se déplièrent des tentes de fête, éprouvai-je le futur et que je serais ainsi, j'aimais le parfum des vagabonds, vers eux à oublier mes camarades. Aucun cri de chœurs par la déchirure, ni tirade loin, le drame requérant l'heure sainte des quinquets, je souhaitais de parler avec un môme trop vacillant pour figurer parmi sa race, au bonnet de nuit taillé comme le chaperon de Dante; qui rentrait en soi, sous l'aspect d'une tartine de fromage mou, déjà la neige des cimes, le lys ou autre blancheur constitutive d'ailes au dedans: je l'eusse prié de m'admettre à son repas supérieur, partagé vite avec quelque aîné fameux jailli contre une proche toile en train des tours de force et banalités alliables au jour.

Mallarmé's is not the facile way of neologism or odd words but rather the exploitation of unusual syntax. The inversion *se déplièrent* means "if tents were erected"; the inversion *éprouvai-je* follows an initial sentence element, as it would in sixteenth-century style or in modern German. *Vers* has its usual symbolist value of "in a movement toward"; *à oublier* means *en oubliant* rather than *pour oublier*, as it first seems to. The verbless expression (*aucun cri . . .*) indicates that there was no sound of a performance from the tent opening; it is a kind of nominal absolute construction, and the following participle *requérant* has the sense of *car le drame exige*. The child is said to totter (*vacillant*) because he is too young to be an acrobat; *rentrer en soi* is a periphrasis for eating, and the sentence ends elliptically, the participles meaning *s'il n'avait pas été partagé avant* and *qui avait jailli soudain; en train de (faire) des tours* is condensed.

> Nu, de pirouetter dans sa prestesse de maillot à mon avis surprenante, lui, qui d'ailleurs commença: "Tes parents?—Je n'en ai pas.—Allons, si tu savais comme c'est farce un père... même l'autre semaine que bouda la soupe, il faisait des grimaces aussi belles, quand le maître lançait les claques et les coups de pied. Mon cher!" et de triompher en élevant à moi la jambe avec aisance glorieuse, "il nous épate, papa," puis de mordre au régal chaste du très jeune: "Ta maman, tu n'en as pas, peut-être, que tu es seul? la mienne mange de la filasse et le monde bat des mains. Tu ne sais rien, des parents sont des gens drôles, qui font rire." La parade s'exaltait, il partit: moi, je soupirai, déçu tout à coup de n'avoir pas de parents.

Examples of the historical infinitive occur, of which the first would be in normal form *et lui de pirouetter*; the construction is rare save in La Fontaine and writers of the end of the nineteenth century, who were fascinated by this alternative to the *passé simple*. Illiterate syntax shows up in *que bouda* for *qu'il bouda*, rather strangely linking the formal tense with the popular relative pronoun.

In Mallarmé's prose, we see a truly thought-out version of nominalizing style.[8] Whereas others were content with variations on the formula *c'étaient d'impassibles immobilités d'arabes* for *des arabes impassibles se tenaient immobiles*, Mallarmé explored more fruitful possibilities such as the Latinate absolute noun and the historical infinitive. The reduction of the relative clause to the present participle was widespread, but the use of the adjective for a clause as in *blancheur constitutive d'ailes* belonged to a new type of expression. The past participles replacing clauses are elliptic in Mallarmé to an unusual degree. While abundant prepositional phrases mark much late nineteenth-century prose, they seldom have Mallarmé's witty concision as in the metaphoric formula *rentrer en soi la neige sous l'aspect d'une tartine* or *dans sa prestesse de maillot surprenante* for *si prestement dans son maillot*

8. For Mallarmé's style see especially Jacques Scherer, *L'Expression littéraire dans l'œuvre de Mallarmé* (Paris: Droz, 1947), and Norman Paxton, *The Development of Mallarmé's Prose Style* (Geneva: Droz, 1968). For Rimbaud and the prose poem, as well as Mallarmé, see John Porter Houston, *French Symbolism and the Modernist Movement: A Study of Poetic Structures* (Baton Rouge: Louisiana State University Press, 1980).

qu'il me surprit. It is always clear in Mallarmé's prose that some effect is gained by singular grammar; here the somewhat awkward, hesitant, solemn tone contrasts with the light, argotic syntax of the *aîné fameux.* Elsewhere, Mallarmé achieves a quality of maniacal precision, as in "La Déclaration foraine," or the elaborately gallant and cryptic manner of "Le Nénuphar blanc."

It is interesting that the obscurity of Mallarmé's prose can be considered a virtue and has classical antecedents, like some of his constructions. Quintilian reports that a rhetorician of Livy's day always enjoined his pupils to obscure the sense of their language, "skótison!" anticipating Mallarmé's "Attendez, par pudeur, que j'y ajoute, du moins, un peu d'obscurité." When one has examined the range of peculiarities in late nineteenth-century art-prose, in the Goncourts, in Moréas, with his *impollués vocables* as he called his characteristic words, and in other lesser writers, it becomes clear that whatever difficulties reading them involves are comparatively minor matters of vocabulary, whereas Mallarmé is genuinely and fruitfully obscure. In Mallarmé's prose poem we have the sense of a mysterious world; in the Goncourts' novels there is simply the ordinary world somewhat oddly described. The banal in Mallarmé seems full of suggestiveness.

The suffusing effect of mystery—the term is his—in Mallarmé's prose demands that we differentiate it from other styles we have examined: the strange or impressive detail does not stand out in Mallarmé's writing, according to the theory of decadent style, which provokes a sense of disintegration of the fabric of the whole to the advantage of particular parts. Rather, Mallarmé's prose is so consistent, from phrase to phrase, in its qualities of concision, metaphoricness, and *écart* from ordinary usage, that he achieves that continuity of effect which is the opposite of the decadent. Furthermore, Mallarmé's concern for general mystery is incompatible with the sensory directness and intensity which, as we have seen, is derived from the conception of the late and decayed nervous system: Mallarmé represents everything bathing evenly in a certain cryptic remoteness. Finally, the tissue of figurative language—such as the conceit of the cheese making one soar inwardly like an acrobat—introduces a play of ideas that takes precedence over effects of descriptive immediacy. In sum, Mallarmé managed, taking the element of linguistic irregularity proper to decadent prose, to create something beyond the decadent esthetic.

The conception of the decadent artist as having extraordinary technical skills is a relevant one as we look back over the lexical richness of Huysmans, for example, or Mallarmé's ability to fashion a new kind of prose syntax. The automatism of such skills is illustrated by the Goncourt style, wherein we perceive a discrepancy between the newness of the verbal means and the less distinctive character of the narrative material. In Proust, we see a quite unprecedented verbal technique put at the service of one of the most characteristic decadent effects, the conveyance of complex sensorial perceptions.

> . . . et le feu cuisant comme une pâte les appétissantes odeurs dont l'air était tout grumeleux et qu'avait déjà fait travailler et "lever" la fraîcheur humide et ensoleillée du matin, il les feuilletait, les dorait, les godait, les boursouflait, en faisant un invisible et palpable gâteau provincial, un immense "chausson" où, à peine goûtés les aromes plus croustillants, plus fins, plus réputés, mais plus secs aussi du placard, de la commode, du papier à ramages, je revenais toujours avec une convoitise inavouée m'engluer dans l'odeur médiane, poisseuse, fade, indigeste, et fruitée du couvre-lit à fleurs.

We observe that Proust's grammatical means are not at all those associated with late nineteenth-century art-prose: the sentence is constructed with strong clausal articulations emphasizing verbs; the traditional adjective rather than combinations of nouns, as in *écriture artiste*, constitutes a principle resource. We note a characteristic joining of balanced *A and B* constructions with asyndetic ones, of series ranging in number of elements from two to five. Finally, hypotaxis rather than a more linear sentence structure is Proust's usual way of tying together sensations or ideas.

In the ordered, rational-seeming sentences that make up Proust's narrative, the actual substance of perceptions often passes completely beyond the bounds of real phenomena into the mythic; here is Legrandin revealing involuntarily his desire to know the Guermantes: "Mais, à ce nom de Guermantes, je vis au milieu des yeux bleus de notre ami se ficher une petite encoche brune comme s'ils venaient d'être percés par une pointe invisible, tandis que le reste de la prunelle réagissait en sécrétant des flots d'azur. Le cerne de sa

paupière noircit, s'abaissa. Et sa bouche marquée d'un pli amer se re-
saisissant plus vite sourit, tandis que le regard restait douloureux,
comme celui d'un beau martyr dont le corps est hérissé de flèches:
'Non, je ne les connais pas,' dit-il . . ." Eyes in reality do not shift
color so readily to betray inner thoughts: Proust has taken the hyper-
sensitive mode of decadent description and carried it into a purely
imaginary domain, with the most striking effects. Like the syn-
esthesia common in the late nineteenth century and represented by
Proust's giving the name Guermantes an orange sound, the super-
perception belongs to some ideal symbolic world where all spiritual
phenomena have physical correspondences; it is the final form taken
by the decadent descriptiveness of romantic literature.

Proust's sentence structure is intended to bind together the most
varied material into new wholes, new total impressions, where the
accessory is as essential as the main object of contemplation.

> De ma chambre, je ne pouvais apercevoir que sa base [that of the steeple]
> qui avait été recouverte d'ardoises; mais quand, le dimanche, je les voyais,
> par une chaude matinée d'été, flamboyer comme un soleil noir, je me
> disais: "Mon Dieu, neuf heures! il faut se préparer pour aller à la grand'-
> messe si je veux avoir le temps d'aller embrasser tante Léonie avant," et je
> savais exactement la couleur qu'avait le soleil sur la place, la chaleur et la
> poussière du marché, l'ombre que faisait le store du magasin où maman
> entrerait peut-être avant la messe, dans une odeur de toile écrue, faire em-
> plette de quelque mouchoir que lui ferait montrer, en cambrant la taille, le
> patron qui, tout en se préparant à fermer, venait d'aller dans l'arrière-
> boutique passer sa veste du dimanche et se savonner les mains qu'il avait
> l'habitude, toutes les cinq minutes, même dans les circonstances les plus
> mélancoliques, de frotter l'une contre l'autre d'un air d'entreprise, de par-
> tie fine et de réussite.

Technically, the sentence concludes with five levels of subordination:
the relative clauses are each elaborated by a following one, and the
historical analogue would be the descending, accretive period of the
sixteenth century. Whereas the latter, however, often seems weak
through an inadequate logical justification for its later clausal incre-
ments, Proust's additive sentence has no pretense to logic, and the
justification for the details about the shop is a purely imaginative
one. For Proust, all ideas and memories are accompanied by a wealth

of incidental material, without which they would be abstract and dead, the product of pure intellection.[9]

The passage on Sunday morning in Combray is characterized by two further effects in sentence structure. There are a good many parenthetical descriptive phrases, especially with prepositions or participles—*dans une odeur de toile écrue, en cambrant la taille*—which, as in renaissance prose, diminish the impression of natural word order by destroying strong syntactic sequentiality. Next, the arrangement of the four main clauses and the eight subordinate clauses offers no sense of symmetry. These aspects of Proust's prose create a rhythmic structure characteristic not only of his work but of the Goncourts' prose, of Mallarmé's, and of other late nineteenth-century writers': there are, on the one hand, no grand climaxes as in Chateaubriand's prose, for the syntax militates against them; on the other, the colloquial spontaneity aimed at often in romantic prose is lacking. This prose is often clarified in its structure by being read aloud; the periods are not silent reading ones as in Amyot and others. At the same time, elaborate syntactico-rhythmic effects, pronounced isocolon or contrasts, striking *chutes de phrase*, are not prominent. These writers sought a middle way between the artful and oratorical manner and the impression of colloquial improvisation.

In Proust, the decadent display of sensitivity, or even, as it often turns out to be, the decadent myth of sensitivity, is unconnected with any belief that the modern age is one of biological decay, for Proust conceived of society and life as moving in cycles. The biological realm is not the one of true life, which is art, but it has no peculiar historical status of decline. The Goncourts, on the other hand, believed in the decadence of their age, and so did Mallarmé, without making a major theme of it; at the same time, decadence does not seem in their writings to add up to a great deal more than earlier romantic laments over one's own time. In other words, decadent traits of style do not always imply a well-worked-out, comprehensive historical view. Where we do find one is in Huysmans, but erotic, religious, and social decay are

9. For Proust's style see Jean Mouton, *Le Style de Marcel Proust* (Paris: Corrêa, 1948); Yvette Louria, *La Convergeance stylistique chez Proust* (Geneva: Droz, 1957); Jean Milly, *La Phrase de Proust* (Paris: Larousse, 1975).

opposed to the new fullness of art in the declining age, so that the notion of decadence turns out to be a somewhat paradoxical one. Zola, on the other hand, took a more relative view of the esthetic ideals of his age: "Ma conviction a fini par être que le jargon de notre époque, cette partie du style purement de mode et qui doit vieillir, restera comme un des plus monstrueux jargons de la langue française."[10] Much as he liked "tous nos raffinements d'écrivains nerveux," the style "chargé d'ornements de toutes sortes," a certain feeling prevailed in him of the cyclic nature of such matters, and he expected new generations would find "brighter," "more solid" styles. We see, in short, that the exact combination of diverse notions of decadence—historical, biological-sensory, stylistic—changes from writer to writer, and in the poets we would find still other variations.

10. Zola, *Oeuvres*, XXXVI, 302–303.

13 English Styles and French Theory

When we look at European romantic prose for points of comparison with French styles, we find that English prose, both in Britain and America, offers the most distinctive examples of highly individual inventors of styles in the service of some particular genre. Lamb's informal essay is a handy place to begin.

> And here I must have leave, in the fullness of my soul, to regret the abolition, and doing-away-with altogether, of those consolatory interstices, and sprinklings of freedom, through the four seasons,—the *rèd-letter days*, now become, to all intents and purposes, *dead-letter days*. There was Paul, and Stephen, and Barnabas—Andrew and John, men famous in old times—we were used to keep all their days holy, as long back as I was at school at Christ's. I remember their effigies, by the same token, in the old *Basket* Prayer Book. There hung Peter in his uneasy posture—holy Bartlemy in the troublesome act of flaying, after the famous Marsyas by Spagnoletti.— I honoured them all, and could almost have wept the defalcation of Iscariot—so much did we love to keep holy memories sacred:—only methought I a little grudged at the coalition of the *better Jude* with Simon— clubbing (as it were) their sanctities together, to make up one poor gaudy-day between them." ("Oxford in the Vacation")

Lamb's peculiar tone holds together the most diverse elements: Latinate and English expressions side by side (*consolatory . . . freedom*); pun; quotation, allusion immediate and remote; the legal term *defalcation*; and the archaic *methought* with the subsequent word order— all strung together in the loosest of punctuation. The heteroclite vocabulary suggests in principle the kind of decadent taste for striking detail which French theorists observed, except that hints of the older language dominate and the effect is a humorous one: the feeling for the archaism, for rhetoric of an earlier stage of style, is somewhat dif-

draw on colloquial sentence movement and how much closer Michelet's language is to that of the twentieth century. These English heightened styles of the romantic and Victorian eras, through their use of older poetic rhetoric, achieve intensity at the risk of appearing as fanciful accidents in the evolving history of the language, much as do French decadent mannerisms of vocabulary. The one attenuating circumstance is the persistent consciousness of English Biblical language, which gives an element of continuity to archaisms; in Ruskin, we are especially aware of the Bible-reading and preaching traditions of the English-speaking world. Here is Ruskin, with his customary gnomic effect, speaking of Titian and Tintoretto's landscapes.

> From the window of Titian's house at Venice, the chain of the Tyrolese Alps is seen lifted in spectral power above the tufted plain of Treviso; every dawn that reddens the towers of Murano lights also a line of pyramidal fires along that colossal ridge; but there is, so far as I know, no evidence in any of the master's works of his ever having beheld, much less felt, the majesty of their burning. The dark firmament and saddened light of Tintoret are sufficient for their end; but the sun never plunges behind San Giorgio in Aliga without such retinue of radiant cloud, such rest of zoned light on the green lagoon, as never received image from his hand. (*Modern Painters* I, Part ii, Section 1, Chapter 7)

By stylistic means, what is essentially a comment on the subject matter of painting becomes filled with moralistic overtones. The use of *every, ever,* and *never* tends to make every statement have an exemplary, monitory ring; the omission of articles (*such retinue, such rest, received image*) is one of Ruskin's especially frequent archaisms that give solemn authority to the prose. In the regularity of epithets, finally, we see another device for conveying a sermonlike, commanding dignity. The persuasive element is so pronounced that we expect a volley of imperatives to be coming up, a form Ruskin does use in his discussions for heightening moral-esthetic immediacy.

It appears, from our samplings of English style, that prose in which the individual word or ornament attracts considerable attention, decadent prose by the criteria of French theorists, was cultivated relatively early in the nineteenth century and with considerable distinction. Its reference to earlier tradition—Melville, for example, often suggests Shakespeare, Browne, or Johnson's ornament—legitimizes

it, and a certain playful consciousness of effect often comes to attenu-
ate extravagance of rhetoric. That these forms of prose tend to constitute a *genus grande* is evident, as is their peculiar adjustment to particular genres. The styles we have been looking at, however, are
brilliant performances, and the uneven or inferior versions of the
same modes inspire doubt about the soundness of the general drift of
nineteenth-century writing in English. The novel, in particular, fitfully written in the case of Dickens or downright badly written, as is,
say, Hawthorne's *Marble Faun*, proved a difficult genre. At the end of
the Victorian period we find attempts at high style in Hardy: "As she
thought again of her dusty boots she almost pitied those habiliments
for the quizzing to which they had been subjected." *Those habiliments*
is rather startling, as is this image: "You could see the skeleton behind the man, and almost the ghost behind the skeleton. He matched
Crivelli's dead *Christus.*" These sentences from *Tess of the d'Urbervilles*
would perhaps be more satisfactory if the whole context were on a
similar plane of embellishment, but it is not. Saintsbury summarized
the problems of Victorian prose as "undue aiming at pictorial effect;
gaudiness of unnatural ornament; preference of gross and glaring
effects."[1] These stylistic vices are, however, merely the beauties of
major prose writers gone wrong; the basic esthetic that led to gross
and glaring effects is the decadent one that had abundantly proved its
validity.

When we compare, even summarily, the history of nineteenth-
century prose in France and in the English-speaking world, decadent
rhetoric seems like a briefer, more limited episode in French literature
than it might otherwise, and more than one aspect of French style
emerges with greater clarity. De Quincey observed: "That particular
fault of style which in English books is all but universal [cumbrous
and unwieldy style] absolutely has not an existence in the French.
. . . The secret lies here; beyond all nations, by constitutional vivacity,
the French are a nation of talkers, and the model of their sentences is
moulded by that fact."[2] The reader of Victorian prose often finds sen-

1. George Saintsbury, quoted in Travis R. Merritt, "Taste, Opinion, and Theory in
the Rise of Victorian Prose Stylism," *The Art of Victorian Prose*, ed. George Levine and
William Madden (New York: Oxford University Press, 1968), 27.
2. Thomas De Quincey, *Selected Essays on Rhetoric*, ed. Frederick Burwick (Carbon-
dale: Southern Illinois University Press, 1967), 154–55.

tences that are neither natural nor beautiful, like this one, again from *Tess of the d'Urbervilles*: "His father, too, was shocked to see him, so reduced was that figure from its former contours by worry and the bad season that Clare had experienced in the climate to which he had so rashly hurried in his first aversion to the mockery of events at home." Hardy is trying to say too much in one sentence, with the result that the idiom is thoroughly strained; it is extremely rare to encounter in French such awkward relations between narrative matter and its expression. By the early twentieth century, English Victorian prose style came to seem alien to some writers. While the gospel of French prose had already been expounded by Pater and Saintsbury, a more effective renovation of English prose along the lines of French was brought about by the efforts of Ford Madox Ford and Ezra Pound. Stendhal, Flaubert, and Maupassant became models, and while from the French point of view their styles are rather different, one can see how, either in translation or to one whose French is imperfect, they exhibit such common characteristics as to conceal divergencies. One finds in them an admirable concision, discrimination in choice of detail, understatement, and homogeneity of texture. Here, for example, is a passage, chosen at random, from "Un Cœur simple."

> There were differences of level between the rooms which made you stumble. A narrow hall divided the kitchen from the parlor where Mme Aubain spent her day, sitting in a wicker easy chair by the window. Against the panels, which were painted white, was a row of eight mahogany chairs. On an old piano under the barometer a heap of wooden and cardboard boxes rose like a pyramid. An armchair stood on either side of the Louis-Quinze chimney mantel, which was in yellow marble with a clock in the middle of it modelled like a temple of Vesta. The whole room was a little musty as the floor was lower than the garden.

The general technique is exemplary: there is no odd vocabulary, for Flaubert came increasingly to avoid that kind of particularity; the figurative element is unobtrusive and severely functional; and we find no explanations, shifts of tone, undue colloquialisms, or humor breaking the mood. Lexical neutrality gives an illusion of impersonality; the weight is on nouns rather than adjectives. In other words,

Flaubert's tendency toward a classicizing unity of effect reaches full expression.

In unity of effect we see that profound similarity between Flaubert and Stendhal which from within the French tradition is likely to escape us, so different are the details of their prose. Stendhal has a peculiar homogeneity of narration and dialogue, cast in a language that is precise with just the right degree of restrained emphasis.

> The carriage was moving all this time at a slow trot. When they saw in the distance the yellow barriers striped with black which indicated the beginning of Austrian territory, the old woman said to Fabrizio: "You would do best to cross the frontier with Giletti's passport in your pocket; as for us, we shall stop for a minute, on the excuse of making ourselves tidy. And besides, the *dogana* will want to look at our things. . . . The police are as sharp as the devil in Austrian states; they will pretty soon know there has been a man killed; you are traveling with a passport which is not yours, that is more than enough to get you two years in prison. Make for the Po on your right after you leave the town, hire a boat and get away to Ravenna or Ferrara; get clear of Austrian parts as quickly as you can. With a couple of louis you should be able to buy another passport from some *doganiere*; it would be fatal to use this one; don't forget you have killed the man."

This is one of the most dramatic moments in *La Chartreuse de Parme*, yet no figurative embellishment marks it. From the standpoint of grammar and vocabulary Stendhal, if anything, drops the tone. This homogeneous, understated kind of prose was the object of much thought by Hemingway, who attempted to explain its effect in this way: "If a writer of prose knows enough about what he is writing about he may omit things that he knows and the reader, if the writer is writing truly enough, will have a feeling of those things as strongly as though the writer had stated them. The dignity of movement of an ice-berg is due to only one-eighth of it being above water. A writer who omits things because he does not know them only makes hollow places in his writing" (*Death in the Afternoon* 16). *La Chartreuse de Parme* in general relies very much on the submerged part of style.

French influence on a post-Victorian conception of prose is evident in such a writer as Dos Passos, with his merger of narrative voice with the character's consciousness, but it achieves its most influential form in Hemingway's style. The opening of *A Farewell to Arms* is a concentrated example of a Flaubert-like concern for beauty of sentence structures.

> In the late summer of that year we lived in a house in a village that looked across the river and the plain to the mountains. In the bed of the river there were pebbles and boulders, dry and white in the sun, and the water was clear and swiftly moving and blue in the channels. Troops went by the house and down the road and the dust they raised powdered the leaves of the trees. The trunks of the trees were dusty and the leaves fell early that year and we saw the troops marching along the road and the dust rising and leaves, stirred by the breeze, falling and the soldiers marching and afterward the road bare and white except for the leaves.

The complexity in the use of simple means comes in part from the various functions of *and*, beginning with joined prepositional and predicate complements, and followed by paired adjectives. The *and* first occurs in *A and B* constructions, then is found in a triplet, and finally occurs in a polysyndetic fivefold complement to the verb *saw*. With great elegance the sequence *troops/road/dust/leaves* in the penultimate sentence is expanded in the last main clause to *troops/road/dust/leaves/breeze/soldiers/road/leaves*; the prose is conceived of as having beauty in its pattern, quite aside from the function of the description in the novel. This is the kind of art of prose Flaubert believed in and astonished Turgenev with. Zola used to inquire of English and German writers whether narrative prose in their language had a discipline and rhetoric comparable to what Flaubert taught and he and others had elaborated; the answer was always negative.

French art-prose, however, did not draw everyone who knew it into its field of influence. The scenic novel in the manner of Flaubert or Zola, with its highly visual qualities and imitative rhythms, did not, notably, win over Henry James, a writer certainly concerned with matters of style but emphatically not a follower of Flaubert. James favors the *analyse psychologique* texture and devises for it a heavy and sometimes quite obscure vocabulary on the order of *this thing, that conception, the thought of which,* all combining in a sequence of mental actions whose content is not always precisely clear: "It was not till many days had passed that the Princess began to accept the idea of having done, a little, something she was not always doing, or indeed that of having listened to any inward voice that spoke in a new tone. Yet these instinctive postponements of reflection were the fruit, positively, of recognitions and perceptions already active; of the sense, above all, that she had made, at a particular hour, made by the mere touch of her hand, a difference in the situation so long present to her as practically inattackable" (*The Golden Bowl*, Chapter 25). Here *something*, *reflection*, *recognition*, and the *situation* allude to an adultery—or as some critics would have it, a mere possibility or suspicion of adultery—on the Prince's part. Since even close readers of James are not in absolute agreement about the content of "the situation," we may take ambiguity to be a dominant stylistic method. This is, of course, not even a really obscure example of James's late style; it shows quite adequately, however, the juxtaposition of abstractions with concrete details like the indications of time and the touch of the hand, the clashes of *postponements of reflection* and *recognitions* and *perceptions*, the general ugliness of James's style judged by the ordinary criteria of coherence and euphony.

James not uncharacteristically follows his abstract style with an image: "This situation had been occupying, for months and months, the very center of the garden of her life, but it had reared itself there like some strange, tall tower of ivory, or perhaps rather some wonderful, beautiful, but outlandish pagoda, a structure plated with hard, bright porcelain, colored and figured and adorned, at the overhanging eaves, with silver bells that tinkled, ever so charmingly, when stirred by chance airs." James is obviously unconcerned about the disparity in style between these two passages, and, indeed, taken as part of the whole of *The Golden Bowl*, there is no incoherency. But on the microstylistic level Flaubert was accustomed to concern himself with, the image is too obtrusive and gaudy, and the psychological vocabulary verges on jargon. James knew of the French naturalists' minute strictures of style but felt it was merely part of English to have repetitious effects of vocabulary. As for figurative language, he does not seem to have concerned himself with French ideas of imagery at all.

Joyce, equally familiar with French literature, used lyric style in parts of *A Portrait of the Artist*, and similar effects in *Ulysses*, especially in Stephen's thoughts: "A cloud began to cover the sun slowly, shadowing the bay in deeper green. It lay behind him, a bowl of bitter waters." But we always remember the comment on colors and adjectives at the beginning ("A new art color for our Irish poets: snot-green"), and a certain irony clings to the poetic and evocative in the novel. But Joyce came ultimately, like James, to think of fiction as other than a prose poem in the French fashion. Flaubert had identified beauty with euphonic values and lyrical imagery; his scenic conception of the novel is not to be separated from this. James and Joyce, on the other hand, were aware of realms of expressiveness that had nothing to do with so traditional and poetic a rhetorical conception. James's ambiguities or the range of styles in *Ulysses*, including the silly and sentimental ("Nausicaa") or the ponderous and dreary ("Eumaeus"), are highly crafted examples of language but not of art-prose. They are a kind of writing that it is almost impossible to conceive of in the higher tradition of the French novel in the later nineteenth century and earlier twentieth, where even in unsuccessful efforts, like the Goncourts', style was intended to represent the most exquisite form of expression.

Conclusion

Sartre, in a discussion of Faulkner, compared the obscurity of the American novelist to the *idées claires* of French tradition and to Proust's lucid remarks on time in particular.[1] Sartre himself, without remarking on the fact, created in *La Nausée* one of the most striking examples of the elegant French use of *idées claires* in fiction. We must not confuse *A la recherche*, *La Nausée*, or any comparable French novels in which there is intellectual content with the old *romans à thèse* like Bourget's *Le Disciple* or Barrès' *Les Déracinés* or with the inferior genre called the novel of ideas in English: Proust, Gide, Mauriac, Malraux, Sartre, and Camus used ideas as part of an intellectual, moral, and psychological complex, and their command of distinctly fictional qualities is sufficient to keep their work on a high imaginative plane. At the same time, some may feel that there is something more purely novelistic about the turbid Christian reference of *Light in August* in comparison with the elegant theology of Mauriac's *Le Baiser au lépreux*; when we read *La Condition humaine*, the initial sense of mystery is soon dispelled, whereas in Faulkner, the effect of mystery, of an unevenly lit, half-concealed story, may persist throughout the whole book. We can scarcely imagine outside the French tradition the stylish remarks of Malraux's characters: "Reconnaître la liberté d'un autre, c'est lui donner raison contre sa propre souffrance"; "L'idéal d'un dieu, n'est-ce pas, c'est de devenir homme en sachant qu'il retrouvera sa puissance; et le rêve de l'homme, de devenir dieu sans perdre sa personnalité." Roquentin is very careful to explore and summarize the ideas springing from experience in *La Nausée*; Camus' tendency toward overt intellectual content led ultimately to *La Chute*,

---

1. Jean-Paul Sartre, *Situations I* (Paris: Gallimard, 1947), 77.

which is primarily a display of analytical intelligence. Furthermore, we feel a strong element of literary reference in the French novel: Nietzsche seems always present, whether by allusion (the title of *L'Immoraliste*) and quotation (as in *Le Baiser au lépreux*) or through the question Tchen asks in *La Condition humaine* and which underlies Sartre and Camus' work: "Que faire d'une âme s'il n'y a Dieu ni Christ?"

I have quoted examples of Malraux's aphoristic language, and in general, in Gide, Proust, Mauriac, Sartre, and Camus there is a use of abstract psychological language far more penetrating than any in the late nineteenth-century realist-naturalist novel.

> L'angoisse que je venais d'éprouver, je pensais que Swann s'en serait bien moqué s'il avait lu ma lettre et en avait deviné le but; or, au contraire, comme je l'ai appris plus tard, une angoisse semblable fut le tourment de longues années de sa vie, et personne aussi bien que lui peut-être n'aurait pu me comprendre; lui, cette angoisse qu'il y a à sentir l'être qu'on aime dans un lieu de plaisir où l'on n'est pas, où l'on ne peut pas le rejoindre, c'est l'amour qui la lui a fait connaître, l'amour, auquel elle est en quelque sorte prédestinée, par lequel elle sera accaparée, spécialisée; mais quand, comme pour moi, elle est entrée en nous avant qu'il ait encore fait son apparition dans notre vie, elle flotte en l'attendant, vague et libre, sans affectation déterminée, au service un jour d'un sentiment, le lendemain d'un autre, tantôt de la tendresse filiale ou de l'amitié pour un camarade. (*Du côté de chez Swann*, "Combray")

But there is another side to the style of these novelists; in these stories of isolated existence, the imagistic and lyrical plays an important role in alternance or combination with the abstract, *moraliste* language.

> Légers, très élevés, les nuages passaient au-dessus des pins sombres et se résorbaient peu à peu dans le ciel; et il lui sembla qu'un de leurs groupes, celui-là précisément, exprimait les hommes qu'il avait connus ou aimés, et qui étaient morts. L'humanité était épaisse et lourde, lourde de chair, de sang, de souffrance, éternellement collée à elle-même comme tout ce qui meurt; mais même le sang, même la chair, même la douleur, même la mort se résorbaient là-haut dans la lumière comme la musique dans la nuit silencieuse: il pensa à celle de Kama et la douleur humaine lui sembla monter et se perdre comme le chant même de la terre; sur la paix frémissante et cachée en lui comme son cœur, la douleur possédée refermait lentement ses bras inhumains. (*La Condition humaine*, Septième Partie)

Camus' evocations of North Africa or Amsterdam are as familiar as his metaphysical questions, and in *La Nausée,* Sartre seems deliberately to have set out to expand metaphoric language.

> Ce qui vient d'arriver, c'est que la Nausée a disparu. Quand la voix s'est élevée, dans le silence, j'ai senti mon corps se durcir et la Nausée s'est évanouie. D'un coup: c'était presque pénible de devenir ainsi tout dur, tout rutilant. En même temps la durée de la musique se dilatait, s'enflait comme une trombe. Elle emplissait la salle de sa transparence métallique, en écrasant contre les murs notre temps misérable. Je suis *dans* la musique. Dans les glaces roulent des globes de feu; des anneaux de fumée les encerclent et tournent, voilant et dévoilant le dur sourire de la lumière. Mon verre de bière s'est rapetissé, il se tasse sur la table: il a l'air dense, indispensable.

Proust actually formulated a theory of the novelistic texture blending the intellectual-sententious with the sensory-lyrical; for him the ideas of the novel were a setting, in the jeweler's sense, for the imagery of experience. But the descriptions of these novelists are sufficiently intermittent that the work gives an impression of contained lyricism, of holding back. Of course, we recognize in all these writers the cult of the beautiful sentence, imagistic or aphoristic, an idea of art-prose which, however different from that of the late nineteenth century, still belongs clearly to a peculiarly French conception of the language of fiction. Even when there is a certain nervous brevity as in Malraux, or an element of the colloquial as in Sartre, the intenser lyrical effects are quite perceptible. In this respect, we see how the major novels of the twenties, thirties, and forties continue the nineteenth-century tradition and are equally open to Robbe-Grillet's criticism of previous fiction as an anthropomorphizing definition of the character's relation to the external world, with its "tragic complicity."

The novelists of the earlier twentieth century, with the exception of Proust, are not such experimenters with fictional technique as more recent writers or as writers in German and English of their own day. It has been said of Camus and others that the novel form was not entirely adequate for what they wanted to say and that they needed the scope of several genres.[2] Gide, Malraux, Sartre, and Mauriac all

2. Wilbur M. Frohock, *Style and Temper: Studies in French Fiction, 1825–1960* (Cambridge: Harvard University Press, 1967), xiv–xv.

tended to write, during or after writing their novels, books that further clarified their thought, and Proust, of course, found a way of incorporating the essay into the novel. Sometimes devices like the journal (in Gide's novels, *La Nausée*, and *La Peste*) add an element of expository prose; at other times, the third-person novelist may use a technique by which fiction is a kind of meditation, the characters part of an authorial reflection on life.[3] Such is often the case in Mauriac, as at the end of the wedding night passage in *Le Baiser au lépreux*: "Elle était pareille à une martyre endormie. Les cheveux collés au front, comme dans l'agonie, rendaient plus mince son visage d'enfant battu. Les mains en croix contre sa gorge innocente, serraient le scapulaire un peu déteint et les médailles bénites. Il aurait fallu baiser ses pieds, saisir ce tendre corps, sans l'éveiller, courir, le tenant ainsi, vers la haute mer, le livrer à la chaste écume" (Chapter 5). Often the work is divided not into large scenic chapters but, as in *Le Baiser au lépreux*, *La Nausée*, *La Condition humaine*, into short episodes conducive to the meditational style. French fiction between the times of Gide and Camus is often compared to the *moralistes* for its content, and this again suggests why it is only fitfully scenic and why the real era of fictional experiment begins only more recently. These writers created, by and large, a less purely novelistic kind of work than Flaubert or the one Percy Lubbock was proposing to the English-speaking world in *The Craft of Fiction*. Returning to our point of departure, Faulkner, we can see how he seems more truly a novelist than his French contemporaries.

I have dwelled at some length on the aphoristic, descriptional, and meditative character of French fiction of the earlier twentieth century because it constitutes a much admired phase of French prose and one whose connections with tradition are now clear. Twenty-five years ago, Mauriac, Malraux, Sartre, and Camus seemed like very different writers, engaged as they were in polemics over literature and politics. Now, after Beckett's fiction, the *Nouveau Roman*, and the *Tel Quel* tendencies represented by Philippe Sollers or Marcelin Pleynet, we

3. Malraux said, "I never wrote a novel in order to write a novel. I continued a sort of uninterrupted meditation which took successive forms, one of which was fiction." Quoted in Rima Drell Reck, *Literature and Responsibility: The French Novelist in the Twentieth Century* (Baton Rouge: Louisiana State University Press, 1969), 269.

see the common grounds of earlier fiction and its historical unity. It would seem today that the dominant form of prose in French intellectual life is frankly the essay, and that its stylistic habits derive from the neologistic manner first attempted by Sartre in his expository works. But the precise extent of this stage of prose is as yet unclear.

Appendix I
The Variables of the French Period

This summary can be conveniently divided into syntactic, periodic, and phonetic structures, all of which are relevant to rhetorical analysis.

Phrase, clause, and sentence are the units of grammar. Our first concern is the simple sentence, one with no subordinate clauses. Here word order is the principal variation:

natural word order:

J'en ai vu la fin avec une sorte de regret;

separation of subject and verb:

Emma, avec une sorte de regret, en vit la fin;

separation of verb and object:

J'en ai vu, avec une sorte de regret, la fin;

separation of the verbal complex:

Elle l'a, quoique involontairement, aimé.

The pertinent concepts here are natural word order and sequentiality of syntax as opposed to hyperbaton, suspension, and the use of *incises*.

When enough material precedes, a final verb strikes one by its position:

Le silence éternel de ces espaces infinis m'effraie.

The reprise or anticipatory pronouns (*Emma, je la vois* or *Je la vois, Emma*) are of most significance in long sentences, although they are, of course, found in simple ones. They provide another variation in word order.

An important aspect of periodic theory is that of natural subordination of meaning. The choice between coordinated verbs and subordination is an important variation:

Emma le vit et elle s'étonna.

Quand elle le vit, elle s'étonna.

The paratactic sentence form with coordinated, equal main verbs is, by the standards of ordinary written language, a slightly emphatic, stylistically distinctive handling of the relation of sense and grammar. There is, of course, variation according to language and historical period in the comparative use of parataxis and hypotaxis. We may, however, consider the sentence with the subordinate clause as normal and neutral.

The above subordinating clausal arrangement can be contrasted with the more suspenseful, forward moving classical pattern:

Emma, quand elle le vit, s'étonna

and with the order having no tension at all:

Elle s'étonna quand elle le vit.

In the classical arrangement of the clauses, the period "aspires toward the end." While such an effect is limited by grammatical considerations in French, there are periods wherein we see a strong pull toward the last words; nonsequentiality of syntax is the device here:

Alors Albertine, qui s'en était aperçue, s'opposa, malgré tout ce qu'elle avait dit le jour auparavant, à ce que je rendisse visite à Mme Verdurin.

In the following example, the reference of the participles is slightly forced to produce a dramatic aspiration to the end:

Là, enchaîné sur un lit comme Prométhée sur son rocher, recevant les coups d'un martinet en effet planté de clous que lui infligeait Maurice, je vis, déjà tout en sang, et couvert d'ecchymoses qui prouvaient que le supplice n'avait pas lieu pour la première fois, je vis devant moi M. de Charlus.

The following period, in a letter from the Archbishop of Parma to Fabrice, is called Ciceronian by Stendhal because the main clause and conclusion is so lengthily postponed:

Quoique la procédure soit environnée du plus profond mystère, et dirigé par le fiscal général Rassi, dont la seule charité chrétienne peut m'empêcher de dire du mal, mais qui a fait sa fortune en s'acharnant après les malheureux accusés comme le chien de chasse après le lièvre; quoique le Rassi, dis-je, dont votre imagination ne saurait s'exagérer la turpitude et la vénalité, ait été chargé de la direction du procès par un prince irrité, j'ai pu lire les trois dépositions du veturino.

Our three examples are quite different in syntactic structure, but all illustrate the capacities of French, when a sufficient occasion arises, for assuming a periodic form similar in effect to that of Latin.

In the Latin ideal of an expository period, all subordinates would refer more or less directly to the main clause. The periods in which clause is added to clause at the end, without any concern for subordination of ideas, are variously called accretive, loose, or descending. The ideal form of the period is less likely to be achieved with a weak main verb than with a strong one. The narrative or progressive period forms an exception to the principle of strict subordination in sense of secondary clauses to the main one; in French, as contrasted with Latin, much more extreme examples are found of periods that move forward leaving the matter of the main clause far behind.

The period is defined as a structure consisting of two or more cola. These are a unit of sense such as a verb (finite form, infinitive, or participle) with another element, or a noun and adjective, or two nouns. The two elements of the colon could, recast if necessary, make a single-clause sentence. The equivalence of various syntactic constructions for the purpose of analyzing cola may be illustrated by the following sentences:

Après qu'il s'y fut rendu,/il trouva ce qu'il cherchait,/de sorte qu'il en revint très content.

Après s'y être rendu,/il trouva ce qu'il cherchait,/et en revint très content. The equivalence is complete between phrase and clause, main clause and subordinate clause. What is, from the standpoint of grouping by verbal nexus, the same kind of three-colon sentence, may be much more complex in syntactic relations:

L'angoisse que je venais d'éprouver,/je pensais que Swann s'en serait bien moquée/s'il avait lu ma lettre.

The use of the noun with reprise pronoun in creating grammatical tension is nicely illustrated, and the end point *si*-clause is much more tightly connected to the main section than many adverbial clauses, because it completes the conditional of the main verbal complex. Some writers tend at times toward highly clausal periods where another might have broken the idea into parallel clauses and nominal constructions:

Il me plaisait que cette habitude quasi-monacale me préservât d'un monde qui, du reste, m'attirait peu, et qu'il m'eût suffi qu'Alissa pût craindre pour m'apparaître aussitôt haïssable.

Le monde m'attirait très peu et mes habitudes, en cela conformes à mon goût, m'en préservaient. J'aurais, d'ailleurs, trouvé aussitôt haïssable toute société crainte par Alissa.

Brief noun and adjective cola are illustrated by *Le silence eternel/de ces espaces infinis.* A single independent clause can thus be a period. In the following example, one word, equivalent to a phrase, is a colon:

Il eut ordre de ramener Frédéric, définitivement.

Il eut ordre de ramener Frédéric, malgré sa résistance.

The apposition is a characteristic device of rather formal prose and can consist of one or more cola:

Elle aimait qu'on lui en fît des leçons sincères: marque assurée d'une âme forte que ses fautes ne dominent pas et qui ne craint pas de les envisager de près.

We can see that a strong apposition like this one of Bossuet's is close in function to an independent clause: *c'est la marque assurée.*

The length of the cola in the preceding examples varies. Seven to ten syllables is common in French. The hexameter or alexandrine length, which Cicero suggests is frequent, can be found (as in *J'aurais . . . haïssable* above) but does not occur so much in a language less polysyllabic than Latin.

Sentence connection or the lack of it, sentence asyndeton, is an important aspect of stylistic texture. Ancient prose has modest sentence connectives (the *de* customary in Greek, and *enim, tamen,* and so forth in Latin), and medieval French had its *si.* The sustaining effect they give is imitated by the use of *et, mais, car,* and *de sorte que,* but such words create a certain ambiguity about the division into sentences, since they are used as well within compound sentences. One must sometimes have recourse to the idea of the period covering more than one punctuational sentence in analyzing their effect. Renaissance French prose also likes heavy sentence links on the order of *quoi voyant, lesquelles choses faites, quoi qu'il en soit.* The use of prominent sentence connectives often goes with elaborate hypotaxis to produce an ostentatiously articulated texture.

Sentence asyndeton, on the other hand, is frequently used with sentences consisting of one main clause or having little subordination. These were joined into periods after the development of expressive punctuation: whereas the semicolon becomes a neutral mark, the colon indicates cause, result, and so forth. Even more elaborate sentences at times are found tied together in what one might call a punctuational period.

The comma is usually a shorter unit than the colon and more fragmentary in meaning, such as an adverb or some other intercalated expression: *d'ailleurs* or *dit-on* are examples. A rhythmic break marks the comma. In Saint Augustine's sample analyses of prose (*De Doctrina Christiana*, IV), the term *caesa* (commata) is used for a series of parallel words or expressions: *In journeying often, in perils of waters, in perils of robbers, in perils from my own nation*. A French example would be *Il est enjoué, grand rieur, impatient, présomptueux, colère*. Commata may occur within the period or without: in the latter case, they are often exclamations or brief questions. In classical periodic texture, it is common to find periods alternating with commata and independent cola or one-phrase sentences.

A phonetic aspect of periodic structure is the relation of length among cola: between the extremes of isocolon and pronounced heterocolon there are the harmonious but not symmetrical relations of 1 to 2/3 or 1 to 3/4; these create concinnity or pleasing proportion as much as isocolon. Increasing colon length (the *Gesetz der wachsenden Glieder*) or diminution also constitute a form of concinnity. In doublings or series of words or phrases, there is also a potential element of concinnity or irregularity: *A and B* is often more balanced seeming than *A,B*; *A,B,C* is as balanced but more formal than *A,B, and C*, but with longer series great variation is possible. Even with *A and B*, dissymmetry can occur if the elements are of varying kind or length: *un panorama ravissant et dont il n'avait jamais vu le pareil*.

The intonational phrases of phonetic analysis create the rhythm of a period and generally correspond to cola. The intonational drop at the end of the sentence varies in length. Other phonetic variables are polysyllabism, the presence of blank alexandrines in prose, assonance and alliteration, homeoteleuthon or similar endings (*les passions et affections*), and the choice of words that are weighty in comparison with their alternatives (subject *lequel* for *qui*, *nonobstant que* for *quoique*). It should be remembered that counting syllables does

not always exactly represent what one perceives in phrase length because of variables like long vowels and syllables or sequences of
monosyllabic words. Thus it has been demonstrated that even a practiced ear cannot in every case distinguish twelve syllables from
eleven or thirteen.

Appendix II
Technical Terms

AETIOLOGICAL MYTH: a story told to account for the origins of a name or situation

AMPLIFICATION: in classical rhetoric, heightening; in medieval rhetoric, lengthening

ANACOLUTHON: a stylistically effective grammatical misconstruction, often through some kind of ellipsis

ANAPHORA: a succession of phrases beginning with the same word

ANASTROPHE: see HYPERBATON

APOSIOPESIS: breaking off a sentence before the grammatical structure is complete: "Why I . . ."

APOTHEGM: maxim

ASYNDETON: avoidance of connective words (such as *thus*) between sentences or omission of connectives (*and, or*) between two or more parallel nouns, adjectives, or verbs

COLON: see APPENDIX I

COMMA: see APPENDIX I

CONCINNITY: the quality of a harmonious structure

DEICTIC: pertaining to demonstrative constructions, such as "this heart" for "my heart"

DELIBERATIVE RHETORIC: in literature, the representation of the attempt to make up one's mind in a doubtful situation. Self-addressed questions characterize it.

EPIC SIMILE: a lengthy simile, as is first found in Homer

EPIDEICTIC RHETORIC: the nonpractical or purely literary branch of rhetoric, focusing in its origins on praise or blame

EPITHETON: the systematic use of epithets

EXORDIUM: the opening, often in the form of a generality, of a formal composition

FIGURES OF SOUND AND THOUGHT: Sound figures, such as isocolon, anaphora, or alliteration, are unrelated to sense; figures of thought, such as antithesis or metaphor, concern the intellectual elaboration of style.

273

GESETZ DER WACHSENDEN GLIEDER: the principle of arranging words, phrases, or clauses according to increasing length

GORGIAN PERIOD: a period with simultaneous isocolon, homeoteleuthon, and antithesis: "Life hath variety; death hath monotony."

HOMEOTELEUTHON: the use of words with identical or similar endings, as in Rimbaud's "L'élégance, la science, la violence!"

HYPERBATON: a word order contrary to the normal one or the separation of words with close grammatical ties

HYPOPHORA: the device of asking a question and answering it oneself

HYPOTAXIS: the use of subordination, particularly of subordinate clauses containing finite verbs

ISOCOLON: the use of phrases of identical or similar length

METAPHORE FILEE: an extended metaphor

NATURAL WORD ORDER: the basic declarative word order, such as French subject-(adjective)-verb-(adverb)-object-(adjective)

PARATAXIS: constructing sentences without subordinate clauses

PERIOD: see APPENDIX I

POLYPTOTON: the use of words containing the same root: "You do not need to encourage the courageous."

POLYSYNDETON: the use of *and* or *or* between all members of a series

PROSOPOPOEIA: the representation of an abstraction or absent person as speaking

PROTASIS AND APODASIS: The protasis is an *if* or other subordinate clause to which the apodasis or main clause is the conclusion.

SYNDETON: linkage between sentences or members of a series

SYNECDOCHE: designating the whole by a part

Index

QUEEN MARY
COLLEGE
LIBRARY

WITHDRAWN
FROM STOCK
QMUL LIBRARY